THE RENEWED CHURCH OF THE
UNITED BRETHREN, 1722-1930

PUBLISHED FOR THE
CHURCH HISTORICAL SOCIETY

New Series

1. ST. AUGUSTINE'S CONVERSION. An outline of his development to the time of his Ordination. By W. J. SPARROW SIMPSON, D.D. Cloth boards, 10s. 6d. net.

2. A HISTORY OF THE ICONOCLASTIC CONTROVERSY. By EDWARD JAMES MARTIN, D.D. Cloth boards, 16s. net.

3 THE CARTHUSIAN ORDER IN ENGLAND. By E. MARGARET THOMPSON, Cloth boards. 21s. net.

4. THE NEW COMMANDMENT. An inquiry into the Social Precept and Practice of the Ancient Church. By C. S. PHILLIPS, M.A., D.D. Cloth boards. 6s. net.

5. STUDIES IN ENGLISH PURITANISM FROM THE RESTORATION TO THE REVOLUTION, 1660-1688. By C. E. WHITING, D.D., B.C.L. Cloth boards. 21s. net.

6. SITTING FOR THE PSALMS. An Historical Study. By CLEMENT F. ROGERS, M.A. Paper Cover. 1s. net.

7. A HISTORY OF THE CHURCH IN BLACKBURNSHIRE. By JOHN EYRE WINSTANLEY WALLIS, M.A. 7s. 6d. net.

8. EXORCISM AND THE HEALING OF THE SICK. By REGINALD MAXWELL WOOLLEY, D.D. 3s. 6d. net.

9. THE RENEWED CHURCH OF THE UNITED BRETHREN, 1722–1930. By WILLIAM GEORGE ADDISON, Ph.D. 12s. 6d. net.

S.P.C.K., LONDON

THE RENEWED CHURCH
OF THE
UNITED BRETHREN
1722-1930

BY

WILLIAM GEORGE ADDISON
(M.A. Camb., B.D., Ph.D. Lond.)

(Thesis approved for the Degree of Doctor of Philosophy in the University of London)

Published for the Church Historical Society

LONDON
SOCIETY FOR PROMOTING
CHRISTIAN KNOWLEDGE
NORTHUMBERLAND AVENUE, W.C. 2
NEW YORK AND TORONTO: THE MACMILLAN CO.
1932

PRINTED IN GREAT BRITAIN BY THE EDINBURGH PRESS, EDINBURGH

The Wise will remember that Frailty is
inseparable from Humanity.

BENHAM, *Memoirs of James Hutton.*

The lesson-book of the Ecclesia, and of every
Ecclesia, is not a Law but a History.

F. J. A. HORT, *The Christian Ecclesia.*

CONTENTS

CHAPTER III

THE ENGLISH PROVINCE: ORIGINS AND EARLY DEVELOPMENT

CHAPTER IV

THE GROWTH OF PROVINCIAL INDEPENDENCE, 1760–1899

CHAPTER V

THE UNITAS FRATRUM AND THE CHURCH OF ENGLAND

APPENDICES

INTRODUCTORY NOTE

PLAINLY the following pages are not an attempt to present even a summary version of the History of the Renewed Church of the Brethren. The main events of that history are, it is hoped, sufficiently noted, and as far as is possible, stated in due chronological sequence. But the purpose of this essay is the more modest and more definite one of selecting such aspects as are likely to attract the student of ecclesiastical history who approaches his subject motived by the conviction that the study of the past has its own specific contribution to make to the great reunion movement of our day. Our aim is to take the history of the renewed *Unitas Fratrum* and, by the light of two centuries of development, to illustrate the evolution of the dominant ideal and intention of its " Renewer," viz.: the ideal of assisting the movement from " a plurality of churches " to " the unity of the children of God."

We shall see how the early idealisms of one gifted individual were forced, by the recalcitrancy of events, the opposition of enemies and the divergent interests of colleagues, to undergo serious modification. Throughout we shall concentrate our attention on the British Province of the Renewed Unitas, partly because only so could we cope with our material, partly because, as it happens, the relations between that Province and the National Church in a land where religious toleration came earlier than in Germany, and where the " Moravians " awoke much earlier to their right to the status of an independent Free Church, are of peculiar interest to one who tries to retain a lively appreciation both of the advantage to Church and State of a National Church Establishment, and also of the fervent zeal for the purity and freedom of the spiritual society expressed in the aphorism " A Free Church in a Free State ".

Finally, as pointing the relevance of the story of the past to matters of moment in our own day, we shall take some note of official contacts between the Moravian and Anglican Churches, in pursuance of that end of Christian unity so central in the circumstances of the Brethren's re-emergence as an institutional body in the second quarter of the eighteenth century.

. . . . .

Reading and Research.—The work itself indicates the exact references to the manuscripts, pamphlets and periodical literature consulted in its composition, at Herrnhut, Fetter Lane, and Lambeth Palace Library. This material has, for the most part, been utilized in Chapter III, the marrow of the essay and that portion of it which is most likely to interest the student of English religious history. Here, too, Daniel Benham's *Memoirs of James Hutton*, London, 1856, has been invaluable, all the more so since its author was no professional historian but an amazingly industrious compiler of facts. Dr G. A. Wauer's Dissertation on *The Beginnings of the Brethren's Church in England*, translated by J. Elliott, 1901, is most useful. For Zinzendorf's personality and ideas, Otto Uttendörfer's *Zinzendorf's Weltbetrachtung*, Herrnhut, 1929, affords an exhaustive and systematic examination. Similarly, for Chapter II, there is available the specialist study by Dr J. T. Müller, until recently Archivar at Herrnhut, and probably the highest authority on Moravian History, *Zinzendorf als Erneuerer der alten Brüder Kirche*, Leipzig, 1900. Ritschl's account of German Pietism, and of Zinzendorf and the Brüdergemeine, is in his *Geschichte des Pietismus*, Band III (esp. Buch 8, Par. 48–55). For personal details and chronology Jackson's abridged translation of Spangenberg's *Life*, London, 1838, has proved adequate and convenient. Zinzendorf's intercourse with Cardinal Noailles and his lifelong zeal for Christian Unity suggests the study of that topic in two earlier eirenical efforts : Leibnitz, *Œuvres*, *Notes et Introduction*, par Foucher de Careil, Tomes I, II. . . . *Pour la Réunion des Protestants et des Catholiques*, Paris, 1859 ; and, *Archbishop Wake and the Project of Union* (1717–1720) *between the Gallican and Anglican Churches*, J. H. Lupton, Bell, 1896.

The full references of the four general Histories frequently quoted are : J. E. Hutton, *A History of the Moravian Church*,

2nd Edn., London, 1909 ; J. Taylor Hamilton, *A History of the Church known as the Moravian Church or The Unitas Fratrum, During the Eighteenth and Nineteenth Centuries*, Bethlehem, Pa., 1900 ; John Holmes, *History of the Protestant Church of the United Brethren*, 2 Vols., London, 1825, 1830 ; David Crantz, *Ancient and Modern History of the Brethren*, trans. B. La Trobe, London, 1780. G. Burkhardt, *Die Brüdergemeine*, Gnadau, 1905, is a compact summary of the Unity's history, Ancient and Renewed ; lighter, popular and pictorial is the general survey of past and present, *Die Brüder*, O. Uttendörfer and W. Schmidt, Herrnhut, 1922. Other literature is noted in the text *seriatim* ; it seems needless to repeat the titles in a necessarily inadequate bibliography. This applies particularly to the English background of Chapter III—the social and religious condition of the nation, the Religious Societies, early Methodism, the quality and attitudes of various Anglican prelates. The standard General and Ecclesiastical Histories of the period provide convenient and classified lists, *e.g.* Dr H. W. V. Temperley's in *Camb. Mod. Hist.*, Vol. VI ; or, more specialist, in Abbey and Overton, *The English Church in the Eighteenth Century*, Longmans, 1887. The footnotes indicate what selection has been made from such lists, though not all books thus used have necessarily received mention. Less well known but most apposite for our background are three academic theses : S. G. Dimond, *The Psychology of the Methodist Revival*, London, 1928 ; N. Sykes, *Edmund Gibson, Bishop of London*, 1669–1748, O.U.P., 1926 ; A. L. Cross, *The Anglican Episcopate and the American Colonies*, Harvard, 1902.

Chapter IV has the least pretensions to originality but some account of the later constitutional development seemed necessary as a bridge between the eighteenth century and the Moravian-Anglican negotiations now in progress. The further fact that in this section the writer finds himself most inclined to differ from the interpretation of later Moravian history as presented in the two modern general Histories of the Brethren's Church may perhaps be noted as evidence of the exercise of "independent critical judgment." Articles in *Ency. Brit.*, *Dic. Nat. Biog.*, and Hastings' *Dic. Ref. and Ethics* have also been consulted. See also Supplementary Note to Chapter V, *c*, for literature on Christian Reunion.

. . . . .

The writer is indebted to the Rev. Canon Claude Jenkins, D.D., Lambeth Librarian, who is responsible for the initial impulse to attempt this survey of English Moravianism. The writer is conscious of certain disabilities due to his small acquaintanceship among ministers or members of the Moravian Church. But much has been learned in conversations with the Rev. H. Mumford, Ex-Principal of the Moravian College, Fairfield, Manchester, and with the Rev. J. N. Libbey, a member of the Provincial Board, Fetter Lane, London, E.C. A greater debt is owing to Dr Henri Roy, Ex-Principal of the Theological Seminary at Herrnhut, for much kind guidance among the shelves of the Unity's Archives and for some assistance in translation.

Acknowledgment should be made to the Committees, both of the Publication Fund of the University of London and of the Church Historical Society, for their financial assistance in making it possible to publish the results of these researches.

W. G. A.

Chapter I

THE RENEWER OF THE OLD BRÜDER KIRCHE

A. "His exceeding great Regard for Christ"

"NICOLAS LEWIS, Count and Lord of Zinzendorf and Pottendorf . . . Aulic and Judicial Counsellor to the Elector of Saxony, Bishop, Advocate, Ordinary, and Representative of the Church of the Bohemian and Moravian Brethren," must be reckoned among those memorable men who found their life-work and earned their posthumous renown by what might seem accidental circumstances rather than by conscious deliberation and choice. Better perhaps to say that he was one of those fortunate souls whom events present with a vocation to a great task which they are the better able to fulfil by reason of a preparation grounded deep in the circumstances of early training, temperamental predilection, and specific principles wrought out in the stress and strain of youth and young manhood.

To delay upon one obvious illustration, the wide-flung missionary activity of the Moravian Church today runs back by a definite process of events to the rest and refuge the Moravian exiles found on the Bethelsdorf estate, and to the nursing care of the infant community by the young Saxon aristocrat. The flame of the old Unity awoke from the embers fanned by the breath of Zinzendorf's solicitude for the unknown refugees. Yet for a space of five years (June 1722–July 1727) he was ignorant of the true character of the Revival he was fostering, or indeed that it was a renewal at all. Zinzendorf was undoubtedly a man of spiritual genius and none can say what, without the Brethren, he might have contributed to the religious life of his age. What is certain is that by his leadership of the renewed Brüdergemeine he ploughed a well-defined channel along which has flowed a stream, running ever more deeply, of evangelistic labours among the heathen. To that destiny Zinzendorf was drawn and surrendered, led whither he knew not. As Gambold wrote to Spangenberg in 1750 :—

> It was wholly accidental and by him unsought, that he has been entrusted with the Direction of a particular Church.

The Count's connection with the Brethren, Gambold goes on to explain (not, we may assume, for Spangenberg's information, but for the benefit of the British public), was the result of a Divine leading, not of any deliberate seeking on the part of the human instrument. The exiles had settled on Zinzendorf's estate, and he was compelled from due regard to public order to look into their tenets ;

> whereupon his own former convictions concurred to make him support, cherish, and prosecute their Ecclesiastical Platform ; believing it might become an extensive Instrument for bringing many souls to a fuller enjoyment of the New Testament Privileges than hitherto.[1]

It is, of course, that " accidental " " Direction of a particular Church " which constitutes Zinzendorf's main title to a place in modern ecclesiastical history. Versatile as he was and surprisingly modern as were certain of his ideas (*e.g.* in point of the application of practical psychology to educational methods), a bare catalogue of the Count's interests and ideas would be of small value. We are not here attempting an essay in biography ; our concern is with the man only in relation to the community, and even that with the added restriction that we shall confine ourselves to such aspects of his personality and career as may shed light upon the discipline and polity of the Renewed Church of the Brethren. Discussion of Zinzendorf's theology and philosophy is beyond our scope and *a fortiori* must we omit consideration of the multifarious schemes which engaged him in act and speech and writing. His formal treatises, discourses, diaries, and correspondence, compass a

[1] *An essay towards Giving some just ideas of the Personal Character of Count Zinzendorf, the Present Advocate and Ordinary of the Brethren's Church.* (James Hutton, MDCCLV, Lambeth, III. H. 13.)

wide territory. In the breadth of his mental range and in facility for committing his thoughts to paper, Zinzendorf anticipated that " capacity for copiousness " which distinguishes the giants of Victorian England. It is understood that the unpublished sermons by him still reposing in the Unity's archives run into hundreds, and though it may well be that the quality and permanent value of Zinzendorf's published and unpublished remains vary enormously, though much may be ephemeral, there is also much gold, and of the latter not a little will be found to be current coin in the controversies of our own day. The literature which has grown around his memory is formidable in quantity, but fortunately there is now available for the study of one of the most prolific and fecund minds of the eighteenth century, a work by the present Direktor of the Unity, *Zinzendorf's Weltbetrachtung*, von Otto Uttendörfer, 1929, offering an examination of the founder of the Brüdergemeine, as philosopher, theologian and ecclesiastical statesman. Well buttressed with citations from the Diaries, Discourses and Correspondence, the book forms an indispensable aid to the study of the background of Zinzendorf's attitudes on the Church, on politics, on education, on the pastoral office, and, not least, on the organization of the Community with which his name is inseparably associated.

It is the last of those interests with which we are concerned, but it seems right to delay to note one factor in Zinzendorf's *Weltbetrachtung* more central even than his passion for the Unity of the Church. The peculiar cast of the Count's theology is not our concern, but inasmuch as his mental texture and religious experience appear, on every re-reading of his aims and acts, as far more closely knit, coherent and consistent than critics like Ritschl have allowed, it would not be satisfactory to treat of his zeal and ardour in the cause of Christian Unity without turning aside to make some reference to that overruling devotion to the Person of Christ which dominated this and all his other activities.

Bishop Gambold's pamphlet already referred to ends by noting that the keynote of Zinzendorf's character and career was that he kept one point only before him, viz.: " the meritorious Sufferings of our Creator "—" a point for the sake of which alone Christians are distinguished from Deists." From that "one point only" are to be deduced the master motives of Zinzendorf's zeal in the pursuit of those varied schemes to which he set his hand, schemes which range from the inculcation of personal holiness in his own household to the reunion of the four great Branches of the Saviour's Church. The stories of his early conversations with, and letters despatched to, Christ his Brother, of dreams troubled by atheistical doubt, of a precocious mind brooding over the Chorales of Paul Erhardt, the daily reading of the Gospel story with his aunt Henrietta in the old castle at Gross Hennersdorf, are all of a piece with the more mature deliverances of later age. In accents reminiscent of Newman's account of *his* early certitude, he said:

> I was (as a boy) as certain that the Son of God was my Lord, as of the existence of my five fingers (Hutton, p. 179, cf. p. 328).
>
> From childhood his whole nature had been permeated by a well-nigh fanatical loving devotion to the person of Jesus which supplied him with a mainspring of thought and action which he would else have lacked (Wauer, p. 46).

Zinzendorf read, marked, learned and inwardly digested the Gospel story and "was not careful" to formulate his creed in the cry of adoration, "My Lord and my God."

Some have held that much of Zinzendorf's language echoes the accents of that brand of Modalistic Monarchianism associated with Praxeas and Noetus of Smyrna. (Denying the pre-existence of the Son as Incarnate, the Modalists held that the Eternal Father is or becomes the Incarnate Son; hence He suffered in or with the Son; hence the name Patripassian.) Zinzendorf certainly, like them, started from "a high view of the simplicity of the Divine Nature," and expresses himself with stark emphasis. But without estimating the Count's possible lapse from orthodox exactitude, and recalling Dr Sanday's remark: "Patripassianism is much the best of all the heresies," it may be asserted that the danger that a future generation might label his Christology "Patripassian" was not likely to avail with one who had looked at Calvary and seen

Godhead at its divinest, Deity in its most characteristic act, God in Christ suffering and making expiation for the world's sin. Here was Gambold's " one point only " which distinguished the real Christian from Socinian, Unitarian, Deist.

> Unto the Lamb which was slain and hath redeemed us to God by His blood, out of every kindred and tongue and people and nation ; to Him be glory at all times in that church which waiteth for Him, and in that which is about Him, from everlasting to everlasting ! Amen.

So at Bethelsdorf ten years after Zinzendorf's passing, David Crantz, the first historian of the renewed United Brethren, wrote as he laid down his pen. There rings the true Zinzendorfian note of a doctrine of the person of Christ, Johannine rather than Pauline, a faith and a love rooted in the Incarnation as interpreted in a mind in which was fused the mystic's quest for God and the evangelist's passion for souls. To the eighteenth-century Pietist as to the author of the Fourth Gospel, the Son is *homoousios* with the Father ; to both, the Son dominates human history in virtue of their own previous experience and reflection upon the significance of the Man Jesus. Both were disciples first and theologians and philosophers later, and what has been said of the formulation of the Logos doctrine is eminently pointed in its application to Zinzendorf : " It was the overmastering impression of Jesus that he (the evangelist) was trying to make intelligible to himself and others (Garvie, *Christian Apologetics*, p. 112).

Zinzendorf was a Lutheran of Luther's stamp in more ways than one ; each perhaps in his own sphere might be described as a progressive conservative, searching for ways to graft the new upon the old and reluctant to welcome change whether in doctrine, ceremony or the constitution of society. Both passed almost reluctantly from profound interior spiritual experiences to the task of embodying the new doctrinal conceptions there attained in new ecclesiastical institutions. Like his great predecessor Zinzendorf is not seen at his most characteristic work in improvising the new mould into which to run the spiritual emotion he himself had done so much to arouse. (The antithesis, Luther—Calvin, readily suggests the parallel one, Zinzendorf—Wesley.) But in nothing is Zinzendorf so like Luther as in his fundamental position that only in and through Jesus the Christ men find God ; other and lesser ways to certainty, to pardon and peace are a superfluous snare. Luther's " We ought to learn to recognize God in Christ " may be set alongside a report of Dr Doddridge of a conversation with the Count :

> He has an exceeding great regard for Christ, and thinks our business is much more with Him than with the Father, that He is God and that His Father has given Him this world as His property (Benham, p. 61).

Like Luther, too, Zinzendorf saw that it was the Cross which makes the Gospel story " the power of God unto Salvation " ; the famous " Blood and Wounds " theology and even the dubious phraseology to which it gave birth, lead straight back to all that followed from Luther's acceptance of Staupitz's advice, " begin from the wounds of Christ."

The first fact, then, to be noted concerning the Renewer of the Brethren's Church is the Christocentric quality of his personal religion. His is the true prophetic-evangelical type of piety characteristic of German Protestantism, with its instinct for homely colloquy with God, for the preaching of the Word, for simple converse and spiritual exercises in company with like-minded souls, above all, for its warm and cheerful devotion to Jesus the Lord and Saviour.[1]

[1] 1. For further illustrations of Zinzendorf's emphasis on the centrality of the Person and Death of Christ, see Hutton, p. 248 (his instructions to missionaries), p. 257 (the story of his conversion of the Jew), pp. 264–5 (the one adequate basis of confessional unity). Also Zinzendorf to Doddridge, Benham, p. 51 : " Geneva is turning from philosophy to tolerate the ignominy of the Cross." . . . " I disapprove of the conduct of the Brethren who philosophize rather than evangelize " ; also Müller, p. 98, on *der Ausgangspunkt von Zinzendorf's Thätigkeit* ; Zinzendorf to the Conference of 1750, " From a child he had no other plan than to get into personal contact with the Saviour, and to obey His words like a slave, to proclaim the Person of the Saviour throughout the world, not in a formal way, but in the way of the Spirit's illumination and power, and to remove everything which might hinder the coming of the Saviour to the heart.

B. His Detachment from Pietism

Bearing in mind, then, that crucial point of Zinzendorf's experiential theology, we may pass on to note two consequences, or series of consequences, of his dogmatic emphasis, which affected his development in early manhood and much of his activity thence onwards. The first is his break with the then current movement of German Pietism, his emancipation from the personal influence and doctrinal attitudes of A. H. Francke and the University of Halle.

The young Zinzendorf was a plant of Pietistic planting and tendance. The family traditions and the personal attentions of his grandmother, his aunt, his tutor, of Spener himself, moulded his infant mind; the boy of ten was sent to Halle, where Francke's institutions and methods, by their compassionate philanthropies, were proving to the world "the advantage of religion to societies." When at sixteen years of age the young nobleman was transferred to a more orthodox Lutheran environment, he did not discard his earlier loyalties, but set himself to make peace between Wittenberg and Halle. Forced by his family into the State appointment at Dresden, he used his leisure in the work of lay-evangelization, finding a justification in that conception which was to play no inconsiderable part in his own future and which owed its origin to no less a personage than the father of Pietism—Philip Jacob Spener—if indeed it had not a more august parentage in Luther himself, viz., the conception of *Ecclesiolæ in Ecclesia* as the way of renewal and revival.[1]

Everything else, even the formation of the Children of God into a *Gemeingang*, however dear that was to him, was only accessory."

2. For Zinzendorf's character, personal habits and impression made upon colleagues, see:

(*a*) Spangenberg's *Life*, Preface, pp. 24–5, a very revealing piece of self-portraiture. "I am a very happy man . . . but I am not a light or a gay man."

(*b*) Benham, pp. 364–7, and Appendix III, excellent personalia by an ardent disciple.

(*c*) Holmes, I, 426–9: "He was . . . an Original."

[1] That conception will engage our attention in due course; at the moment, following the chronology of events, we note that one consideration in the purchase of the Bethelsdorf estate was that its young master would

Briefly, then, it may be said that from babyhood to his majority Zinzendorf lived and moved within the circle of that genuine spiritual movement in Germany which sought to inaugurate a new reformation based, not on exactitude in dogmatic definition, but on the spread of true godliness and the cultivation of personal piety in intimate fellowship. Of the three major influences upon Zinzendorf's early life—home, school and university—the first two were thoroughly in sympathy with the fundamental ideals of this new revival. Naturally the impress of these early environmental influences never entirely faded, yet nevertheless, within a few years, as travel and contacts with scholars and statesmen of other schools widened his horizon, and as his own individual genius asserted itself, the inevitable happened.

By 1724, when Zinzendorf, now in possession of Bethelsdorf and wishing to secure Francke's approbation of his projects relating to the estate, visited Halle, the sense of strain was acute and a future parting of the ways only a matter of time. The old master and his former disciple held different ideas as to the degree of dependence of the local centres of revival upon the fountain-head at Halle. After that year, and especially after Francke's death, divergences turned to avowed hostility.[1] The rift was deeper than merely personal antipathies or matters of jurisdictional allegiance. It was not likely that one with Zinzendorf's mental range and spiritual orientation should find in contemporary Pietism a permanent home. As the history of Christendom abundantly testifies, where primary principles diverge it is impossible to expect collaboration, even in the practical pursuit of allied ends. When Zinzendorf had worked his way to new emphases in his doctrinal outlook, occasions for controversy with his early preceptors inevitably

be able to apply Pietistic ideals to the poorer brethren, "to promote goodness along the lines of activity suggested by the Pietistic movement." Hamilton, p. 24; Hutton, p. 189, quotes the clause in the Smalkald Articles on which Zinzendorf relied.

[1] Cf. Hamilton, p. 32, "Francke would have been better pleased had Bethelsdorf been distinctly tributary to Halle."

The Gotha Synod of 1740 sent a solemn deputation "to ask pardon of the institution at Halle which was thought to have been aggrieved in several ways; but as it was not accepted, the desired effect was not attained" (Crantz, p. 132).

presented themselves. Moreover, the Pietistic Movement before the middle of the century seemed to be drifting perilously near to bondage to those "beggarly elements" of a new Protestant scholasticism—dogmatism, legalism, and a dry moralism—against which in its origin it had been a protest. For the message of the sweetness and light of a life of Christian faith and love—the *Pia Desideria* of Paul Gerhardt and P. J. Spener—Pietism was in process of substituting the conception of an invariable, necessary and painful struggle for repentance as the one unalterable method of achieving reconciliation with a just and angry Deity. While this was becoming the accent of Halle, Zinzendorf at Herrnhut was preaching the process of salvation, not as one of pain and distress induced by a subjective conviction of sin and guilt, but as an immediate and joyful apprehension of a loving Father, persistently yet gently leading His child into a new life of happy companionship with Himself. Moreover, the growth within Pietistic circles of a methodistic moralism—always, whether in Germany or England, alien to Zinzendorf's inculcation by precept and example of a godly cheerfulness in all innocent social intercourse—hastened the inevitable *Spaltung* between Halle and Herrnhut. Zinzendorf's emancipation from the theological and social rigidities of "Hallensian Pietism" marks a stage in his progress towards the fulfilment of the vocation laid upon him, and it was perhaps inevitable, if regrettable, that at various points of his career the freedom won had to be paid for in the "obstructive tactics of the Hallensian party against anything and everything identified with Herrnhut."[1]

[1] 1. Hamilton, pp. 79 and 190. The Luther—Spener—Zinzendorf problem is most concisely treated in Müller; Section V, pp. 96–98, is especially valuable. The ingrained subjective character of Zinzendorf's religion—which he owed to Pietism—was not helpful to him in his capacity of renewer of an ancient historical Church-Fellowship. And Zinzendorf's antipathy to Separatism made the difficulty the more acute, since "to the Pietist the Church dissolves into a totality of converted and unconverted individuals. Therefore to those who do not wish to progress from Pietism to Separatism it is hard to achieve a positive relationship to the Church." The use of the Lot, too, is encouraged by the Pietistic attitude. On the other hand, Pietistic individualism *did* facilitate the work among the heathen.

2. Cf. Goethe's *Wilhelm Meister's Apprenticeship*, Bk. VI, "Confessions

C. The Unity of the Children of God

The other series of consequences of Zinzendorf's devotion to the Son and Saviour, to which reference was made as being regulative for his thought and action, was his lifelong pursuit of the ideal of the reunion in one "ecclesiastical constitution" of all who profess and call themselves Christians.

Here without doubt Zinzendorf has most to offer to our own age. His doctrinal standpoint, its expression along his characteristic lines, his diplomacy, even definite moral attitudes, may not all commend themselves to the approval of a later century; it remains true that our own generation has much to learn from a man whose unflagging energy was directed to the actualization of the ideal unity of all the children of God. At the least we may learn the right point of departure; this eighteenth-century reunionist awoke and sustained his enthusiasm by virtue of a deep devotion to the Person of the Church's Founder and a passion for the realization of His desire, "That they all may be one," that "My house shall be a house of prayer for all the nations." The ideals of the young aristocrat completing his education by foreign travel remained, chastened perhaps but not forgotten, to the very end; on his death-bed Zinzendorf conversed with the watchers about various matters and "especially the accomplishment of the testament of Jesus, John xvii., 'That they all may be one'" (Crantz, p. 498). Reserving till later an account of the somewhat intricate process by which Zinzendorf reconciled his renewal of the Unitas with his idea of the Church as an invisible Body, a mystical entity transcending all ecclesiastical divisions, it will be of distinct value for an understanding of some later passages in the history both of the man and of the community, to delay to remark upon one episode in his early years. The interviews and correspondence of the young Saxon nobleman and the Cardinal de Noailles, Archbishop of Paris, have other obvious interests

of a Beautiful Soul," for delineation of an experience similar to Zinzendorf's in respect of the *Busskampf*:

"With reluctance I finally adopted the Hallean principle of conversion, though my natural feelings were not wholly in harmony with it."

but concern us chiefly as illuminative of the early convictions held by the younger man before and in the few years following his acquaintance with the Bohemian refugees.[1]

If it is indeed, as the editor of the correspondence suggests, " extraordinary that a young student of nineteen years should feel impelled to concern himself with the state of the Christian Church," a sufficient explanation will be found in the environment of his infancy and adolescence. " Infantile sensitivity to environmental influences " will account for the permanent mark left upon Zinzendorf by his grandmother, Henrietta Catherine, " one of those people who concern themselves with everything to do with the Saviour, irrespective of Church-allegiance." From her, he says, he learned that it is devotion to the Person of the Saviour, it is union with Christ which makes all who call themselves disciples, members of one family. To the propagation of that truth he would like to devote all his energies ; to preach it among Lutherans in Germany, Reformed in France and Holland, Anglicans in England, among Jansenists and Salzburg refugees, to the Coptic Patriarch in Cairo, to the Pope himself. The very glow and warmth of the phraseology of these letters, however attributable to the enthusiasm of youth, is at least indicative of this author's firm grasp of the simple, if sometimes forgotten, truth that the only ground for the existence of a Church is that it may create and promote fellowship among souls who live in a state of ardent love and obedience to the Saviour. Among such souls, unity is already a fact, whatever their confessional allegiance—Roman, Lutheran or Reformed.

> What, Monsignor, would you say to me if instead of quoting Protestant controversial writings, I offered you in all simplicity the Church, Universal and Catholic, as the bond of our brotherhood ? You would say " Good " and retire unto the bosom of the Roman Church, your

[1] *La Catholicité du Monde Chretien d'après la correspondance inédite du conte Louis de Zinzendorf avec le cardinal de Noailles et les évêques appelants*, 1719–1728, par A. Saloman, Paris, 1929 : a selection from two collections in the Herrnhut archives. A further selection is promised, to be devoted to Zinzendorf's correspondence with the Jansenists. The italics in our citations are the original writers'.

> mother, as it was that of your ancestors. To which I reply, "No," that far from falling into sectarianism, I have rescued myself from it, perceiving that the Kingdom is neither here nor there, but quite to the contrary, it is within us. I appoint as your *rendezvous* the heart of our Saviour, and, for guide, His holy life (Zinzendorf to Noailles, 24.9.1723).

Death, he writes in the same letter, is a great simplifier of our problems, and in face of that mystery, the thousand prejudices, imaginations, and misconceptions with which men fill their minds will vanish. Will a man at that moment seek consolation in the cleverest controversial writers ? No, he will turn only to the merits of Jesus Christ, where alone his soul can rest in his sickness and find sure healing.

> I do not believe, Monsignor, that your priests know a better, nor that they commend any other in the hour of death. That being so, would it not be most fair and seemly to leave there all our controversies, and to reunite in the *wounds of our Saviour ?*

It is more profitable to talk of virtue and morality and health of soul than to turn to controversy : "So brotherly love does not suffer and the union of hearts is effected more easily." As St Paul taught, in the final judgment, neither greater accuracy in exegesis, nor prophecy, nor even faith, but only Love, will avail. So the Lutheran will pray with the Catholic :

> Thus, Monsignor, I pray for you, to the Lord Jesus, not staying over those writers, which you as Cardinal of the Roman Church have quoted, who indeed do me no good but only distract me. We will end this interchange and speak only of the spouse of our souls. . . . I leave you, Monsignor, to this good Master ; I honour you in the highest, but I love you much more (30.1.1722).

Such sentiments, however admirable and true, are yet scarcely an adequate equipment wherewith to encounter the actual situation of the post-Reformation divisions in the visible Church. It was inevitable that the correspondence should come nearer to the personal positions and problems of the two men.

A careful and somewhat lengthy letter from the Cardinal (15.12.1725) evoked an elaborate and even longer rejoinder. According to the Cardinal's reading of the situation Zinzendorf has now formed for himself a little flock, separated from the Lutherans, thereby following Luther's bad example in cutting himself off from the august communion of the Catholic Church. If Zinzendorf argues that he has a right to do what Luther did, Noailles will reply that a claim to such a liberty is repugnant to Christian piety and contrary to what has always been believed in the Church of Jesus Christ. Can you bear, he asks, with tranquillity to reject what the Church has taught since the time of the Apostles? Do you feel on firm ground, when you reflect on the one hand that your position is based on principles which Christians rejected in the centuries nearest to the Apostles, and which have led you today to believe yourself solitary and separated from almost the whole Christian world? "*Are you not afraid of your solitude and your situation?*"

The gage of battle thus thrown down Zinzendorf picks up with exhilaration and is not sparing in argument, justifying equally his theoretical loyalty to the church of his baptism and his acts as the lord of the Bethelsdorf estate. The argument runs through the familiar heads of the controversy he would fain deprecate; the nature of Salvation, the obligations of Corporate Religion, the authority of Bishops, the organization of the Primitive Church, together with explanations of the peculiar character and status of the little community the writer has gathered around him at Herrnhut. The familiar note of assurance of the rightness of his own position is not lacking:

> I am persuaded that the opinions of the Church agree with my system in proportion as the Church returns to the times of Jesus Christ and His Apostles.

So far from becoming the leader of a little sect Zinzendorf finds himself a member of a world-wide fellowship of which the little group at Herrnhut is a microcosm. Nay, he pities Noailles who, by reason of his bondage to Rome and

> to that college of Cardinals which he hates, and which is assuredly unworthy of such a colleague,

is denied a free and fruitful access to the wider fellowship. Noailles errs greatly in supposing that Zinzendorf is confined to one little corner of Germany and his Communion restricted thereto. On the contrary :

> I see myself as a member of the great body of that majestic fulness—the God-man—which fills the Universe. I find myself included along with a Pius V, an Innocent XI, a Fénelon, a Quesnel—and close beside my dear Cardinal de Noailles. . . .

At Herrnhut there is fellowship and a common life shot through with the spirit of the Gospel, but there is also liberty of conscience, of worship, of belief, and these are enjoyed by Lutherans, Reformed, Roman Catholics, and various lesser groups. Here, in fact, is a lesson, not in theory, but in life, worthy of the notice and emulation of the greater world. The motive-power is not love of licence, or innovation, or contradiction ; the principle of his actions is " the establishment of *Salvation from Above* which alone can change the heart, and *lead men to act in accord with their Creator* " ; a work beyond the power of any ordinary mortal, but one to which Zinzendorf has set his hand to carry through in all the Churches as in his own, " *without mixing myself up in anything to do with the Ritual and external laws of these Churches*."

Such, he is convinced, is the Saviour's way. He respects Antiquity—but that means getting back in organization and spirit to the times nearest Jesus Christ and His disciples. He is strongly disposed to recognize the necessity of bishops, provided that " all ecclesiastics holding jurisdiction " may be so called. The Catholic Church is a fact, but does not find its centre in Rome. In fact, the word " church " is equivocal and must be defined more closely ; for his part, though he dislikes the formation of diverse sects, a rigorous interpretation of the word would lead to the position that there are as many churches as there are assemblies where the Gospel is preached, and the test then becomes whether that preaching approaches or declines from the Truth as taught by the Lord and His Apostles.

In that interpretation " the assembly which meets every

> Sunday in my house to talk over the Pastor's (morning) sermon is as much a church as that of Rome."

If, however, we are thinking of the One Universal Church, then we must mean the entire body of which Christ is the Husband and Head,

> the Church recognized under the great names of the mystical Body of Jesus Christ, the Spiritual Assembly of God, the Fulness of Him who fills the Universe.

And neither the Lutheran nor Reformed nor Anabaptist nor other community can properly claim that lofty title.

> For my part I call members of the true Church only *those who are Christians . . . because they are born of God.* (Zinzendorf to Noailles, 9.3.1726.)

It is not perhaps surprising that at such high discourse the Roman Cardinal falls back from argument to appeal.

> Can I see you heading for certain shipwreck and not invite you, urge you, and implore you, to come aboard that ship which alone can bring you to port (Noailles to Zinzendorf, 23.4.1726).

And that, too, seems as unanswerable! It is not true that "Rome does not change," neither was it likely that the earnest outpourings of a young, eager and dogmatic mind should have made much impression on a dignitary grown old in the service of the Roman Church. Zinzendorf, for his part, was neither deficient in the conviction of the truth of his own position nor forgetful of his dignity as a nobleman, a patron and protector of humbler folk, as to make his "conversion" at all easy. Each went his own way; Noailles to tread the path of submission to a centralized ecclesiastical authority; Zinzendorf to more and more intimate relations with that little colony of Protestant refugees who were enjoying the protection of his civil authority, and in connection with whom he was to devote his life to an attempt at exhibiting to the world, first at Herrnhut and then on a wider stage, his conviction that varying ecclesiastical traditions and even doctrinal diversity need not impede the gathering together into one Body all the true children of God.

D. The Many Churches

No doubt it would be unhistorical to represent Zinzendorf as having reached maturity in his views on the divisions of Christendom when he despatched his last letter to Cardinal Noailles. Without question there shines through that correspondence the younger man's "chivalrous glow, his brotherly love, his aspirations for the unity of the Christian Church," and most decidedly "the whole religious scheme of the future founder of the Moravian Brethren is in these letters sketched in outline" (Introduction to Correspondence, p. 9). No doubt life and experience and meditation were yet to do much in the way of addition and modification; perhaps, indeed, of "exaggeration and deformation." Yet none the less in that department of his thought which is our special concern, it seems possible to affirm that to the end there was no loss of intellectual interest or slackening of arduous activity in pursuing the ideal of unity on the same simple basis that the Saviour yearns to see all members of His family dwelling under one roof. However, in face of apathy or hostility, and by virtue of the more concrete precipitation of his ideas as he moved from thought to action, the Count, and still more, the Brethren's Ordinary, found himself committed to the task of almost unintermittent explication of the corollaries of those early ideals and principles.

Both the permanence of his principles and their fuller unfolding in the stress of argument and controversy will, it is believed, become apparent in the quotations now to be given.

> There is nothing easier, he said only a year before his death, than to hold the true Faith (Glaube). To have no faith at all is natural, but when a man has one, it is most natural to have the right one. What is the cause that there are some eighty faiths in Christendom of which, however, no more than one can be true—one more or less, since perhaps none is completely correct, though one is nearer the truth than the others, so that if they are all mixed up

> and the related ideas compared, out of the eighty faiths one would be the better? How is it that this does not happen, though it would be so easy and presents so little difficulty?
>
> Answer: Because the mass of Christian men never yield without reservation to the Creator, to the Holy Spirit and His illumination and guidance; they always and in all ways get out of the pupilage by the Holy Ghost—not indeed so much openly as by mental reservation in the spirit of their minds. One holds to some preconceived opinion, in another the motive is fleshly . . . a third will not take the trouble (Uttendörfer, p. 78).

Both the Protestant Confessions suffer from a spirit of dissidence, the spirit of a crude, rough handling of truth, a spirit of contrariness. They strive merely from defiance and uphold what formerly had not been upheld or even had been denied. It was this love of contradiction for its own sake, or from motives of sectarian jealousy, which was to be lamented, not necessarily and absolutely the fact that Christians of different temperament, education and tradition, allied themselves in different bodies for the culture of the spiritual life.

The modes of apprehending the one truth as it is in Jesus, and its expression in organization and worship, are as diverse as we might deduce from a survey of the difference in the racial, national, and social traditions and customs. Zinzendorf would have applauded heartily—indeed, the verbal similarity is striking—the sentiment of the author of the *Religio Medici*, that there is "a geography of religion as well as of lands," and that reformations in every country have proceeded "according as their national interest, together with their constitution and clime, inclined them." Thus in 1746 he observes:

> The Religions (*i.e.* the Christian Churches) are facts of nationality (Nationalsachen) adapted to the customary temperamental disposition of the people.

With greater elaboration he says in 1744:

> Religions are God's economy, machinery to bring Truth and the Love of His Son to men according to their capacity,

> and according to the temperature and atmosphere of the country. For England the English Religion is suitable; in the Spanish and Portuguese atmosphere, the Catholic; for the French temperament the last is not quite so fitting; hence the Gallican Church, a *misch-masch* of Catholic and Reformed with more Freedom than in other Catholic countries. Protestantism suits Germany and still more the northern lands. The Saviour has all the Religions under His protection and will not let them be destroyed. So that even were the Catholic religion abolished in a country where it now is, it would not be Lutheranism but Atheism that would take its place. There is a little Italian city where the Catholic Church was abolished, but in its place has come no Protestant community, but Arianism and Socinianism—the Italians when they have freedom to reason do not turn to Spener but to Servetus and Socinius (*Ibid.*, p. 79).

God's dealings with man, that is to say, vary according to epochs, generations, countries, even climates; the truth of the Gospel is one, yet is mediated through the varying personalities of prophets (who are men of some one definite time and place) and through "the quality of the rulers of this world." To recognize thus plainly the facts of history and experience can do no harm but good, provided always that all the sons of men recognize, too, their community of spirit as members of one species, and "educate themselves towards an identity of feeling."[1]

That summary must serve to represent the main tenor of Zinzendorf's theoretical answer to the actual presence of the confessional divisions of the Europe of his day. Later we shall see the problem of the churches as "Nationalsachen" filling a large space in his thought and diplomatic activity, and we are now to examine one of his favourite "Ground-Ideas" by means of which he trusted to overcome the divisive effects of nationality. Yet before passing from these higher ranges to a more mundane level, it is not valueless to reflect that there

[1] For further illustrations of Zinzendorf's valuations of the different church-constitutions, see Uttendörfer, II. 2. d., Die Wertung der verschiedenen Kirchen und Richtungen, pp. 80–88.

is never an age when mankind does not need seers and teachers who, like Zinzendorf, will remind it of those higher levels and of the " Community of Spirits " where lesser matters of tradition and custom no longer divide. His biographer has said of Lord Bryce (*Life*, I, 324) that " with a mind nurtured in elemental pieties " he was both a staunch Presbyterian and also " one of those rare beings, an undenominational Christian." Reading Lutheran for Presbyterian, the antithesis is true of Zinzendorf; and if the attribute of " undenominationality " may to some savour of blame rather than of praise, there are others who, while upholding with warmth and affection the peculiar excellence of their own church-constitution, are content to find in the Book of Common Prayer a warrant for an attitude of respectful toleration towards other great Confessional Communions, including (by submission to the spirit rather than to the letter) such as would not or could not describe themselves as National Churches.

> And in these our doings we condemn no other Nations nor prescribe anything but to our own people only: For we think it convenient that every country should use such ceremonies as they think best to the setting forth of God's honour and glory, and to the reducing of the people to a most perfect and godly living, without error or superstition (B.C.P., " Of Ceremonies ").

The words are a text on which the Brethren's Ordinary was to preach many sermons.

E. Das Tropenprinzip

In attacking the problem presented by the unhappy divisions of Christendom, Zinzendorf relied much and often on a conception of his own, variously referred to as *Das Tropenprinzip*, *Die Tropenidee*, *The Tropus-Idea*. This conception he continuously offers as presenting a method, first of softening and ultimately of eliminating the barriers between one " religion " and another. The term occurs frequently in Zinzendorf's own discourses and in the apologetic pamphlets put forth by the English Brethren. Largely by the assistance of the ideas grouped under the term he was able to re-orientate his position, and to continue to act as the Patron and Ordinary of the Unitas when it became apparent that the members were bent on attaining the status of an organized and self-standing church-polity. Some elucidation of the phrase is therefore necessary to a due comprehension of the relations of Zinzendorf to the Brethren, and of both to the Lutheran, Anglican and Reformed Churches.[1] By *das Tropenprinzip*, says Wauer, Zinzendorf meant

> that as the unity of the spirit can be kept in spite of the diversity of creeds and liturgies, so the peculiar Moravian genius (τρόπος) of the emigrants could retain the old Moravian discipline and forms of worship, while the other members of the community might as rightly retain the Lutheran or Reformed ritual they had been accustomed to (p. 52).

But it should be added that the idea had reference to things deeper, wider and more pervasive than questions of ritual and worship ; τρόπος is a way, a manner of life, a habit, a temper, a character ; it is the " conversation " of the true children of light, who, bearing with one another's different emphases and tolerating each the other's incomplete apprehension of God's whole truth, endeavour to keep the unity of the spirit in the bond of peace. The Tropos (or Tropus : Zinzendorf's usage varies) in its simplest essence is first a school in which to learn the lesson of Unity ; when the lesson has been learned the school will be done away. The scheme of instituting the various Tropoi (Tropi) is not therefore an end in itself ; it is a piece of ecclesiastical machinery adapted, like other processes of education (tropoi paideias), to the capacity of the learner as he or she grows to maturity.

[1] The term so transliterated is in classical usage definable as (i) direction or way ; (ii) manner, fashion or mode ; (iii) a way of life, habit, custom, character, temper. (So Liddell and Scott.) For the N.T., see Matt. xxiii. 37 ; Acts xv. 11 ; 2 Thess. ii. 3, and iii. 16 ; Phil. i. 18 ; Jude 7, and Heb. xiii. 5 ; where A.V. has " conversation " and R.V. marg. " your turn of mind."

Uttendörfer, II. 2. b. provides citations showing Zinzendorf's long-continued attempts to make plain to his disciples his own understanding of the term.

In 1751, St Paul is noted as the best exponent of *die Tropenidee :* " To the Greeks I became as a Greek, to the Jews as a Jew, that I might win many." Since we cannot assume the Apostle chose deliberately to become a hypocrite, this must mean :

> If I come to Paul, I submit myself to Paul's method and manner ; if to Peter, likewise ; if I am alone, I can hold the truth as I wish.

Yet this is not to become an indifferentist, to tolerate a *General-religion* ; the Tropoi are means to guard against that very error ; all human institutions have their infiltration of error and the Tropoi prevent its spread from one community to another. St Paul means that men have many ways of measuring truth, and all—Lutheran, Reformed, Pietist, Brother—must be allowed to use that method apposite to their own individual case. The actual constitution of the human mind necessitates that the Ultimate Truth must be viewed by different bodies of men from different angles ; both Logic and Charity, therefore, will prevent adherents of one group condemning members of another or even endeavouring to entice them from their present allegiance.

> The difference of the " religions " is a divine wisdom, not to be overthrown by any one " religion " ; all ideas, however, bear the impress of their human origin and of them one can say : " Men did not so think for 300 or 500 or 1000 years." There is only One of Whom it is to be affirmed " Yesterday, today and for ever," and His Church rests there. (1746; Uttendörfer, pp. 75–6.)

What is deducible from an analysis of the human mind is supported by our (partial) understanding of the intention of the Divine Mind. In 1758 Zinzendorf, protesting that he has founded no other religion than that of the Saviour is, nevertheless, firmly of opinion,

> that in the plurality and multiplicity of the various schools of Christ's religion lies one of the deepest intentions of God, whereby His spiritual Empire and Unity are not dissipated but where there may afresh arise a universal

political Church-Empire (ein allgemeines politisches Kirchenreich) which hides itself behind the forces friendly or hostile which please the temporarily most powerful and important Party. To that predominant opinion Christianity may attach itself for 50, 20, or even 10 years, and the fashion of that ecclesiastical dress and livery may change as often as suits the Powers-that-be, so that the Church in one age must become Arian, Monothelite, Eutychian, Nestorian, and that opinion alone is termed orthodox which is dominant at the moment (*Ibid.*, p. 77).

If this seems to take us too near to Gibbon's dictum, that the saints are those whose views ultimately prevailed, a corrective will be found in the larger lesson stressed by Zinzendorf throughout his voluminous discourses, that the Christian seeking assurance and certitude need not faint in weariness and despair, and that the restful finality of faith, when attained, will be found to be none other than the simple "original religion of the Saviour" which men must seek for diligently, humbly and in co-operation one with another. *Das Tropenprinzip* he put forward as a scheme leading to that necessary and fructiferous co-operation.

Chapter II

THE RENEWAL: KIRCHE ODER GEMEINE?

A. The Ancient Unitas Fratrum

FROM our all too incomplete study of the "Renewer" of the Brüdergemeine we turn to survey some salient points in the process of Renewal, to watch the human agent as he seeks to actualize his Church-ideas first in Germany and, later and with more detailed attention, in our own country. One large sphere of his extensive interests we must leave almost without notice. His attempts to transplant his ecclesiastical ideas across the Atlantic can be only mentioned. In face of the spectacle of the chaos of creeds and the vast populations lacking any spiritual ministrations presented by American life in the first half of the eighteenth century, the optimism and energy of one ardent soul bent on unity were foredoomed to failure. Zinzendorf was too much a child of the old world, with its family pieties, its attachment to the State Church, its leadership based on birth and ancient tradition, to have become a successful propagandist, even of ideas less original than his own, among the heterogeneous mass of exiles, rebels, sectaries then slowly finding their way to a loose and undefined nationhood.[1] In point of fact, the events of the next 150 years were to show the American Branch of the Unity leading the Anglo-Saxon protest against the limitations imposed upon the Brethren by the patron to whom under God they owed their resuscitation. That protest has not been unsuccessful and successive Synods of the nineteenth century mark, by their constitutional rearrangements, increasing dilutions of the Zinzendorfian ideas with the freer and more independent spirit of American and British Moravianism. The Renewer of the Brethren was not the first nor the last idealogue to find himself defeated in action

[1] S. G. Dimond, pp. 21–23. On American Moravianism, Bishop Hamilton's bulky volume is a mine of information.

by the opposition of counter opinions held as tenaciously as his own and having behind them the forces of the ideas and movements which were destined to mould the ideas and institutions of the future.

While, then, remembering that today far the most numerous of the Provinces of the Renewed Moravian Church is the American, and that the story of its institutional development is at least as full of romance and significance as the history of its sister-Province in Great Britain, it is on affairs this side of the ocean that we now concentrate. And first, some attempt must be made to understand the real character of the " Moravian " exiles, their traditions and past history, their hopes and intentions, the political and ecclesiastical circumstances attending their settlement on Zinzendorf's estate.

Our concern, indeed, is with them and with their spiritual descendants and with their first patron only as they reflect certain phases of his ideals and aspirations. The Moravian Church in Great Britain today rightly claims spiritual descent from an ancient episcopal Church whose fathers made their protest against the Church of Rome before ever the great German Reformer nailed his theses on the door of the Castle Church of Wittenberg. The very name " Moravian " carries us back to the valleys and villages of old Bohemia, to the land and times of John Huss, of Ziska the warrior, of Peter of Chelçic the Christian pacifist, of Gregory the Patriarch who leaving his monastery was later to become the founder of the Church of the Brethren in the valley of Kunwald, back to Luke of Prague and the inflow of German members and German influence into a Czech environment. There are *two* historic spots in Moravian history bearing the name of Fulneck. Yet to trace that long spiritual ancestry is not our task ; we must concentrate on certain points in the later story at which the fundamental convictions of the " Renewer " came into contact with the dim memories, the sparse literary relics, the vague traditions of the first exiles, indicating the subsequent modification of both viewpoints as the twofold stream of influence flowed out into the wider fields of Continental and Anglo-Saxon life. It is a far cry from the prosperous colony of godly artisans and small merchants at Herrnhut about 1760 to the semi-

Utraquist Böhmische-Brüder isolated in the Kunwald valley, and farther still from either to the modern Moravian Church House " in streaming London's central roar."

We must perforce relinquish any full examination of the significance of the old Bohemian Brüder-Kirche and the character of the influence it exerted, a century after its practical extinction, upon the " Renewed Church of the Brethren." We should have to trace with more detail than is here possible, the process of its evolution from a company of " Gospel-Christians " to an independent church with an ethos, tradition, cultus and polity of its own—exactly the same process as was repeated throughout the eighteenth and nineteenth centuries in the case of the communities associated with the career of Count Zinzendorf. Further comparisons and contrasts suggest themselves, each with its significance in relation to the disease and cure of Christian disunity.

The fundamental feature for our purpose is the fact, common to both histories, Ancient and Renewed, that neither begins as the history of a " church " but as the history of a Gemeinschaft, a Unität, a Brüderverein—a Fellowship, a Unity, a Brotherhood. Such designations, drawn from the " Ancient " history, are yet quite apposite and customary in describing the " renewed " Church or Brüdergemeine until, at any rate, the constitutional changes of the later nineteenth century and the further effects of the Great War had come to slow fruition.[1]

The ancient Unitas was perhaps more markedly a product of nationality than the renewed, but of both it is true that the key to the characteristic quality of its being lies within the circle of the idea of a " *Gemeine* " as applied to the local group, with the honoured and expressive title, *Unitas Fratrum*, as its corollary wherewith to indicate the whole membership. Each Gemeine will be seen at its characteristic function in embodying the ideal of the unity of the true children of God, cultivating their spiritual life within a religious " Gemeinschaft " of those who have found in Christ their Saviour and

[1] The reservation should be noted. Hutton, pp. 70, 71, insists on the full ecclesiastical standing of the original Bohemian Brethren—" Unitas Fratrum " is a misleading translation and its common use by the Brethren later is due to an excusable error. This opinion is, of course, quite contrary to that maintained in these pages.

Lord. Among both ancient and renewed Brethren, this eirenical ideal was pursued with ardour; it was only after bitter and repeated discouragements that they capitulated to the stress of circumstances, seceded from the national reformed churches, and became "eine selbständige kirche." In the case of the old Brüder Kirche the two contributory causes which led to the impossibility of maintaining its "Unions-charakter" were, as is well known, the ruthless persecutions of the Counter Reformation and the internal dissensions of the reformed churches at the same period. In the case of the renewed Gemeine the story of the reluctant acceptations of the same status is less harrowing if more intricate.

B. Herrnhut, 1722–1729: Three Statutory Documents

That the young owner of the Bethelsdorf estate did not know whither events were taking him when he allowed the exiles to settle beneath the Hutberg is not surprising. He certainly was without information as to the true character of the old Bohemian Brethren; to him the successive bands which Christian David guided over the mountains were merely so many persecuted Protestants who would desire nothing better than to be allowed to worship God in peace and quietness, always, of course, paying due deference to himself as Lord of the Manor. Loyalty to the Lutheran Church and to the Augsburg Confession was not so much commanded as assumed.[1] With the Lutheran pastor's assistance, the Count was at first fully occupied in dovetailing the new settlement into the parish organization, with schemes for schools, printing-shops and similar social ventures. Apparently Herrnhut was left very much to its own devices under the kindly supervision of pastor and steward, until dissension and schism evoked two administrative *acta*:[2]

[1] The details of the composition of the first family-groups to settle at Herrnhut are most easily accessible from the Rev. J. E. Hutton's graphic narrative of Christian David's epical journeys (*e.g.* pp. 194–202). That active itinerant himself, of course, shared Zinzendorf's ignorance of the old Unitas. It was only the third group (the Nitschmanns) who represented the old stock; they intended to seek out their fellow-Brethren in Polish Lissa (p. 196, note, p. 200).

[2] Printed in Müller, Appendices I and II; cf. pp. 23–25.

(*a*) Herrschafliche Gebote und Verbote: published and signed 12th May and 15th June 1727:

(*b*) Brüderlicher Verein und Wilkür in Herrnhut: 4th July 1727.

The first, the *Manorial Injunctions and Prohibitions*, was compulsory and therefore signed in a corporate character by all the inhabitants of the new settlement. The second, the *Brotherly Union and Compact* (the so-called *Statutes*), was voluntary and was signed singly when and as the signatories wished to enter a free, inner, religious Gemeine. The one was civil, the other moral, in its compulsions, and while the first included inhabitants of Herrnhut, the second was not so embracive, and was, moreover, signed by a few non-residents. The important point to be noted is, however, that under neither document was there any idea of confining the authority of the document to Moravian members of the community. Even the voluntary compact was directed to the perfecting of such Christian folk as, according to Luther's phrase, are "Christians who mean the word with earnestness" and therefore bind themselves together for mutual assistance in spiritual progress. Naturally it was recognized (Par. 4) that the Moravians, as descendants of the ancient Brotherhood and possessed of their ideal of fellowship, have given the first impulse to the founding of this Brüderverein. The Brotherly Union went no further than the creation of a voluntary society of persons who, as individuals, added an agreed mode of communal life to their precedent obligations of loyalty to the greater society; in this case, the Lutheran Landeskirche. As to the Manorial Injunctions, they simply inaugurated a village constitution differing little from that obtaining on many another Saxon noble's estate.

The whole series of events with its issue in these two documents was only a local application of the famous formula: *Cuius regio eius religio*, with perhaps a more democratic tinge to the proceedings than other landowners would have tolerated. In the eyes of the lord of Bethelsdorf, two happy results had been attained:

> As the lord of the manor he had crushed the design to form a separate sect; and as Spener's disciple he had persuaded the descendants of the Bohemian Brethren to form another "Church within the Church" (Hutton, p. 207).

It is true that these remarks refer to the period before Zinzendorf's discovery of the ancient Brethren's *Ratio Disciplinæ* in Comenius' Latin version. So far, the Count had been entertaining Brethren unawares, and the discovery in the Zittau library did, in fact, shed some light on the path his feet were treading and on the quality of the guests he was entertaining. Yet it is obvious that the mere recognition of a connection between the new community and the old did not have that revolutionary effect upon his aims and intentions which subsequent generations of the spiritual heirs of the old Brüder Kirche have imagined. The very similarity of his own legislation to the ancient discipline would tend to conceal the fact that here was a renewed community rising from the ashes of the old. The organization and social communism of early Herrnhut might be strikingly similar to the discipline of 300 years before, but that must not be taken to imply an identity of the two bodies.[1]

Acquaintance with the *Ratio Disciplinæ*, great as was its effect in opening Zinzendorf's eyes to the true character of the old Brüder Kirche, did little or nothing to shake his conviction that the new Brotherhood was not meant to be, and should not become, an autonomous "church"; they were to be nothing more than a Communion, a Fellowship, a Gemeinschaft, organized, indeed, for its own special ends, but always within the confines of the National Church. From that conviction he never wavered. Indeed, it was after the discovery of Comenius' work, and after his instruction by Buddæus in the history of the Bohemian Brethren, that the Count's vacillation culminated in the proposal to abolish the new regulations and to merge the new settlement in the general civil and ecclesiastical discipline of the Manor.

[1] Cf. Hutton, p. 225. Also Müller, pp. 26–8. The latter discusses the affinities and differences of the old Bohemian organization to and from the "Statuten," and concludes that the resemblances spring "not from any direct copying but simply out of the similar character of two (communities)."

The discovery in the Zittau library had probably a greater effect upon the exiles than upon himself in so far as it led to a greater pride and enhanced loyalty to the traditions of their fathers. But whatever deductions *they* might be disposed to draw from the similarity of the Statutes to the Ratio, *he* persisted in his error in holding that the Bohemian Brethren were never strictly a *Church* but only a *Society* within a Church, and that his position could and should be upheld. In his eyes all that had been done so far was that the new Gemeine had unwittingly renewed the complete organization of the Bohemian Brethren, "with the sole exception that while their Fathers had been with the Reformed Church, they were henceforth joined to the Lutheran" (Müller, p. 28). That was not true, and the mistake was of deeper origin than mere confusion of "reformed" and "Reformed" (the former being employed in the sixteenth century in a mere general anti-Catholic sense, and not, like the latter, as a definite Confessional designation). "Zinzendorf was so far right that *in Bohemia*" (not in Moravia nor in Poland), "the Brüder Kirche after 1609 had formed a Gemeinschaft inside the national Evangelical Church, with the same Creed but with its own constitution and discipline" (Müller, p. 31). But (apart from these two important territorial reservations) this alliance was political in origin and not representative of the essential features of the Brethren's spirit and polity. In any case, much water had flowed under the bridges since 1609; it was not by relying on the authority of the (misconceived) example of the ancient Brethren, but under the impulse of his own preconceived and doctrinaire notions that Zinzendorf went forward with his plans for the institution of a Gemeine inside the Lutheran Church, to which it was to be bound by the terms of its constitution and by doctrinal loyalty to the Augsburg Confession.

. . . . .

One other document of this first stage here falls under notice. To official criticism that he was founding a new church, Zinzendorf felt there was already a sufficient answer in the *Notariats-Instrument* (August 1729). Here in legal form had been amicably settled the relationship of the new settlement to the civil and ecclesiastical authorities, as represented by himself and the Lutheran incumbent. On the basis of this document, it could be shown :

(1) There was no intention of founding a new sect ; the process is rather the renewal of an ancient Gemeine (Pars. 1, 2).

(2) The Moravian exiles are not to be compelled to renounce the constitution they have inherited from their forefathers—that of 1457 granted by King George Podiebrad (4, 9). For doctrinal standards, they retain the declaration given by the Faculty of Wittenberg, 1575 (11). For historical justification they turn to Buddæus and Comenius (13).

(3) They will cultivate fellowship with other Brethren and other Gemeinen, but only with such as attain the Lutheran standards of Church-membership : "We know no visible Gemeine-Christi save where the word of God is taught purely and plainly and men through it live holy as children of God" (5, 6).

(4) As to Bethelsdorf, *i.e.* to the Lutheran parochial system, it is agreed that the exiles join the public worship there "so long as our freedom in the Lord is not restricted" (10). (Müller, pp. 37–39.)

Zinzendorf and Rothe issued a complementary Declaration in the same month, and these positions became the basis of the new community. So long as the inhabitants of Herrnhut continue in a simple, peaceable and non-schismatic behaviour and temper, they are to be allowed to enjoy religious freedom, to pursue their extra-parochial exercises and are acknowledged as descendants of the ancient Bohemian Brethren.

Both sides no doubt viewed the interchange with satisfaction. The Moravian position was now much stronger : the Gemeine in Herrnhut, though it must not develop sectarian tendencies, is recognized as the natural outgrowth of an ancient polity ; moreover, it is no longer dependent for its justification on any utterances of Luther respecting the nature of the visible church. Zinzendorf, for his part, having conceded the retention of the old name and discipline could believe he had merely recognized these descendants of Bohemian Brethren as Brethren still, fit material for a Gemeine in his sense: *ecclesiola in ecclesia*. He did not at all concede, in so doing, that the old Brethren had been a "church," "an historic ecclesiastical entity, with its own Confession, Cultus and Constitution" (Müller, pp. 40 f.).

Had the Count thought otherwise he could not have acted as he did in the beginning of 1731. Nor indeed could the two hundred or so inhabitants of Herrnhut have possibly developed a very ardent "church-consciousness" or they would not have received his suggestion of the abrogation of their new liberties with such submissive equanimity. It is questionable whether they would have felt this was quite the sort of issue for the decision of the Lot. No more need be said on that transaction than that Zinzendorf's proposal was certainly one method of achieving organizational unity! But it was a method more reminiscent of modern Ultramontanism than of eighteenth-century Pietism; the success of the proposal would have spelled, not a true unity of diversities, but absorption of the less into the greater. In any case the Lot said No, and the events immediately following called both the settlers and their patron to fix their eyes on wider horizons. The links between them were reinforced by the opportunity and the duty to undertake in co-operation certain heroic enterprises of which all the world has since heard. The fundamental differences of which we have spoken in these paragraphs, were never entirely dissipated, but they rose to the surface only on intermittent occasions of crisis and were then more or less satisfactorily adjusted until, finally, Zinzendorf had passed from the scene.

Only so much can we delay to note of this first period of contact between Zinzendorf and the Moravian exiles. It is perhaps enough to have shown the gradual dissipation of the Count's ignorance of the old Bohemian Brethren, how slowly and haltingly he came to his always partial understanding of their few descendants, and how the vacillation of his direction arose from the conflict of their desire for self-realization as a community with a noble lineage and his own definite Lutheran antecedents. The "Tropenidee" may be regarded as in part the result of that conflict, and that development of his thought in turn may serve to illuminate the transition from the community on his personal estate into the *Unitas Fratrum* of the later decades. To that wider field of activity and controversy we now turn. So far as the first home of the renewed Unitas on the Bethelsdorf estate is concerned, the formative period of transition extended for another twenty years or so, during which time it was ecclesiastically united with the parish church a mile away. Steadily developing "communal, liturgical and doctrinal features of its own" the new settlement on the Zittau high-road achieved practical independence, and two years before the Count's death a legal agreement in this sense was effected between himself as representing the Brethren and the authorities of the State Church. This emancipation of the new settlement from the old parish organization affords a not inapt analogy to the wider and longer process by which at last, within the present decade (1922), the Moravian community has in the land of its renewal finally attained a position of legalized independence and autonomy. The problem, both in Germany, and in the country of the third migration, the British Isles, is the perennial one of the adaptability of the living organism to a new environment. The renewed Unitas had now to succeed, as in the storms of the Counter Reformation it had not succeeded in either Bohemia or Poland, in the twofold task, first that of creating an organization, stable enough to conserve its own distinctive ethos and, secondly, elastic enough to provide opportunities for assimilating into itself such elements of the populations in the new fields whither it spread as were likely to be attracted to its particular type of spiritual culture.

Some phases of that twofold process of consolidation and adaptation amid a Lutheran environment are now to be noted; parallel events moving to the same end in our own country will receive fuller treatment in the following chapter.

C. Community-building, 1732–41

(i) *External Opposition*

"The characteristic features of our Church," says a modern Moravian apologist (the Rev. C. H. Shawe, *The Moravian Church and what it stands for*, 1927), "are to be regarded rather as the impress of its long and eventful history than as the expression of any deliberately adopted doctrinal view or ecclesiastical theory." But the supersession of a theory in the course of the years is not the same as its absence at the beginning. If what is meant is that at its Renewal there was no intention on the part of the chief agent to organize a new independent ecclesiastical organization, the statement is true enough. That, however, is not likely to have been the writer's intention. The fact is, surely, that the characteristic features of the modern Moravian polity and much of its doctrinal emphasis are the results of definite tendencies, long and earnestly deliberated upon, during the last two centuries. The true situation is that the triumph of those tendencies has necessarily pushed into the background the very definite "ecclesiastical theory" of Zinzendorf himself and, it may be added, of such stalwarts of the first age as J. de Watteville, Gambold, Hutton, and La Trobe. That portion of the "long and eventful history" during which Zinzendorf was guiding the community's destiny presents at frequent intervals the conflict between two very deliberate and definitely held conceptions of the place and function of the new society in Christendom.

The persevering attempt of the Brethren's Ordinary to reconcile what he himself saw clearly enough to be two complementary, if not contradictory, ends, may surely evoke our admiration even though we may also feel that that task of reconciliation was an impossible one. His own death and the firm and gentle rule of that great soul, August Gottlieb Spangenberg, "in his element as an organizer," definitely marks the emergence of a new corporate self-consciousness and the declension of the earlier body of ideas (the *Gemeine-Tropen-Diaspora* scheme). But it was long before the historical development reached its inevitable end and, as we shall see, voices of protestation against the new orientation were raised from time to time by those who felt themselves qualified to speak, both as true and faithful disciples of "the late Ordinary" and as students of their Church's origins.

To recall these facts does not, of course, imply any unwillingness to accept the fact of the existence of a strong and self-reliant and independent Moravian Church in the present, and as we review the history of the renewal of the old Unitas, we can distinguish two main streams of influences running contrary to the original plan of the Renewer: so far it *is* true that the characteristic features of the existing Church present the impress of the experiences of the past.

(i) The traditions of their Fathers in the old Bohemian Brüder Kirche.

(ii) The hostility of the civil and ecclesiastical authorities who, either from misunderstanding or incredulity, refused to countenance Zinzendorf's community-building.

To these a third may be perhaps added: the natural desire for local and national freedom in a community or group of communities, becoming conscious of possessing qualities and experiences inexpressibly dear to themselves and likely to be equally profitable to those whom they might attract into their fellowship. This third impulse, however, in the early years, became closely related to the first, and led to greater emphasis upon the identity of the new regulations with the *Ratio Disciplinæ*.

Before, then, we come to the actual content of the communal organization (in fact or in supposition inherited from the ancient Brethren), let us delay to note the impulse given towards organization by that further circumstance in respect of which the new and the old Gemeine were alike, namely, hostility from without. When, following the official examination by the Commission of 1732, the Theological Faculty of Tübingen had returned an emphatic affirmative in reply to the twofold query: (*a*) as to the identity of the new Moravian Brethren with the old Brüder Kirche; and (*b*) whether, that admitted, the renewed community could rightly maintain their 300-years-old institutions within the Lutheran Church, the Brethren confidently expected that the work of rebuilding the walls might be put in hand forthwith.[1] But " Put not your trust in princes " was an exhortation with equal point in Bohemia under the Counter Reformation and in the German states of the days of Frederick the Great. The *Unitas Fratrum* was reborn in persecution and that, not only in respect of the appearance of the harassed refugees under Christian David, but also in respect of the definite Gemeine-polity organized at first tentatively within and then, with increasing momentum, outside of, the State Church. It was the disapprobation of the National Church, including many of the Pietist party, together with the ill-concealed economic utilitarianism of the civil power (each developing after the apparently happy issue of the Tübingen enquiry) which impelled Zinzendorf and his colleagues stage by stage to a more definite and independent organization. The quality of this impetus should not be lost sight of in any endeavour rightly to appraise the development of Zinzendorf's ideas on Christian Unity in their contact with the renewal of the Unitas. As he once said, it was not the friends but the enemies of the Moravians who were responsible for the new constitution. That fact illuminates much of his own conduct and gives a certain emphasis to the Moravian view of their polity and place among the modern Church systems. Ritschl, strong Lutheran as he was, found one cause of his dislike of the Brüdergemeine in his suspicions that this " Gemeingrundung " of Zinzendorf was an attempt to transplant Catholic monasticism into the Protestant world, where there was no need for any such monastic or semi-monastic " orders " independent of the ordinary pastoral discipline (Müller, p. 17). The criticism is interesting, but its error is obvious; the analogy lacks finesse and appreciation

[1] Zinzendorf's view is put in the later, *Plain Case of the Representatives of the Unitas Fratrum*, London, 1754 (Lambeth, 112 f. 16). P. 2 quotes " The Responsum of the Divines at Tübingen," " the Purport of which was, that the Brethren, dropping for a while the use of, though not renouncing their Peculiar Church Form in public, ought on the other hand to be welcome guests in the Presbyterian Churches, and be hindered by nobody from exercising all the Branches of their Discipline in private."

of the first elements of Zinzendorf's system. The Moravian Committee for negotiating with the Anglican Church are strictly historical in rejecting the conception of their position as analogous to that of a special "order" within the greater society like the Cistercians or Franciscans within the Mediæval Church-Empire, or like Port Royal within the Gallican Church. Before the troublous times and the needs of an expanding community turned Zinzendorf to the creation of a constitution, he was able to claim that so far as he had fostered a new organization, he had done nothing more than what Luther himself had advocated—"das bekannte Projekt Luthers, das dieser in seiner Deutschen Messe entwirft"—and that along with the Lutheran pastor, Rothe, he had only brought into existence a little community of small groups, united in a voluntary social and religious Brotherhood, that he had only carried into effect a scheme envisaged by Luther himself in looking expectantly towards a time when "die Christen, so mit Ernst das Wort meinen, sich selbst finden und anhalten" (quoted Müller, p. 18). If now, so Zinzendorf argued, we have come to the Kingdom at such a time as Luther envisaged we may not deny the Divine leading at the frown of those who do *not* "mean the word with earnestness," and who have decided to neglect this very element in the Reformer's teaching. As for the fact that the Herrnhuters were largely descendants of a pre-Lutheran Gesellschaft or Brüdergemeine, that did not seem to him any warrant for their exclusion from the scope of Luther's "Projekt." Moreover, in 1733 he could point to the deliberate judgment of an unimpeachable Lutheran Theological Faculty that the Moravian Brüder-Gemeine could both hold to its ancient institutions and yet remain in church-fellowship with the Evangelical churches of the Augsburg Confession.[1]

[1] Müller, pp. 46–7. Cf. Zinzendorf's *Exposition or True State* of the matters objected to in England to the people known by the name of the Unitas Fratrum, Part II, 1755; Lambeth, 112 f., 15: "I have a real attachment to the spirit of Luther" . . . "I have never intended publicly or privately to profess any Doctrine contrary to the Augsburg Confession . . . and *am not conscious that I hold any tenet* contrary to that Confession" (p. 2). "My brethren of the *Lutheran Tropus* and I have no other doctrine than what is taught by that school" (p. 3).

Thus as Zinzendorf saw the position, he was engaged in upholding the true teaching of the German Reformer against those who refused to act on what Luther had himself hoped for. How far the Lutheran authorities in Dresden were justified in their view of the situation is not our concern. What is to our purpose is to note that in encountering their opposition, their opponent found his own mind supplied with an adequate theoretical justification and grew more rigid in insisting on his own large liberty, his rightful heritage, in the fostering of the new community. That point clear, we need not carefully discuss the nice point of detail (examined by Müller, pp. 12–13) whether Halle, with its Christian social compassions, or Ebersdorf, with its family devotional groups, most correctly transmitted to the young noble the ideas of a *Gemeine Christi* which Spener had learned from Luther.[1]

(ii) *Internal Organization*

In 1738 the Count, by then in Lutheran orders, was temporarily exiled from Saxony. Yet neither that climax of Authority's disapproval nor social ostracism nor Pietist intrigue did anything more than confirm him in his conviction that it

[1] For the sake of clearness we note briefly Müller's summary of what Zinzendorf had in fact accomplished at this stage (1733).

(*a*) *Bethelsdorf*: an ordinary Haus- or Schloss-Gemeine on the Ebersdorf model.

(*b*) *Herrnhut*: a communal religious brotherhood, a Verein, a Gemeine—perhaps here better, *Gemeinde*, as embracing all the inhabitants of the civil parish.

(*c*) *Also at Herrnhut*, but with a few adherents elsewhere, a Moravian Brüdergemeine conscious of its own traditional discipline, now definitely within the Landeskirche but with all the possibilities of becoming more and more an independent church.

"Thus," says Müller on this critical phase, "the institution of the Gemeine in Herrnhut from 12th May 1727, belongs essentially to the original Christian-Community-Foundation side of Zinzendorf's activity, yet is seen in historical perspective as the beginning of the renewal of the Brüderkirche, and the Moravians indeed have from the beginning so held" (p. 17).

That "historical perspective" of two centuries revolves round the two foci: external hostility from Church and State, and the growth of a Church-consciousness within; it is from these two centres that the origin and expansion of the renewed Unity, on its constitutional side, may be most readily understood.

was perfectly possible to assist in the reorganization of the Moravian Church without disloyalty to the Church of his baptism. Before and after his expulsion he was occupied in securing the stability of the new community now under his leadership; hence the importance of the decade following the visit of the Commissioners (1732) in the formulation of the characteristic features of the renewed Unitas as an organized body. Throughout this period there arose stage by stage the external fabric of a Church of the Brethren, with its own Ministry—diaconal, presbyterial, episcopal—Synods, Discipline, Settlement-System and Overseas Mission. In the remarkably short space of ten years or so the process proceeded, the building, fitly framed together, becoming sufficiently firm-knit to survive the autocratic abolition of many of its parts at the hands of its architect at the Hirschberg Synod (1743).

The plan of the edifice was examined and authorized by the first four Synods, 1739–41, those of Ebersdorf, Gotha, Marienborn, and London. Their work in constructing the new Church-institution may, though by no means exhaustively, be noted in respect of the five following elements.

1. *The Synod*

In stressing the place of the Synod in the governmental machinery the modern Moravian is returning to a principle of his Church's renewal. The community over which Zinzendorf presided was never, from its earliest years, without its informal interchange of consultation, and the growth of a corporate consciousness was fostered by more deliberate and formal assembly in Conference and Synod. With Zinzendorf's hearty co-operation, the early years of the renewed church saw the revival of those two healthy elements both of the undivided Catholic Church and of the Brüder Kirche: the episcopate and the synodical participation of clergy and laity in the initiation and execution of policy and in the administration of discipline. And in so doing, Zinzendorf and his colleagues "laid the foundation of modern Moravian Church life." The composition of these early Synods might be doubtful and varied, their powers and authority dubious, their relations to other governmental organs ill defined—witness the events of 1743 on Zinzendorf's return from America—but it was an enormous gain to the future movement towards a systematic ordering of a democratic Church order, that its exponents could point for justification to an early practice which, once begun, remained for future imitation.

2. *Leadership : Clerical and Lay*

(i) Much as was the case in the apostolic church, the "office-bearers" of the renewed Unitas included certain trusted and capable men, administrative officials, who shared with the "spiritual" leaders, the bishops, the oversight and direction of the Church. Their emergence at the Synod of Marienborn (1745) and their subsequent importance as business-managers and intermediaries between the ecclesiastical and the civil authorities would afford an interesting study. Spangenberg recounts their origin:

> The Count . . . proposed for deliberation, whether something which had been formerly customary in the Moravian Church could not be usefully renewed amongst them. He thought, for instance, it might be well if the Brethren had *Seniores Civiles*, who should be commissioned to take charge of the secular affairs of the Church, which did not altogether accord with the duties of the Bishops.[1]

The Synod chose two "principal seniores" and two *con-seniores civiles*, and such names as those of Abraham von Gersdorf and Henry Cossart recall at once how valuable such offices were to prove. The distinction between the episcopate, with its concentration upon spiritual and pastoral oversight, and these officials to whom was entrusted the financial, legal and administrative side of the organization, had obvious practical advantages altogether apart from the impulse of

[1] *Life*, p. 350. But the ancient office had been clerical, not lay. Holmes, I, pp. 67–81, tells us that the ancient Brethren preferred "Senior" to "Bishop" because the Romish bishops had usurped princely authority. "Conseniors" were assistants to the bishops, and both ranks together formed the Ecclesiastical Council which was subordinate only to the General Synod. The other ranks of the ministry were Presbyters, Deacons, Acoluths, and Elders, male and female.

precedent practice, and has been preserved, at least in the German Branch of the Unity, down to the present.

It is to be noted that in actual direction of policy there neither has been nor is any absolute and exclusive separation of the two elements in the leadership; the convenience of committing specific "secular" concerns to the "Elders" has not and does not imply that a Moravian "Bishop" may never be allotted high administrative duties in addition to his spiritual office. The early "Boards" and "Executive Committees" (if so we may refer to, *e.g.* the Herrnhut Elders' Conference, the Board of Arbitrators, the Board of Twelve) were in no case purely clerical or lay—a characteristic feature preserved even when, after 1741, the differentiation of function had become more fixed.

(ii) The kindred question of the place of the *Elder* and his position *vis-à-vis* the Bishop need not long delay us, though that problem is not without its bearing upon the degree of accuracy with which Zinzendorf may be described as the Renewer of the ancient Brüder Kirche. A resolution at the Gotha Synod (1740) seems to give precedence to the Eldership:

> Die Bischöfe sind *über* den Ältesten mit Ausnahme des Generalältesten und des Ältesten in *der* Gemeine, wo der Bischof gerade ist (Müller, p. 72).

Actually their functions were so different, "that the question of *over* or *under* was in practice without significance." What is clear, and germane to our discussion, is that Zinzendorf himself looked to the Eldership to furnish Watchmen and Pastors and to the Bishops for external ordering and jurisdiction. Precisely the opposite was the case at the end of the century, when the supreme jurisdiction lay with the Unity's Elders' Conference and the more pastoral and prophetic ordering was the work of the bishops. If fear of prelacy and papalism was the motive in the attempt to minimize "the office of a bishop" there seemed for a short space a similar danger lest the Chief Elder should become "a Protestant Pope" in his own community, "the Elder of Herrnhut being at the same time General Elder of all other Moravian congregations" (Wauer, p. 49). "He had been elected by Lot, and was therefore supposed to possess Divine authority. . . . He had authority over Zinzendorf himself, over all the Bishops. . . ." (Hutton, p. 266). The danger in Europe at least, was averted by the famous decision in Red Lion Street, London, 16.9.1741: "That the office of General Elder be abolished and be transferred to the Saviour." Thereafter the situation may be stated: either that the Moravian Church was represented by its Bishops, or the *Gemeine Jesu* (of which they are the first-fruits) through the Elders, especially through the Chief Elders. Zinzendorf himself preferred the latter conception as exhibiting more clearly the fraternal quality of the new community. Bishops were necessary *for the time being*, only because the Moravian Church is the (temporary) home of the *Gemeine Jesu*. His attitude was subtle but not therefore incoherent: viz., by the balance of the two offices (Eldership and Episcopate) to further his dominating aim while providing organization which if transient was necessary. All was to conduce to the avoidance of sectarianism and the nurture of a true *Gemeine Christi*.

(iii) In the organization of the Ministry, the liveliest interest naturally hinges round the revival of the *Episcopate* of the ancient Unitas, by the consecration of David Nitschmann (1735) and of Zinzendorf himself (1737). Neither consecration implied separatism. The first, as with Wesley's ordinations, found its motives in the necessities of the work overseas.[1] The second (Zinzendorf's own consecration, under the encouragement of two such diverse advisers as Frederick William I and Archbishop Potter) placed him in the anomalous position of being at once a Lutheran clergyman and a Moravian Bishop. But however difficult posterity may find it to estimate aright the significance in Zinzendorf's own mind of the two

[1] But compare Hamilton's comment on Jablonski's Letters of Consecration to Nitschmann, pp. 70, 71: "In the judgment of Zinzendorf the episcopate which had thus been transferred was intended merely for the foreign missions, and was not in any way to separate Herrnhut from the Lutheran Church or to be significant of independent organization. Yet just these things necessarily resulted. The first ordination performed by Nitschmann was that of John George Waiblinger, not as a missionary, but minister-elect of the settlement at Pilgerruh in Schleswig, 29th July 1735; nor did he afterwards confine his exercise of episcopal functions to the supervision of missions and the ordination of missionaries."

offices, it is at any rate clear that he himself did not conceive that his progress from the status of a Lutheran presbyter to that of a Bishop of the Moravian Church implied any weakening of his adherence to his original plan for the Unitas. Not once only, but many times after his own exercise of his episcopal power to ordain, notably at Hirschberg (1743) and Marienborn (1745), did he insist on the necessity of avoiding sectarianism, and that his aim was *not* to set up an independent Moravian Church but to forward the ideal of gathering all Christians as into one wide and open and equal " Community of Jesus."

This conviction, therefore, must not be lost sight of in discussing the episcopal character of the church order of the Gemeine. A similar warning is necessary in respect of the revival of the subordinate orders.[1] The new Ministers were reminded that they had been called to serve, not the Moravian Church merely, but a wider and more embracive fellowship, the " Church of the Brethren "; their ministry would be exercised among Lutherans, Reformed, and the children of other Confessions who would not change their " religion " in joining the Brethren. In other words, it was on *Das Tropenprinzip* that Zinzendorf relied for his general reply to cynical scoffer and ardent " denominationalist." There were two further lines of defence: the conceptions of the *Pilgergemeine* and of the *Diaspora*.

3. *The Pilgrim Church* (*Pilgergemeine*, *later*, *Pilgerhaus*).

This peculiar element of the early organization took shape at the important Synod of Hirschberg, 1743, and remained a central feature of the administration until Zinzendorf's decease. Ideally, it was

> a union of men and women whose mission it was to proclaim the Saviour in the whole world and who therefore itinerated from place to place in accordance with the needs of the cause.[2]

[1] Deacons and Deaconesses proposed to Synod 1745. There were already " Deacons " in the modern Free Church sense, and also women " labourers." The new order, of both sexes, were now to be ordained by imposition of hands. The ordained Deacon, apparently, was to be qualified to administer the sacraments (Spangenberg, p. 350).

[2] Hamilton, p. 73. The duties of the Committee of Pilgrims are noted in Benham, p. 119.

Its origin, aptly enough, is to be found in the Count's banishment from his own estates (1736).

> From that time (wrote Spangenberg) a company of pilgrims always assembled around him: for wherever he was, the brethren and sisters who were employed in the Lord's service generally made his house their home. When they returned to their destined stations, they conferred with him, and were accompanied by the blessing of the Church, in his house. If he changed his residence the brethren above-mentioned generally accompanied him: and thus himself and his inmates were literally strangers and pilgrims upon earth, according to the expression of the apostle (p. 211).

In more definite terms it was a college of servants, secretaries and agents grouped around Zinzendorf and his closest intimates, whom he directed in the prosecution of the work in Germany, England, America and among the heathen. He appointed its members (with the approval of the Lot) and changes were frequent as the individuals departed on their specific errands. The Headquarters, too, changed from time to time; it began in Wetteravia but operated subsequently in Berlin, Holland, London, Yorkshire and elsewhere. The members received no stated salary and were supported as need arose from gifts mainly from Zinzendorf's own resources. The corporate life of the household was nourished by a round of daily services; and the discourses in which Zinzendorf unfolded his mind to these colleagues were copied by the Schreiber Collegium and transmitted to the Brethren throughout the world. A "Pilgrim" according to Zinzendorf's own definition is "a Philadelphian with a Moravian coat and a Lutheran tongue"; his mission essentially is, first to bring souls to a knowledge of the Saviour and then clothe the souls so saved "in their several religious habits, as Lutherans, Anglicans, Calvinists, Moravians" (Benham, p. 118).

The Pilgergemeine did not endure as a permanent part of the Moravian polity, but some slight notice of it seemed necessary, not only because in his lifetime Zinzendorf found within its intimate fellowship the scene of his most devoted activity, not only because it indicates the happy union in his mind of a strong originality and a deference to scriptural precedent, but also because he found in it a means of reconciling his growing immersion in the oversight of a new ecclesiastical constitution with his simultaneous and repeated affirmations of the transient nature of that new organization and its not distant absorption in the one great church of the Saviour.

4. *The Diaspora Plan*

On the other hand the extension of the pastoral care of the Brethren to the " sojourners of the Dispersion " has remained a lasting result of the Zinzendorfian conception of the Brüdergemeine as the servant of all the Churches. The English and American Provinces have not, save in rare instances, regarded themselves as agents of a deeper spiritual culture ancillary to, and in supplement of, the parochial ministrations provided by the National Church. Such a plan must clearly be far less apposite to a situation such as that of North America, with its ingrained independency and actual welter of multifarious churches and sects, than to the Germany of the eighteenth and nineteenth centuries with its two predominant Protestant systems and its strong repugnance to confessional heterogeneity. In this country, the Diaspora-plan soon fell out of favour but was not without its apologists in the last century. In Germany, despite the effects of the Revolution in loosening the exclusive character of the Lutheran parochial system, the plan still proves its value. A small group forms an inner bond, accepts the moral and devotional standards of the Brüder, and, naturally with the consent of the parish clergy, welcomes the ministrations of the Brethren's agents. This " extra-mural " pastoral activity extends over a wide and religiously diverse territory : the Bavarian Palatinate, the Rhine Valley, Silesia ; and, outside Germany, in Switzerland, Norway, Sweden, and increasingly in the old lands of origin, Moravia and Bohemia.

The relevance of this feature of the early propaganda is sufficiently indicated in some figures provided by a Moravian historian to whom the idea does not greatly appeal ; before the Great War some 120 Diaspora workers were ministering, from 60 or 70 stations, to some 70,000 souls, while yet only six new " congregations " had been organized. " Thus do the German Moravians uphold the Pietist ideals of Zinzendorf."[1]

5. *Classes* (*Choirs*) *and Bands*

The characteristic local unit of the renewed Unitas was, as on the Continent it still is, the *Settlement*. Here Herrnhut and other early centres strike the keynote. Partly as the result of encouragement on the part of prince or landowner who was glad to welcome a small influx of industrious and capable craftsmen, partly to avoid the appearance of competition with the parochial system of the National Church, there developed that "settlement system" which played so large a part in the further expansion of the Unitas. It was a disciplinary system at once economic, social and religious. In a manner not unlike the mediæval monastic settlements, groups of Brethren congregated at such quiet solitudes, remote from the greater centres of population as Niesky, Herrnhaag, Pilgerruh, Marienborn. There, as a few years later in England, a township would arise wherein the civil regulations, the economic occupations and the round of religious observances might subserve the Moravian devotional ideal. Social life and public amusements were so regulated as to promote fellowship and innocence. Suitable business enterprises and occupations were fostered, the sick and aged cared for by the community, hostels provided for the various "Choirs." As it may be put, the regulations of the *Gemeinde* (the civil parish) were directed to the furtherance of the social prosperity and spiritual health of the *Gemeine* (the community of Brethren). Significant, of course, at such settlements as Herrnhut and Niesky, were the training colleges for missionaries and the boarding-schools; both indicated two of the most fruitful lines of development. As has been well said, "wherever the early Brethren built a church they built a school." The "diacony" or the organization of the industrial side of the settlement, has had a chequered history. It suggests by analogy the parallel development in the Jesuit Order which hastened

[1] Hutton, p. 491. The origin of the name is usually given by reference to 1 Pet. i. 1; the idea, though not the word, cannot be better exemplified than in John xi. 52.

its suppression at this very period. Yet here again the Brethren's fortunes in Germany afford a contrast to the situation in Great Britain.

This system of communal settlements will occupy our attention later when we discuss its influence in retarding the numerical increase of the British Province ; we pass on to note how, either within the settlement as within a shell, or as more or less isolated offshoots in the monastic mode, there developed that system of spiritual discipline and moral invigoration which, along with the work of pioneer-evangelism, is the most obvious feature of these early decades. It is true that the system which produced the typical Moravian township of eighteenth- and nineteenth-century Germany, and was transplanted thence across the wide oceans, seems in process of dissipation or even, in England and America, of disappearance. Yet it holds a most honourable place in Moravian history, its influence is by no means exhausted, and it has had, through the Methodists, no inconsiderable influence upon British Nonconformity. The amount of the Methodist debt to the Brethren's Church is a matter for discussion and many of the features of the corporate devotional life founded on the Brotherly Agreement (the basis of the settlement life : see later) have no peculiar Moravian significance—the Prayer Meetings, Singing Meetings, Bible Readings and the like—but are common to most religious revivals. What is peculiar is the system of group-division now to be noted. The details of this system no doubt are changeable and elastic enough to have given rise to much discussion and the exact content of the vocabulary employed in discussing it is sufficiently intricate ; so likewise is the question of its antecedent impulse in Zinzendorf's development—origins as diverse as Roman Catholic or Pietistic influence have been suggested. In any case, we are once again led to notice how Zinzendorf's reluctance to encourage separation shows itself in polity as in theology. He may be said to have anticipated Macaulay in seeing that a great Church, national or international, should be able to welcome and encourage within its own wide borders all kinds of subsidiary associations.

The Classes (later *Choirs*) were compulsory groupings based on sex and age ; the number seems to have varied from seven to eleven, of which today those including children, single men, single sisters, married, widows and widowers still survive at Herrnhut. Hence the fine and spacious *Choir Houses* in the architecture of the typical Moravian settlement on the Continent.

Within the Choirs were the *Bands* (*die Bänden*; after 1736, *Kleine Gesellschaften*), small groups of three to seven persons meeting periodically to

> converse heartily and kindly over their whole hearts with one another . . . for more complete nurture in the Lord.

On the organization of the early Bands, the Count spent much care. Freedom and elasticity seemed to have been his guiding principles: "The souls must not be overdriven." If either a private member or a Helper (Convener, *Bändhalter*) did not derive benefit from one Band he might move to another. Organization is for man and not *vice versa*. The Helpers were subject to the control, and availed themselves of the advice, of the Band Conference. They were like a General Staff on the field.

> Watchful and careful they viewed all points of the battle-array and endeavoured to fix their field-dispositions so as to throw back the enemy. . . . By virtue of their Band-organization, they marked which individuals the enemy sought to alienate from their fellowship. At these points they focussed their cares in prayer, exhortation and punishment and thus very often gave timely assistance to the weak brother and sister (Herrnhut Diarium, 10.3.1735).

The Band system was subjected to outspoken criticism, but it proved its value; it combined a sense of a corporate consciousness with a due emphasis on individual responsibility for the moral health of the whole community; it was a buttress to the weak brother and an opportunity for those gifted with capacity for subordinate leadership to prove their quality. Its success in assisting expansion is undoubted; the diaries of such ardent evangelists as Martin Dober and Peter Böhler show that whenever the seed was sown and took root, there Bands were immediately organized. In or around a single year (1733) the system spread to neighbouring towns and villages like

Zittau, Görlitz, Ebersdorf, Jena, Hennersdorf; even at Tübingen, the students and professors "straightway hastened to organize Bands."

> The Band organization secured friends for Herrnhut from outside, and the Bands were adapted to other localities, . . . whence the Herrnhut influence spread.

Among such localities to which the system was adapted were Oxford and London. The agent was that lovable soul and accomplished "*Bändenhalter*," Peter Böhler. His method of "awakening" was, like St Paul's, to move from place to place leaving behind a group of awakened souls who in fellowship and under a few simple rules might be expected to keep alive the flame of a warm-hearted religion of love and obedience to the Saviour. The two Wesleys watched him at work at Oxford where he formed a Band (Diary, 28.2.1738). Later, 12th May, he meets the older Wesley, back from Oxford, and reports him as one among other Brethren who are of one mind, seeking a nearer fellowship, "and want therefore to begin a Band." "I discoursed with them about the fellowship of the children of God. They received the word with joy and wish so to be and so to remain ever after joined together in union." Here both the vocabulary and the spirit hail from Herrnhut; the Bands are to be distinguished from Classes, and are free Unions open to the more earnest souls seeking a richer fellowship.

The formal organization under the famous *Orders of a Religious Society meeting in Fetter Lane*, 1.5.1737–8, marks the definite crystallization of the London group in the Herrnhut mould. Any differences (and there are several redactions of the Orders) were in the direction of even greater elasticity, *e.g.* the easy transference of membership from one Band to another. Each Band had its convener and every Wednesday there was a general Conference of the whole Fellowship. An agreed contribution was collected every month. The relative contributions of Böhler and John Wesley in these regulations is doubtful. One fact is, however, certain; the system was thoroughly suited to the genius of the nascent Methodist organization and the principles were embodied in the practice of the new United Societies formed by Wesley after 1740, especially at London, Bristol and Newcastle.[1]

D. The Struggle against Separatism

Signor Mussolini once remarked, in disclaiming any responsibility for the subversive activities of German Fascists, some of whom made pilgrimages to Rome to see him as good Catholics came to see the Pope:

> Dass der italienische Faschismus kein Exportartikel ist. We recognize no imitators. We have nothing to do with them. I know no Fascists outside Italy; there are indeed none. (Interview in *Berliner Tageblatt*, 11.5.1930.)

It was a dictum which might be true for diplomacy but not for a social philosophy. No great body of doctrine, political or theological, ever lived in a series of disparate compartments, national, provincial or local. Rome, Canterbury, Geneva, Moscow, cannot but become springs whence flow, open or underground, streams of refreshment to revivify the spirits of their lovers dwelling in dry places or by distant oases. Conversely, unless indeed one excepts Papal Rome, such centres will themselves be subject to influences flowing inwards from the circumference, and the broad outline of the particular faith and doctrine professed, the total genius, ethos or atmosphere, will be the result of the complementary motions. "Canterbury" may serve as a shorthand symbol of Anglicanism, but the policy of the remotest missionary diocese is not without its effect on that rich complex totality, the Anglican Communion.

[1] (1) *The Nature, Design and General Rules of the United Societies*, issued by Wesley in 1744, includes "Rules of the Band-Societies," and they are no other than a short extract from the rules of the Fetter Lane Society.

(2) Detailed examination of the Band system in *Zeitschrift für Brüdergeschichte*, 1909, 2: "Die Bänden oder Gesellschaften im alten Herrnhut," von Gottfried Schmidt.

(3) As to their transference to England, see our later and fuller treatment. Sources in Herrnhut archives, R. 13, A. 19, Englische Ordnungen, Zinzendorfischen Periode, 1737–55; Wesley's *Journal*, Sect. II-IV (1.2.1737–3.9.1741); Hutton, Bk. II, Chap. IX; Wauer, pp. 62–66; Benham, pp. 29–32.

The resuscitation of the ancient *Unitas Fratrum* affords many an instructive illustration of this process of exchange in the interpretation of the general doctrinal position held by all its adherents, near or far. From Herrnhut or from the Pilgergemeine flowed a stream of influence and a series of authoritative injunction throughout the membership in Germany, Great Britain and America. Of the source and character of that influence we have already seen something and shall later see more. There is no need to reiterate that the strongest single impetus in the stream of centrifugal influence was contributed by Zinzendorf himself, and that always he saw the new Brotherhood as a tiny rivulet making its way to join the great ocean of the one wide *Gemeine Christi*, the one Holy Catholic Church. The Moravian embodiment of the ideal universality of the Gospel and the Church was very much, in his view, an " Exportartikel."

But it must not be forgotten that there was a second species of formative influence, the centripetal, flowing from the scattered settlements and societies and personalities who and which, for one reason or another, found themselves in communion with the renewed Brüder Kirche. They were not seldom the exponents of a series of ideas and aims running counter to those prevailing in the inner circle of Zinzendorf and his associates. Motived, usually, either by reminiscences of the traditions of the old Brüder Kirche, or by a natural spirit of independence, their desire and intention was not to see the polity we have just described quickly merged in a wider and more universal communion, but to work out their own corporate salvation, with fear and trembling indeed, but with increasing independence of any other ecclesiastical loyalty. Such men saw themselves laying the foundations of a new " historical-church-organization," having its springs doubtless in the far-off past, but now developing its own Constitution, Worship, Doctrine and Traditions ; their chief saw in all such tendencies treachery to his own deepest convictions, his own task he visualized as that of a man leading a select company of pioneers, who may set up a tent from temporary necessity but know well that soon that modest accommodation will have become unnecessary and inadequate and give place to better.

> Every dweller retain his *Heimatrecht* in the Church in which he was nurtured—and retains it however long or short it be ere he reaffirms his right (Müller, p. 95).

Or the Gemeine may be compared to a war-trumpet or battle-horse which may assist the victory, but is not the victory; the victory will be the triumph of *die Tropenidee*. Then the war-horse may be discharged. Hence it followed that the Gemeine is not a Church; he rejects the appellation as applied to a band of Brothers:

> Es ist ein Corpus, das heisst die *Brüder* (Müller, p. 94).

On the reception of this attitude by his colleagues perhaps the best commentary and summary of the situation until the Count's decease is supplied by his most devoted and able lieutenant. Spangenberg relates how after Zinzendorf had stressed his Tropenidee at Marienborn in 1745,

> He was obliged to suffer himself to be opposed in this, by individuals, who otherwise loved and honoured him, although he felt so assured that it was acceptable to God, that he did not suffer himself to be drawn away from his purpose, and, at length, succeeded in convincing them of the necessity of the thing (p. 349).

The members of the Synod may have been convinced, or may have succumbed, to the force of an ardent protagonist expounding his ideal; but not all the Brethren were at Marienborn, and both practically and argumentatively the opposition manifested itself throughout the remainder of Zinzendorf's life. On his death the question was slowly but inevitably solved by the logic of events, in particular by the increasingly firm demands of the Anglo-Saxon Provinces for some measure of provincial autonomy in respect to Herrnhut, and of definite detachment from any semblance of dependence upon any other church. The circumference closed in upon the centre and the advocates of independency carried their cause.

To confine ourselves for the moment to events in which Zinzendorf was a participant, it will be convenient to distinguish *two* periods of his leadership, broken by a *third*, that of his long residence in England, which receives fuller treatment in the next chapter.

(i) *Before Residence in England*, 1741–1749.

The year 1741 saw Zinzendorf on his way to America and inaugurated a period of eight years of most arduous journeyings in that Continent, in England and in Europe. These diligent peregrinations may fitly symbolize the spread of the Community, both numerically and in extent. Yet however its agents and members might increase, its Ordinary abated none of his determination not to allow it to become a new sect. As the American historian puts it, the Count at the time of his visit and after imagined he had wrought out a method enabling men

> to accede to the desire of Moravians to have the disciplinary features of their ancient Church preserved to them, and at the same time, maintain the connection with the parish organization (Hamilton, p. 36).

That attitude has, of course, been noted before ; what we are now observing is its reaffirmation under conditions much wider in their scope than those of the days when the lord of Bethelsdorf would have no schism on his estate. We are hearing the identical *motif* sounding incessantly through all the varied experiences so briefly alluded to, from the early days of the Herrnhut *ecclesiola* to the " Recognition " of the Brethren by the British Parliament. On that latter occasion, indeed, Zinzendorf announced that he was prepared to lose the Act of Recognition rather than countenance the name " Moravian Brethren " which seemed to him to imply a church-organization based on national characteristics. The religious society which he was asking Parliament to recognize was no church, of Moravia or elsewhere, but a Unity of Brethren whose bond was their grip on real and vital religion. For creed as standard they turned to the Augsburg Confession, and for their great vocation—the preaching of the Gospel—to the Synod of Berne (1532). Both historical references pointed to the reconciliation, and not to the accentuation, of differences.

Neither the name "Moravian" nor the specific discipline it connoted, was essential or desirable (Müller, pp. 91–3).

Before 1749, "the renewer of the old Brüder Kirche" had emphasized his disinclination to accept that rôle, if, by so doing, he found himself involved in the creation of an independent church. His protests increased in vehemence if not in effectiveness as the course of affairs and his absorption in the Tropenidee more and more seemed to him to confirm his faith in his Master's plan to gather into the one fold all His sheep. Thus when in 1741 he visited Geneva, "the proper seat of Calvin and the mother of many Presbyterian Churches," and there met many inclined to separation, he at once did all he could to discourage such—and that at the same time as he was propagating an account of the Brethren's origin, doctrine and discipline. He would permit no strangers to join the "regulated meetings" in his own house and sent his domestics who belonged to the Reformed religion to communion at the Parish Church.[1]

A much more serious exemplification of the theory comes from the American visit. There, between September 1741 and February 1743, the Count, under the style of Mr Von Thurnstein, was indefatigable in works of religion and philanthropy, preaching to Lutheran and Reformed, establishing societies and schools and seminaries, issuing a collection of hymns and an edition of Luther's Smaller Catechism, and, not least, undertaking dangerous and arduous tours among the Indians. Yet amid the partisan and, at times, violent clash of sects and creeds (Crantz, p. 257, enumerates some twenty) Mr Thurnstein could not forget the old world where rank still counted and kings and prelates and superintendents still imposed some measure of ecclesiastical regimentation. He would at least rescue "his beloved Lutherans" from this welter, and if possible, draw them into union with other orthodox Protestants. Hence in Pennsylvania he discarded not only his rank but his Moravian episcopal office in order to appear merely as a Lutheran clergyman. In this capacity he organized a Consistory and, still in line with Luther and Spener, provided

[1] Crantz, p. 252. Spangenberg's picture of this visit illustrates various picturesque features of Zinzendorf's habits, pp. 282–6.

regulations on the model of the *ecclesiolæ in ecclesia.* He preached in Reformed pulpits, but took measures to provide such congregations with ministers of their own Church from Europe. And for six months he laboured at an imposing attempt at Church Reunion, presiding as Syndic over seven General Conferences convened by circular letters to Lutheran, Reformed and other orthodox Confessions. By the fifth conference, the enthusiasm of some had waned ; the remnant, failing to achieve any definite constitutional union, merely bound themselves to a spiritual union of love and fellowship, the *Gemeine Gottes im Geist*, and even that loose confederation could not long maintain itself. It remains an interesting incident in American Church history ; its significance for us lies in the light it casts on the Count's handling of material even less amenable to his own idealistic projects than that with which he was called upon to deal on his return to Europe. That return provides a severely uncompromising expression of his viewpoint.

Back in Herrnhaag (the centre proposed for members of the Reformed Tropus) in April 1743, the Count followed up an epistolary protest sent from Bethlehem by " making himself fully acquainted with the various changes which had taken place in his absence . . . and sought to amend the faults which had been occasionally committed " (Spangenberg, p. 326). This involved correction of the acts of the Board of Twelve in the matter of the " concessions "—those entered into with the Counts of Isenburg, the general concession in Prussia and the special concessions in Silesia and Saxony—as well as the allied problem of submission to the Lutheran consistories. The Synod of Hirschberg (July 1–12) saw these matters settled to Zinzendorf's satisfaction, except in the important field in Silesia, where, it is noteworthy, the Lutheran clergy themselves objected to the inclusion of the Moravian Gemeine (*ibid.*, pp. 330, 338). Elsewhere he succeeded as effectively as Colonel Pride—and with as little permanent success—in purging the Brethren of separatistic tendencies. He reversed the process by which " the idea of confessional unity gave way before economic and industrial improvement." The Prussian Concession, especially, evoked his anathemas as being the outcome of simoniacal bargaining, not of genuine confessional liberality, and as, from the basest motives, leading to a sharp delimitation of the Brüder from the Landes Kirche. Motive and method were equally culpable. As he said roundly at the Synod, "The Brüder are and will remain a Society within the Lutheran Church" (Müller, p. 83). Both worldly prudence and Divine vocation should teach them that they were not, and must not become, a "fourth religion."

The subsequent colloquies between Zinzendorf and his colleagues are of prime importance in estimating his future position, theoretical and practical. They ended (11.21.1743) in the solemn vocation given by the Brethren to him to become "the Servant of the Protestant Moravian Church invested with full power." Almost a year elapsed before Zinzendorf answered the call, and the delay may well be due, as Müller (p. 84) suggests, to the contradictory position in which he found himself. He saw the necessity of some measure of independence; equally he was aware that his own convictions would not permit him to assist in establishing a new constitution over against the existing "religions." The way out of his difficulties appeared in his written acceptance; he would accept the position of "authorized servant" (bevollmächtigen Diener) if they on their part would accept his Tropenidee and incorporate that conception within the constitution of the Brüdergemeine (Müller, p. 85). His own deep preference is for the Lutheran faith—"Ich habe die Grundprincipia Lutheri"—but nevertheless the threefold Moravian constitution is a wonder of Divine grace (ein gottliches Gnadenwunder) and he will gladly spend himself with joy in its service. To this the "labourers" of the "strict Moravian Tropus" offer observations indicative of a due admixture of firmness, humility and, perhaps, of mystification. They do not, they said, share Zinzendorf's predilection for Lutheranism, its theologians have not been especially pleasant to him despite his moderation. So they rejoice to learn that the three Tropoi are not to be mixed; their conservation will prevent a shameful *misch-masch* of principles among Brethren who are indeed united in love and the pursuit of true blessedness, but have been born and reared in, and hold firmly to, different traditions. (Müller, pp. 86–87.) It may be here added that in accordance with the proviso relating to the constitution, Zinzendorf secured from the Synod of Marienborn, 1744, the appointment of an *Antistes* at the head of each of the three Tropoi with special care for the members of his own Confession. The first three holders of the office were, Polycarp Müller (Moravian), Fredk. de Watteville (Reformed), and Zinzendorf. But the office lasted only until 1789, when Synod nominated the last *Administratores Troporum*.[1]

The theoretical scheme was not capable of actualization; there was no escape from the two alternatives: division into three separate sects, *or* fusion into the one Gemeine on the basis of the common element—the idea of brotherhood as expressed in the history of the past and experienced in the living fellowship of the present, the old Brethren's way being none other than the new plan of Herrnhut. It was the latter alternative which triumphed and the renewed Brüder Kirche, not the Moravian Tropus, came into being. No longer were there Lutheran and Reformed and Moravian Brethren, but simply Brüder and Brüder-Bishops. The basis of the constitution was *der Brüdercharakter* and it was pre-eminently in virtue of that deep simplicity that the renewed *Unitas Fratrum* could go forward to fulfil its wide commission, "das Apostolat für alle Welt, sonderlich die Heidenwelt," or, in Lord Granville's phrase which Zinzendorf so heartily approved, "to cast the Net over all Christendom" (Müller, p. 99).

[1] See *A Brief History of the Protestant Episcopal Church, known by the name of Unitas Fratrum or United Brethren*, London, MDCCL, Lambeth, III, H. 13 (3), a small pamphlet, being reports of the speeches in the House of Commons from 8.2.1749 to 26.5.1749. At the end is a note explaining the vouchers printed in the Report of the Committee of the House. Among other explanations,

> is shown the reason why the Unitas Fratrum speak beside of some United Brethren; namely because there being many persons from other Protestant professions, chiefly not episcopal, who enjoy fellowship with the brethren's church, she, not being willing to encroach upon the former constitution of the others, made a provision for them by means of Tropus's and accordingly invested some of the most considerable divines of the Lutheran and reformed church, with their superintendency (p. 31).

(ii) *The Last Five Years*, 1755–1760

From the beginning of 1749 to 1755 Zinzendorf lived chiefly, though by no means continuously, in London, first at Northampton House, Bloomsbury, and later at Lindsey House, Chelsea. The first year saw the successful conclusion of the appeal to Parliament, the next a visit to Herrnhut and Barby to restore order and discipline after the confusions of "the Sifting Time"; the period 1751–1755 (March), though broken by another tour in Germany, were occupied in the oversight of the Brethren's increasing membership in this country, the supervision of the settlements, the extrication from the financial crash, and the provision of apologetic literature.

In 1755 Zinzendorf returned to Herrnhut and entered upon the last and serenest phase. What the fortunes of the Moravian Church in this country might have been had there been no Zinzendorf nor Pilgrim Congregation at Lindsey House it would be unprofitable to discuss. The variety and value of the services he rendered here are indubitable, yet the period of his London residence had its full measure of trial and disillusionment as well as its tale of triumphs—the virulence and vulgarity of external attacks, the business mismanagement and the consequent financial disaster, the internal jealousies and divisions, "the care of all the churches." To this catalogue there must be added the presence of misgiving in the Ordinary's mind as to whether, after all, he was making much progress towards realizing his ideals and convictions, even in the minds of some of the most energetic of his new supporters. Yet in face of these discouragements, there was even in England, as we shall see, no diplomatic withdrawal from the *Gemeine-Tropen-Diaspora* outlook. Much more from the Schloss at Bethelsdorf and other German centres, the utterances in speech and by pen continued steadily to insist on the fact that the events we have narrated, culminating in the appointment of the Tropus-Bishops, had brought the renewed Unitas to a position whence it could move forward with vigour and confidence to its task of gathering together in one all the children of God. In particular (so runs the argument), now that the Tropenidee had received clearer elucidation and incorporation in the constitution, the Brüder Kirche is so much the more fitted to become a beacon-light set on a hill for the guidance of the other " religions " which as yet do not possess the note of Universality. If the great Lutheran Church was, by the hostility of its theologians, partly responsible for the rise of the new organization, the Brethren would heap coals of fire upon their head by offering them an actual embodiment of Christian fellowship and ecclesiastical unity in which differences of creed and tradition and worship were resolved by the spirit of the Saviour into a rich harmony.

The variations on this theme during these closing years deserve closer study than we can afford. In no other respect is the underlying consistency of this remarkable personality so evident as in the identity of motive operating within him from the beginning to the end. That motive, put at its simplest, is that of attaining and retaining a lively experience of fellowship with the Saviour, to serve Him " like a slave," and to preach Him throughout the world. To return to the great formative eight or fifty days after the Resurrection is more to be desired than to return only as far as to the Corinthian or Ephesian or Colossian " Gemeine." (The phraseology is Zinzendorf's, of the year 1752, Müller, p. 98.) There must be " a family of the Saviour," but it is the Saviour and not the family who comes first in all his plans. There must be concreteness (Religionsform) or there can be no family, but its worth he values as merely the best visible embodiment under existing circumstances of the Gemeine of which the Saviour is the Head and Indwelling Presence. At the moment the Moravian " Constitution " is a better home for the Gemeine Jesu than the State Church, but the Saviour is not confined to this one instrument and may create another Gemeine still more universalistic, or, for Zinzendorf is not afraid of the word, still more Catholic (Herrnhut Diarium, 12.5.1755, Müller, p. 102).

How much of this high-spirited idealism and its historio-philosophical explication found an entrance into the minds or an echo in the hearts of his lieutenants will be the subject of further note. Zinzendorf's death, like that of his great

Methodist contemporary, released forces hitherto held in suspense. So long as they lived, neither, for all their lovableness, could have tolerated a Mayor of the Palace. From the time the London Synod of 1741 had commissioned him "after mature deliberation to take charge of the affairs of the Brethren and their missions, with unlimited authority" (Spangenberg, p. 340), Zinzendorf and his personal entourage became the focus of all the Unity's activities, evangelistic, financial, and literary. He himself achieved and maintained the status of a benevolent autocrat and for the most part his authority was unchallenged. Criticism of the whole scheme of the Tropoi there was, and its originator had to grapple with objection and reluctance in this central point. Yet even here his personal predominance prevailed. The subordinate leaders never carried their opposition to any point approaching dissolution of partnership. The greatest of them, A. G. Spangenberg, unable to follow his leader in every step, remained, nevertheless, consistently loyal and devoted; he was, in any case, in charge of the American work till recalled after Zinzendorf's decease. Bishop John de Watteville, upon whom in Zinzendorf's illnesses the burden of the European work seems to have fallen, "differed from his father-in-law in some things and acted from other views"; but agreement was re-established before the Count's death (Spangenberg, pp. 407, 497). As for the rest, it is no reflection upon them to say that their Ordinary was easily their superior in rank, wealth, fecundity of invention, breadth of vision and knowledge of the world. For the most part, it was only in the energy of sacrificial evangelism that they could aspire to be his rivals.

The personal interest of these final years must not detain us. Periods of physical weakness and retirement alternated with episcopal visits carried through a war-racked countryside. From Bethelsdorf or Gross Hennersdorf the Count travelled round to the settlements or centres, Barby, Niesky, Ebersdorf, Gnadenberg, to Switzerland or Holland, addressing conferences, commissioning missionaries, reorganizing classes and bands, blessing new choir-houses. And all the while the diligent pen was at work, annotating archives (noting "what might and ought to have been done"), compiling heads of suggested schemes of conduct and teaching, extracting liturgies from the ancient Fathers; in this last he characteristically rejoices to see "how frequently the Eastern Church referred to the incarnation of Christ," and regrets "not meeting with more upon the sufferings of Jesus." So, in sickness resigned to the Divine Will, and in health active and diligent as ever in project and performance, the Count occupied these last five years. On 9th May 1760, he died "well satisfied with the ways of his Lord."[1]

Zinzendorf's death left two administrative bodies in control: *Die Raths-Conferenz*, which undertook general direction, and the *Board of Directors*, founded by the late Ordinary in 1757, which continued supervision in its appointed field (business management, especially of the diaconies). Until the Seven Years' War permitted the holding of a representative Synod, authority lay in the hands of a Provisional Board (the Small Conference or Inner Council) located at Herrnhut and including Spangenberg, recalled from America. "The first General Representative Synod of the Renewed Church of the Brethren" met at Marienborn, 1764; there were present 11 bishops, 7 seniores, 15 presbyters, 24 deacons. As will be noted later its deliberations were of supreme importance for the course of events during a century. For the moment we merely note its creation of the three Departments respectively supervised by *Directory* (general oversight), *Syndics* (external relations), *Wardens* (finance). The three Boards were responsible to the General Synod and in the interim exercised supreme executive authority. Their membership was entirely German. So far as Zinzendorf's place could be filled, this was done by appointing Count Henry XXVIII Reuss, Advocate of the

[1] Quite in keeping with the original and characteristic feature of the renewed Church is the summary of the situation of the Unity "at the death of its resuscitator" in Hamilton, pp. 198–9: Its influence is not to be measured by the number of avowed constituents but by the impress of its spirit upon that "far larger number" who remained "adherents of the principal Confessional Churches." In 1756 he estimates 17,000 persons in Germany alone, belonging to other communions but identified with the Diaspora Societies. Other societies were established in Denmark, Norway, Sweden, Switzerland, France, in the Baltic Provinces, and in Great Britain and North America.

Brethren. Administrators of a Lutheran and Reformed Tropus were also nominated.

Whatever the price to be paid later, therefore, the Unity of the Brethren (*Unitas Fratrum*) was reaffirmed; Herrnhut, forty years before woodland and marsh, attained its unique position as the focus of the whole Community and the seat of the Directing Authority. As we return upon our story to trace the fortunes of the Gemeine in our own country, it may be permitted to surmise what might have been the fortunes of Anglo-Saxon Moravianism had Zinzendorf remained five years longer in London and Lindsey House become the seat of the Unity's Directory.

CHAPTER III

THE ENGLISH PROVINCE: ORIGINS AND EARLY DEVELOPMENT

A. THE ASSOCIATIONAL PRINCIPLE IN THE EARLY EIGHTEENTH CENTURY

(i) *Group Life and the Sovereign State*

THERE seems little necessity to preface our survey of the origins of English Moravianism with a necessarily inadequate sketch of the background, the general social, political and religious conditions of the fourth decade of the eighteenth century. Apart from the general histories (see Bibliography), the specialist studies to which reference will be made are usually so prefaced. There is, however, one feature of the post-Revolution English Church which does call for notice. It is a feature which may count as a white square on " that chess-board character " which, by an obvious metaphor, suggests one manner of regarding the period. The extraordinary number and variety of those associations for the culture of true religion and for the reformation of public morals to which attention is now directed assists in the rehabilitation of the period under discussion in the eyes of " the genuine Anglican " who need no longer turn away in sorrowful shame from an unrelieved spectacle of Erastianism, slovenliness, pluralism and absenteeism. Another end, too, than the pursuit of historical veracity is served in noting this outburst of the associational instinct. Tillotson, so Mark Pattison reminds us (*Essays and Reviews*, p. 274), has a sermon, " On the Advantages of Religion to Societies." His own times would have supplied familiar and adequate illustrations had the preacher discoursed instead on the Advantages of Societies to Religion. Conceivably, two centuries would not have exhausted the value and relevance of such a discourse, since it is clear that the twentieth century is becoming more and more preoccupied with the exploration and explication of the functions and status of the Group in relation to the complex life of man in Society.[1]

In the England of the early eighteenth century there were certain phenomena in the political, social and religious life of the nation which might have made this conception less strange than in Tudor or Stuart England, *e.g.* the Constitutionalism resulting from the Revolution of 1688, the Toleration Act of 1689, the mere presence of nonconforming Churches, and, especially, the existence of a series of religious associations which for the most part acted as friendly auxiliaries of the official parochial machinery. There was, indeed, a plenitude of rigidity and despotism in the England of Walpole and George I, but there were not wanting qualities, both personal and corporate, which might have assisted the process of the recognition of the inherent sanctity, the non-concessionary character, of small societies. On the Continent, too, alike in Catholic France and Protestant Germany, the same associational principle was finding expression in the late seventeenth and early eighteenth centuries. We have seen how Zinzendorf's society-founding had been inspired by Spener and Francke, and the English societies have been compared to those associated with the work of St Vincent de Paul and M. de Renty in France, in the preceding century (*Caritas Anglicana*, pp. 22–26).

Across the Channel, however, any associations, local, cultural or religious, were as little likely to enjoy uninterrupted growth in a congenial soil as they would be in the Russia of today. If any such associations might survive it could only be by virtue of their obscurity or their pliability to the supreme authority. The age of " enlightened despotism " was likely

[1] The four lectures by Neville Figgis, *Churches in the Modern State*, remain as a most valuable summary of the argument against the doctrine of " the Great Leviathan " and an exposition of the case for " the reality of small societies "—that fundamental axiom of all fruitful discussion of the problem presented by the intricate heterogeneity of the modern world. The relevance of the conception of the Church (as also, of course, of the State) as in itself a grouping of lesser, but not necessarily inferior, societies or associations, to the Reunion problem, needs only to be indicated.

to tolerate subordinate groupings only so far as their existence was held to imply no derogation of the " absolute " sovereignty of the Omnicompetent National State. The cynical disregard of the rights of the smaller nationalities and the general dragooning of minorities represents an attitude in which the inherent rights of the smaller society within the State were likely to receive short shrift. " Administrative despotism," however " benevolent," was inspired by that " passion for State absolutism, which is the child of the Renaissance and Reform," and was not, therefore, likely to lead men's minds to a theory of Society as itself a Society of Societies wherein each lesser unit was the focus of the loyalty of individuals, few or many, whose more intimate affiliation to the smaller group fostered rather than hindered their loyalty to the Great Society.

Nor was the prevailing ecclesiastical temper on the Continent any the more conducive to a perception of the true relationship of societies to Society. The Roman Catholic Church was either only too willing to extend the current ideas of uniformity and rigidity to the spiritual sphere (as the fate of the Jansenists showed) or was itself to become a victim of absolutist ideas applied by the secular state to the internal concerns of a spiritual society (as is seen in the successive blows which fell upon the very champions of absolutism in the Church, the Jesuit Order, or in the reforms of Joseph II later in the century). Protestantism was in no better case ; *Cuius regio eius religio* is merely a summarized version of the theory of a centralized autocracy. Lutheranism of the eighteenth century (in the bosom of which the Moravian Church was reborn) was certainly not in a position to offer any escape from the current adherence to the doctrines that the National State is the Source of all authority, that the Church itself possesses only delegated and conceded rights, that Society consists of a mass of unrelated units set over against a Supreme Head and Governor. Neither the Lutheran Church nor the Anglican was prepared to witness with equanimity the efflorescence of a diversified group-life within the National Church system.

The circumstances connected with the renewal of the ancient *Unitas Fratrum* are not noted in the general histories of the second quarter of the century; history has other movements of more moment and stir to record. Yet if we may hold that the significance of events is not to be assessed in terms of their general public interest, we may be justified in regarding this renewal as an episode affording its own contribution to the solution of a problem now, after some two hundred years, again compelling the attention of students alike of Social Theory and of Church Unity. That contribution is fitly symbolized in the more accurate designation of "the Moravians" as a "Unity of Brethren"; among themselves they were a Community of Communities; in respect of the National Churches, though they were not Separatists, they *were* Dissenters—from the concessionary theory; they did assert in word and act their own "inherent spontaneity of life, and that as communal societies they had their own rights and liberty" (Figgis, p. 76). That assertion, at first possibly more instinctive than the result of conscious deliberation, became later more deliberate, and at last, in company with the general body of English Nonconformity, won its way to full success. But, as we now shall notice, immediately on its arrival in this country the "Moravian" organization found itself able to build upon a broad basis of precedent; English religious life had for several decades been familiar with voluntary associations, and was on the eve of witnessing a national revival of religion by which the idea of such voluntary groupings was to become as familiar to rulers and populace as ever Guild or Fraternity had been in the Middle Ages.

(ii) *England, the Earlier Religious Associations*, 1690–1729

As long ago as 1678, Dr Antony Horneck of the Savoy Chapel and Mr Smythies of St Michael's, Cornhill, had organized groups of young men in London for weekly conferences, prayer and Bible-reading. Horneck, "the Friend, or rather Father to these societies from their first rise," though born at Bacharach on the Rhine, had graduated from Oxford, had held successive livings and preferments, and finally attained to burial in Westminster Abbey. The rules of these earliest societies which derive from Horneck as printed by Josiah Woodward, " Minister of Popler," show that in essence they aimed at the application of the " Philadelphian idea " to the attainment of personal virtue and godliness.[1]

Until 1690 the Religious Societies were markedly Anglican (under James II strongly anti-papist in addition), were confined entirely to personal religious progress, and composed only of youths and young men. They were " pious fellowships of Youth," their members, " our associated young men," were supervised by their parish clergyman. Under William and Mary they grew rapidly: by 1698 there were thirty-two groups, and from the metropolis they had spread as far as Cambridge and Dublin.

From 1691, however, " the young men " formed the nucleus of a second type of society, *The Societies for the Reformation of Manners*, of which the objects were not personal but public, and of which the membership was not exclusively Anglican. Assisted by " Senior Friends " who, " like kind fathers," supplied the necessary financial resources, the members of these Societies set themselves to elevate public morals, to stimulate magistrates and police to do their duty, to war against drunkenness, cursing, gaming, debauchery and Sabbath-

[1] The reference is to the " Philadelphians " who gathered round John Pordage (d. 1681) and Jane Leade (d. 1704). See *Dic. Nat. Biog.*, Vol. 2, 32, 46. Both were disciples of Jacob Boehme; there were groups of " theosophists calling themselves Philadelphians " in England, Holland, Germany. See R. Jones, *Spiritual Reformers*, for a discussion of the influence of this school of Behmenist mysticism on groups who meet us in early Moravian history, *e.g.* Memnonites and Schwenkfelders. For Horneck, see *Dic. Nat. Biog.*, Vol. 27; and, more fully, Woodward, *Rise and Progress of the Religious Societies in London*, etc., 2nd edition, 1698. Chap. V, pp. 120 f. gives a specimen of the Orders of the Societies. The influence of Woodward's *Account* in Germany (translated by Jablonski) appears in the interesting letter transcribed in our Appendix A. Cf. Simon, *John Wesley and the Religious Societies*, 1921, p. 26.

The Religious Societies and the Societies for the Reformation of Manners are minutely discussed by G. A. Portus, *Caritas Anglicana*, Mowbray, 1912, a fascinating study based almost entirely on contemporary pamphlet literature. Specimen Rules of the earliest societies (before 1691) in Appendix VI. See Secretan's *Life and Times of the Pious Robert Nelson*, Chap. III, for notice of some of the early leaders of the Rel. Societies, S.R.M., S.P.C.K., S.P.G., and kindred " Church associations," 1700–1714.

breaking, " to discountenance and suppress publick Enormities." Four or five gentlemen, who were both legal and pious, supplied zealous members with Blank Warrants wherewith the reformers could the more securely invoke the aid of the civil power. Encouraged by two Royal Proclamations against immorality, the Societies for the Reformation of Manners prospered and by 1698 there were twenty such societies in and about the city and suburbs, besides those in " Nottingham, Shrewsbury and other parts."

We should note that though Churchman and Dissenter might join in suppressing public vice, the Anglican patrons of both types of Society were extremely anxious to avoid any appearance of encouraging schism. The devotions of the Religious Societies were drawn almost entirely from the Book of Common Prayer and were normally conducted by some pious and orthodox parish minister—and that without reward or salary. As to co-operation in the Societies with Dissenters, the Churchmen claim to have been thus instrumental in leading Quakers, Baptists, and other " Persuasions " to join the Church, while only one Anglican had lapsed in the last twenty years.[1]

B. London: The Fetter Lane Society

(i) *New Wine into Fresh Wineskins*, 1729–1740

The Societies for the Reformation of Manners published their last report in 1738 but had been moribund for some years. We need not enquire whether it was their failure to reach the upper classes, or suspicions of political disaffection, or the popular determination to evade the Gin Acts of 1729

[1] Woodward, Chap. VII, " Objections Answered "; cf. Stoughton, V, 253, 256, on Archbishop Sharpe's refusal to countenance either type. Add Portus, pp. 98–103; also W. H. Hutton, *The English Church*, 1625–1714, pp. 306–7. It may be added that the S.P.C.K. was founded in 1698, and the S.P.G. three years later; the work of the former was largely responsible for the decline of the S.R.M. The various other factors working to the same end need not detain us; later remarks bear upon the parallel decline of the earlier Religious Societies and their transformation to meet new conditions. The causes of the decline of the S.R.M. are examined by Portus, pp. 190 f. In *The Plain Case*, etc., Lambeth, 112 f., 16, the S.P.C.K. appears, p. 6, as " the Society *de propaganda*."

and 1736, or other cause, which led to their decline; with this particular phase of the general movement we have no further concern. The Religious Societies, on the other hand, link on to the rise of Methodism at Oxford, London and Bristol, labouring, however, between that period and the death of Queen Anne under the double criticism of "incipient Jacobitism and self-righteousness" (cf. Portus, p. 193, and Benham, pp. 7 and 9).

But the grapes were ripening for a new vintage; the sun shone at Oxford in that summer of 1730 when that *miles emeritus*, the Rector of Epworth, encouraged his two sons and their associates "to turn the war against the devil" by fasting and prayer, by reading something in practical divinity, and by visiting the poor and sick and imprisoned. The new wine had a better bouquet than the old if we may trust a comparison between Woodward's Specimen Orders—introspective, rigid mechanized—and the far less self-centred, more apostolic, charitable and earnest spirit of such a foundation-document as Wesley's long series of questions issued at the end of 1729 against "the outcry daily increasing" in the colleges at Oxford (*Journal*, Letter to Mr Morgan, Sen. 18th Oct. 1730; Tyerman, *Oxford Methodists*, pp. 8, 9). Our interests, however, lead us, not to Oxford, but to London, and our concern with the great founder of Methodism must be limited to that period only in which the fortunes of John Wesley and of the Moravians were linked together in "the Fetter Lane Society." There we shall find the more permanent home of a voluntary religious association not dissimilar in origin and early characteristics from the other older Societies, but becoming the seed-plot of the British Moravian Church, an *ecclesiola* which became an *ecclesia*.

This Society was not a direct descendant of the earlier Societies; there was an intermediate series of small associations. To detail that development would be to tell the story of the Huttons, father and son (Portus, pp. 197–209; Benham, pp. 8–15). Briefly, James Hutton became the intermediary between the Wesley-Whitefield group and the first bands of Zinzendorf's disciples in London. The latter were either missionaries *en route* for America or more permanent residents, like the group of ten whose simple Society Rules are available (Benham, pp. 25, 26). On his side James had already organized a little group in Nettleton Court, Aldersgate Street, which met every week for mutual edification and now formed a group of " several pious people " who gathered to hear read the correspondence and diaries from Georgia. This was a new grouping though naturally drawn partly from other societies already existing (Benham, p. 12). In connection with it was a *Poor Box Society*, the 200–300 subscribers being " members of different societies which had already existed from the time of King James II," while from it again, arose another " very similar to it, only so arranged that each member attended in his own society on the Sunday " (Benham, p. 12).

These excerpts will be sufficient to indicate the varied character of the associations of which both Methodists and Moravians availed themselves later, and to show how the line runs back to the Anglican societies on the Woodward model. Secondly, they show how the societies of Hutton's time, " the London Societies," were enriched, quickened and multiplied after 1730 by the enthusiasm of those other " associated young men " who have written their names in indelible letters on the later history of the century. Charles Wesley, back from Georgia (1736), was received as a son in the Hutton household. George Whitefield there made contacts with Charles and with others who set him on his career of preacher and philanthropic organizer. Filled with plans for his own journey to Georgia, Whitefield passed on those who came to him for advice to the societies organized by James Hutton and his friends. Whitefield departed, John Wesley returned (1.2.1738) and built on the same foundations. The dramatic preachings to the multitudes by both were another link between the old societies and the new movement. There were others, too, of less force and popular appeal perhaps, but who, like Ingham, Delamotte and Gambold, were preparing their contributions of pastoral diligence and zealous propaganda to the " awakening."

The next intermediate stage is marked by the addition to the careful methodism of Oxford and Georgia of the Moravian contribution from Herrnhut, of that " heart religion," that saving experience of Jesus as Friend and Saviour as contrasted with the "eudæmonistic ethicism" which Wesley and his friends had caught from William Law (Wauer, p. 42). Hutton and his friends "continued after the plan of the Methodists to visit the sick, to pray fervently and frequently, and practise their self-denying austerities," but "this was but half a life, for as yet they knew nothing of Jesus, the sinner's friend" (Benham, pp. 13, 14). That necessary fusion of Law and Grace had for its scene the old meeting-house in Fetter Lane to which, from considerations of convenience, Hutton and his friends had transferred themselves.[1] There, in the "long room" near to the ancient Dissenting chapel, on 1st May 1738, they agreed upon *The Orders of a Religious Society meeting in Fetter Lane, In obedience to the command of God, by St James, and by the advice of Peter Böhler.*[2] Four days later Böhler left for Carolina, and shortly after (August) John Wesley and Ingham journeyed to Herrnhut. The last night of the year, or rather 3 a.m. of the first morning of the New Year, when "the power of God came mightily" upon the little group, may serve to mark the climax of fellowship within the bosom of this Anglican-Moravian-Methodist Religious Society.

For the temporary partnership between the two wings of the army of revival was dissolving throughout 1739 until the final breach in July 1740. On the 20th of that month, at a Sunday evening Love-feast, Wesley withdrew with eighteen or nineteen followers, and Moravian and Methodist went separately on their several ways, to attempt to forward the revival through

[1] Actually they first met in "the Long Room" in one of the courts off Fetter Lane, until they rented the old chapel, 25.3.1740.

[2] See references before given. G. Schmidt (*Zeitschrift*) prints six Rules under three different dates, and summarizes the remainder. Benham prints thirty-three, six under dates as Schmidt. No. 33 empowers admittance of country members who must correspond with the Society at least once a month. Wesley has eleven only, but he professes to give only "our fundamental rules." He omits No. 32, "That no particular Person be allowed to act in any thing contrary to any Order of this Society, but that everyone, without Distinction, submit to the Determination of his Brethren," upon pain of expulsion. The Herrnhut MSS. gives thirty Rules under four different dates; after title-heading it adds, "the members consisting of Persons in communion with the Established Church" (R. 13, A. 19, 2).

the organization of societies within the framework of the National Church. Each carried over into the new crusade much of what they had learned together in the brief period of their alliance.[1] Much might be said in analysing the causes which broke up their fellowship: the personalities of the two leaders, the suspicions of antinomianism on the one side and of self-righteousness and legality on the other, the relative importance attached by the two parties to primitive discipline and ecclesiastical tradition, Molther's exaggerated quietism, Moravian dislike of the "scenes," the Wesleyan postulate of the possibility of sinlessness in this present life—the catalogue might be lengthened, and these and other topics expanded (cf. J. Wesley's *Journal*, the anti-Moravian sections, *e.g.* 12.8.1738, 1.11.1739, 3.9.1741). Or again, how far was the breach irreparable and at what point of time had it so become? There were attempts at reconciliation. It must have been an affecting moment when Wesley and Böhler met with seven of the original ten at a little Love-feast "to confess our faults to one another" and to seek "union in mind" (*Journal*, 1.5.1741, and 6.5.1741). And how earnest must have been the conversation with Böhler and Spangenberg on the day following, when the intractable difficulty was faced of deciding whether the "new man" in conversion (justification) does or does not at once and completely expel "the old heart, corrupt and abominable." One wonders what might have been the turn of events had Böhler not departed to Carolina or Spangenberg's firm hand been on the helm sooner than it was. We, however, leaving Wesley to carry into his United Societies much which, on the administrative side,[2] he had learned from his contacts

[1] For story of *the Disruption*, see Wauer, pp. 69–78; J. E. Hutton, pp. 295–301; Benham, p. 54; Portus, pp. 209–216; also pp. 217–220, the debt of Methodism to the Fetter Lane and to the older Societies; Wesley's *Journal* for 1740, July 2, 4, 9, 15, and 16, the crucial reading of "The Mystic Divinity of Dionysius"; also for 31.12.1739, Wesley's analysis of the differences between himself and P. H. Molther.

[2] Especially "the band system," essentially Moravian, and the backbone of the Methodist Societies. Wesley had formed a distinct Society as early as December 1739 (see *Journal*, 24.12.1739 and cf. Simon, Chap. XXIII).

The fruitless conference between him and Zinzendorf in Gray's Inn Gardens took place 3rd September 1741—not, as Hamilton (p. 133), on

with the Moravians, now turn to see how the latter, under Spangenberg's leadership, succeeded in planting firmly an English counterpart of the Pilgergemeine and in training a devoted band of labourers wherewith to further the revival of "heart-religion" in English, Irish and Scottish towns and villages.

(ii) *Anglican Society to Moravian Congregation, July* 1740–*October* 1742

If the Fetter Lane Society may be said broadly to have remained an ordinary Religious Society for two years following the Disruption (so J. E. Hutton, *Owen's College Essays*, p. 423), that description must be so qualified as to admit the presence of distinctive Moravian elements imported by Molther, Töltschig, Spangenberg (after April 1741), and Englishmen, like Hutton and Holland, whom the Germans had rescued from "the Pelagianism" of the older societies. Its home was now the historic meeting-house. From Hutton's house the original members had removed to the "Long Room" (1738), and now the old chapel was rented (25.3.1740). In 1741 three houses in Goldsmith's Court on the eastern side of the chapel were taken, and here the smaller meetings were held. New leases were taken out in 1748 and 1776. In 1777 both the chapel and No. 32 Fetter Lane were taken on a 400 years' lease. This block of buildings was, therefore, the home of the Fetter Lane Society.

The leadership of the group, for a short while after, as before, the Methodist secession, devolved upon P. H. Molther.[1] James Hutton, now supplied with a Moravian wife, returned to London, accompanied by Bishop David Nitschmann, Anna Nitschmann and Sister Molther (Benham, p. 56).

Zinzendorf's return from America in 1743. Benham, too, is in error in placing the conversation in 1743 (p. 111).

For the *United Societies* (Methodist), see *The Nature, Design and General Rules of the United Societies in London, Bristol, Kingswood and Newcastle-upon-Tyne*, 4th edition, 1744. It subjoins the Rules of the Band Societies by John and Charles Wesley, 1st May 1743.

[1] Benham, pp. 53–4, supplies Molther's own account of his energetic discharge of his duties.

Töltschig was already present, and on 5th April 1741, Spangenberg and his wife joined them. Meanwhile, we may add, Ingham and Delamotte, not as yet in any sense Moravians, were forwarding their work among the "simple people" of Yorkshire.

Spangenberg came with a commission from Synod at Marienborn, and his task in those few but critical months when he was in charge lay along two lines. The first can be no more than barely indicated. In the house in Red Lion Square the auxiliary *Society for the Furtherance of the Gospel* had its birth at a Love-feast on 27th April 1741. In its original form the life of this new Society was short, some ten years only, but it was revived later, and rendered excellent service in the Brethren's mission work overseas. Crantz (p. 274) is hardly correct in stating that "the Ordinary formed at London a Society for the furtherance of the Gospel." The truth is that Zinzendorf found the S.F.G. in existence on his return from America (Spring, 1743), was "very much pleased" with its rules, and renewed old acquaintanceships among its members (Benham, pp. 70–3, 111). The Society's committee co-opted Spangenberg to represent "the congregation abroad" with the status of "Assessor of the Church of the Brethren." Four members of the Committee were to act with two or three of the Moravian Brethren (Rules 5 and 7). All members of the Fetter Lane Society might be admitted to the monthly reading of letters and accounts; this ended, all who were not members of the S.F.G., were to depart (Rule 3). These bare details are sufficient to indicate the constitutional empiricism of the early organization. The S.F.G. stood in much the same relation to the London Society as the latter did to the whole Unitas, auxiliary and with partial identity of membership, but neither were all the members of the S.F.G. members of the Fetter Lane Society nor all members of the latter full members of the S.F.G. Its object was to afford a rallying-point for all sympathizers with the Brethren's work overseas. Hutton, his friends of the Fetter Lane Society, Spangenberg and his associates, "the brethren and sisters in office" dwelling in Red Lion Square, were the core of the new organization (cf. Wauer, p. 84: "Practically the Fetter

Lane Society was the S.F.G."). Thus in the fire of missionary zeal was forged a bond between "Hutton and the society under his care" and Spangenberg, the representative of the Brethren's Church and emissary from her recent Synod.[1]

Secondly, the organization of the English work. The months of August and September following Spangenberg's arrival represent a period of great importance. In August the English Brethren, first providing that the Moravians would not forsake them, elected a President and two Stewards (Hutton, Viney, and Holland). This was a step with a twofold significance: (*a*) The Society had taken measures towards permanence and that under Moravian influence; (*b*) there was an open expression of reluctance to move in this direction if it implied a future withdrawal of the Brethren's fostering care. Even more important, there took place in September 1741, under Zinzendorf's presidency, that Synodal Conference in Red Lion Square which must rank as the crucial constitutional event in this period of transition.

At that Conference, in a full and representative assembly of "labourers," both English and German, the fortunes of the renewed Church of the Brethren for the last nineteen years was surveyed and "the best mode of governing the same" was settled. The enemies of the Brethren subsequently poured much scorn upon the affirmation by the Conference that the office of "Chief Elder," vacant through the resignation of Leonard Dober, be transferred to the Saviour Himself. Of more positive value is the complementary enactment that the

[1] The S.F.G. was renewed in 1766, and one of its first tasks was the translation and printing of Crantz's *History of the Missions of the Brethren in Greenland*. The Herrnhut MSS., R. 13, A. 37, gives twenty-six Rules slightly different from those of the original foundation. They are more definite in regarding the S.F.G. as specifically an auxiliary society to the Brethren's Missions. So the phraseology of the following Minute of a Privy Council (His Majesty being present) of 3.5.1769 :—

His Majesty allowed James Hutton, Benj. La Trobe, Chas. Metcalfe, John Edmonds, Philip Hurlock, John Wollin, and Jeris (?) Haven, "In Trust for the Unitas Fratrum and its Society for the Furtherance of the Gospel, to occupy and possess during His Majesty's pleasure 100,000 acres of land in such part of Eskimaux Bay on the Coast of Labrador as they shall find most suitable to their purpose . . ." (Herrnhut, R. 13, A. 38).

"temporal" government be vested in "*a General Conference* or collegiate *Board of Direction* consisting of twelve persons who should reside at Marienborn and superintend the whole Church of the Brethren" (Benham, p. 75). The English headquarters were transferred to Fulneck, and the London work directed from that remote settlement. On the wisdom of these arrangements there is little need for comment: the practical difficulties, "facilities for travelling being then but few," are obvious. However, they were loyally accepted, and in May 1742, Spangenberg commissioned the appointed "labourers" for the field of war in Yorkshire, where both Ingham and the Methodists had already reaped a valuable harvest. Before that month had expired, Ingham had transferred his societies to the Brethren, who thereupon went forward to gather in numbers of the rough and simple peasantry. Methodist opposition naturally drew more sharply the line of cleavage; the Disruption in London two years before was accentuated by the events in the North.

Meanwhile in London events were shaping themselves so as to lead to an ever nearer identification of the Fetter Lane Society with the Brethren. While we need to beware of allotting too much influence to that Society, or indeed to events in London, as compared with those in the provinces, it is nevertheless obvious that transactions affecting the amorphous relations between the London Society and Spangenberg would naturally exercise enormous influence on the whole character and position of those societies of awakened souls gathered together by the Brethren's labours. Hence the extreme importance of the fact that in October 1742 the Fetter Lane Society was established "a congregation of the Unity of the Brethren" (Benham, p. 89), and organized in accordance with the characteristic Moravian regulations. The congregation numbered 72 souls; 37 men, 35 women. Exactly half were appointed forthwith to positions of greater or lesser dignity and responsibility. William Holland (Congregation Elder) and James Hutton (Warden) are the first two names. After more than one entry occurs the designation, "Dissenter," "Baptist." Other notes imply that the future connection of some with the Society was not of long duration. John Gambold,

"Minister, Stanton Harcourt," appears among the Single Men. He and James Hutton, the two best educationally qualified of the group, were fully aware of the peculiar Zinzendorfian ideas concerning the ecclesiastical status of the Brethren's Church, and would have been able to have explained the exact significance of their corporate metamorphosis into "a Society in the Church of England in union with the Brethren." Whether that ability would have been predicable of all the members of the Society may be questioned.

It is important that we, at any rate, should note the precise character of the change which had come upon the Fetter Lane Society. That association had neither vanished into thin air nor become merged in the renewed Unitas. All its members, save the 72, continued in the same position as was enjoyed by the members of other societies now welcoming the ministrations of the Moravian "labourers," while both the 72 and such of Hutton's friends as were not of that group, continued to regard themselves as loyal Churchmen, and rigorously guarded themselves against schism. It was precisely one year after the birth of "The Congregation of the Lamb . . . as settled in London, Oct. 30th, 1742, O.S." that

> the threat of exclusion was carried into effect upon Br. Hurlock who was turned out of Coleman Street Society, and a rule was made, "That he who will not keep close to the Church of England must not be a member of the Society," October 21st, 1743 (Benham, p. 129).

For similar reasons, it was in the next year (1744) that William Holland and "many of the English Brethren" withdrew from connection with the Brethren in protest against proposals passed at a Synod at Marienborn in July which appeared likely to force them into the position of dissenters from the National Church, "a thing they most of all dreaded." [1]

[1] Benham, p. 153. Most important, too, is *An Extract or Short Account of some few matters relating to the work of the Lord in England*, 1732–45, by William Holland (for Count Z.); Herrnhut, R. 13, A. 2 c. Note at end by later hand: "The name of the author of this Account is W. H. and it is a relation . . . concerning the origin of the English Brethren out of members of religious Societys or Vestry Societys of the Church of

though quite unjustly, the political agitations increased the disturbance of the Brethren's meetings and the ill-treatment of their agents.[1] Two apologetic protests against these attacks may be noted. The first is the "*Declaration of the Societies in England joining the Brethren*," printed for public enlightenment in the *Daily Advertiser*, 2.8.1745. Here, after a glance at the errors of the Methodist way, and a relation of instances in which the Brethren on the Continent have trained and disciplined souls who have since "returned to their respective religions," it is plainly affirmed that the English Brethren wish for no different outcome to their labours.

> We wish for nothing more than that some time or other there might be some bishop or parish minister found of the English Church, to whom, with convenience, and to the good liking of all sides, we could deliver the care of those persons of the English church, who have given themselves to our care (Benham, p. 182).

If one aim and result of this public announcement was to make it plain to all reasonable men that "their main desire was to prevent separation from the established church," the other protest to which we refer was one against themselves being compelled to register as Dissenters. That the illuminative letter from Yorkshire of Wm. Holland and James Charlesworth to the Archbishop of York (see Appendix B) was not a purely personal expression of opinion is confirmed by the fact that at the Ockbrook (Derby) Conference in the Spring of 1744, when a proposition was made to have the meeting-places licensed as Dissenting Chapels, the proposal "was opposed and nothing definite concluded" (Benham, p. 174).

In 1746 Zinzendorf came to England and addressed himself to the task of translating all these protestations into actuality. He came determined that the English members of the Societies should, if they could be at all persuaded, remain within their

[1] Thus Br. Ockershausen was arrested at Ossett after preaching, 19th November 1745, and committed to York Castle by Justice John Burton on the ground "that he is a suspicious and dangerous person and is unable to give any good Account of himself or of his way of life." Herrnhut, A. 5 (4), 118. See also our Appendix B.

original "church-constitutions," that in due course there should be appointed a bishop as superintendent of the Anglican Tropus, and that meanwhile he himself, charged with their oversight, would put down firmly both separatism and proselytism. He persuaded a Synod in September to accept the use of the Book of Common Prayer in the Sunday worship and a scheme for joint-ordination by Anglican and Moravian bishops. But this was too speedy a development; the Archbishop shelved the affair and died next year—a serious blow to Zinzendorf since it removed from the Primacy one who had always shown a friendly sympathy with the *sancta et illustris sedes episcopalis Moravica*, and who was, as the Count once remarked, one of the few prelates in Great Britain really acquainted with Universal History.

(ii) *Parliamentary Recognition*, 1747–1749

The year 1747 brings us within the period during which the whole doctrinal and constitutional justification of the renewed Unitas was lifted on to a more dignified plane, subjected to an official examination and discussion in the National Parliament, whence it emerged with an assured and defined legal status. What is commonly referred to as the "Recognition" of the *Unitas Fratrum* by Parliament in 1749 is, for a study of the transition from the Herrnhut *Gemeine* to the present British Moravian Church, an event of the highest interest. The Recognition marked a stage in that progress from which there has been no looking back. Its effects are to be traced in developments not at all visualized by its prime mover, both in respect of internal polity and of relationships with other ecclesiastical constitutions in these islands. The success of the struggle for national Recognition was not, of course, equivalent to entering the harbour and furling the sails. There still remained a long voyage through cross-currents of theological prejudice and popular suspicion ere the Unitas entered the open sea and, undisturbed by external hostility, could devote itself to its characteristic works of religion, education and philanthropy. Nevertheless, the year 1749 is rightly regarded as marking the culmination of the first great stage of the journey of the renewed Church of the Brethren in England to freedom and independence.[1]

Among the causes which provoked the petition to Parliament, the most urgent was the popular hostility, increasing from 1742 onwards. It would be easy to compile a long list of definite instances of molestation of individuals and of attacks upon meetings thence onwards. Anti-popery riots, threats of impressment, aspersions of immorality, stonings and imprisonment were all employed in London, at Thaxted, Leeds, and elsewhere (see Benham, pp. 129, 135, 180, 187, 198). Such disturbances underlined the necessity for obtaining licences for the meeting-houses and some means of securing magisterial certificates for the "labourers." In turn, those necessities (the result of reluctance to accept a position of a dissenting body) provoked the further necessity of submitting to an official examination of the Unity's doctrinal standards and historical antecedents. That last necessity was eagerly accepted by Zinzendorf, and in the series of doctrinal statements, historical catena, interviews, letters and memoranda submitted to eminent personages, he utilized the magnificent opportunity events had afforded of explicating his reiterated convictions upon the place and witness of the renewed Moravian Church in relation to Christendom in general and to the

[1] *The Recognition of the Unitas Fratrum as an old Protestant Episcopal Church by the Parliament of Great Britain in* 1749, by Bishop J. T. Hamilton, Moravian Historical Society, 1924, details fully the conditions and causes leading to the Act.

In the *Herrnhut Archives*, R. 13, there are :—

A. 22. b. Summaries of the speeches in Lords and Commons, 9.2. to 3.5.1749.
A. 25. b. 4. Catalogue of vouchers produced by witnesses.
b. 6. Report of H. of C. Committee.
b. 11. Copies of the Bill and of the Act.
A. 25. 32. Certificates issued to Charles Metcalfe and J. Hutton.
A. 25. b. 8. Facsimile of issue of *Universal Magazine*, 16 pp.;

"The Privileges granted to the Protestants called the United Brethren in the British Dominions"; the speeches in the House have been "collected from the best authorities and from several Persons who attended," probably Zinzendorf, Nitschmann and Schrautenbach, who must remain the real "original sources," *i.e.* Croeger, Plitt, and other historians run back to these three eye-witnesses. Benham, pp. 204–21, merely translates Plitt's MSS.

Established Church of England in particular. Here the usefulness of our earlier notices of Zinzendorf's church-ideas becomes apparent. Attention was there drawn to the development of his thought at the period when there emerged a drift of opinion among his followers pointing to the inauguration of another independent Church. We saw the difficulties he felt when the tide was running strongly in the direction of the rebuilding of the ancient traditions of the Bohemian-Moravian Church, and how its patron baptized that natural loyalty into his wider ideals of the reunion of Christendom, with *die Tropenidee* as the ideological instrument. By 1747 the Count had apparently welded that concept firmly into the official standpoint of the renewed Church. A later generation will never perhaps be able to estimate the degree of latent reserve and genuine mystification with which the Brethren accepted their Ordinary's ideas on this point. We only catch hints of such reserve in Germany or among the "inner circle," though dissent in England came to the surface on occasion, as *e.g.* in the controversies over "the name" and, in more dramatic fashion, in Viney's "rebellion." In the main, however, at the time we are now considering, Zinzendorf had attained a position of control which in practice was akin to personal absolutism, and if his subordinate colleagues sometimes questioned his wisdom, they normally yielded tacit consent in silence. In such a matter as the Parliamentary petition success depended almost entirely upon his rank, wealth, knowledge of the world and mental energy. Hence this chapter of their story is, from the Brethren's side, very largely a study of the application to the world of affairs of Zinzendorf's characteristic "church-ideas" which we noted earlier.[1]

One other feature of the preparatory circumstances may be noted. Mob-violence no doubt accentuated the sense of urgency but the immediate impulse had a more distant origin, viz., New York, where the Act (1744) directed against "every

[1] Bishop Hamilton euphemistically expresses the situation after Hirschberg, 1743: "Thus the monarchical principle was allowed temporarily to displace the conferential principle . . ." (p. 113). In plain speech, men like the Nitschmanns, Neissers, Dobers and P. Müller "surrendered unconditionally" in 1743 to what was a complete reversal of the traditional policy of the Brethren in the earliest days.

vagrant preacher, Moravian or disguised Papist" had marked down the Brethren for official disapproval and informal persecution. Their situation in America was indeed peculiarly difficult just then. The repercussions of the Franco-British War, the Indian mission-villages, the pacifist tendency, the removal in 1740 to a fresh field, Pennsylvania, "that land of liberty of conscience," the antipathy there excited by the alleged Moravian resemblances to Popery in ritual and their dissemblances from Calvinism in doctrine, even the less respectable dislike of the liquor-sellers—all these offences culminated in Governor Clinton's clumsy Act of 1744. Here is the starting-point of the struggle in the British Legislature. That unfortunate piece of legislation was silently buried and the Brethren were less molested than seemed likely, though certain missionaries were thrown into jail (Hamilton, *The Recognition*, etc., p. 8). One minor result was a hot fit of indignation in the breast of worthy James Hutton, who, filled with shame for his countrymen's reputation, wrote to Zinzendorf suggesting that the time had now come "for bringing our cause publicly before Parliament" (Benham, p. 171). A personal visit to his chief resulted in the appointment of Abraham van Gersdorf (*Deputatus ad Reges*) as Commissioner to the authorities in London. Zinzendorf himself arrived the year following, and thus began the initial stage of securing the sympathetic consideration and practical assistance of well-disposed persons: the Primate, the Court (through the Chevalier Schaub), General Oglethorpe and Penn, Proprietor of Pennsylvania.

Largely by the help of the two latter, it was comparatively easy to secure legislation permitting the Moravian Brethren in all the American Colonies to affirm instead of taking the oath.[1] This exemption, however, was but a minor gain and, moreover, one on what was not an essential point of ethics. Zinzendorf and his advisers were in search of an acknow-

[1] The actual procedure was the emendation of the Naturalization Act of 1740; the privilege therein granted to Quakers was now extended to Moravians. There was no opposition, and the Royal Assent was given on 28.6.1747. The views of the agent, H. Cossart, of Oglethorpe and of Zinzendorf on the exiguous quality of the concession thus obtained are in Benham, p. 207.

ledgment in a much broader and more fundamental sense, both in the Colonies and at home. As he expressed the necessities of his flock in a consultation with Oglethorpe and Penn, "How could the congregations of the Brethren at home and their missionaries abroad, procure a legal standing in the British Empire and the Church of the Brethren be legally acknowledged?"

Their answer was, broadly, "the sanction of Parliament," and though neither was a constitutional lawyer, their further advice on the strategy of the campaign was eminently in accord with the spirit and custom of law-making under the British Constitution. They saw, as the German Count did not, that the British Parliament would not concern itself with a merely abstract examination of the situation; a public enquiry which would give the country in general "a more correct view of our cause" was not the business of that legislative body which "began its life not as a mere 'debating assembly' but as part of the King's 'High Court' of Parliament" (G. M. Trevelyan, *History of England*, p. 253). The way to Parliamentary sanction lay through a Petition for certain concrete objects, a Petition afterwards to be embodied in a Bill which Parliament would turn into an Act. Therefore two definite exemptions were fixed upon: from taking oaths and from bearing arms, the concessions to apply, in the first instance to the Brethren's American Colonists, and next, by logical deduction and legal necessity, to all members of the community under British rule. To this "circuitous way" Zinzendorf, now installed in Northampton House, reluctantly consented; the Colonial necessities of the Brethren were at this moment symbolized by the ship *Irene* in the Thames carrying her "sea-congregation" of 150 brethren and sisters to Pennsylvania. In the event, Oglethorpe's advice was thoroughly justified; a full historical and doctrinal survey of the Unitas was collected, presented, discussed and defended in both Houses (see *Acta Fratrum Unitatis in Anglia* for evidence submitted to the Parliamentary Committee, Lambeth, 118, f. 20). Leave to bring in a Bill was granted on 25th March 1749, the first reading was taken on 28th March and the third on 18th April. In the Lords the Bill was opposed by the

Duke of Newcastle and the Court Party, favoured by Granville, Argyle and his sixteen Presbyterian colleagues, and by the Bishops, including Sherlock of London, who had withdrawn his earlier opposition. Passed 12th May, the Bill received the Royal Assent on 6th June.

The significance of this success has been variously estimated. The immediate practical outcome, the securing of the twofold exemption requested in the Petition, was a definite gain, though, as the debates had shown, neither "conscientious objection" was an integral part of Moravian ethics. It was rather in the implications of the constitutional decision that the friends of the Brethren found their chief source of satisfaction. The legal exemptions, they hoped, would serve as a symbol of the larger fact that after an exhaustive and public investigation, the *Unitas Fratrum* in England and in the Colonies had been acknowledged by Parliament to be an ancient Protestant Episcopal Church, in a true line of descent, through Comenius, with the Bohemian Brethren, and a sister-church of that other Protestant Episcopal Church, the Church of England. Such deductions granted, the result of the Petition was indeed "an event of vital importance."[1] On the other hand, it may be regarded as an empty triumph without real effect upon the fortunes of the English Brethren (so Hutton, p. 345). Official approbation did not silence scoffers and critics, nor lead to any increased security from disturbance. Nor did the Act extricate the Brethren from the necessity, so much disliked, of licensing their rooms and edifices as Dissenting Chapels. More than a century was to elapse before the growth of tolerance brought to an end the reign of religious, social and educational disabilities this position implied. Still, the historian is probably justified in marking the Parliamentary Recognition of the Moravian Church, not only as an interesting point in the evolution of British religious freedom, but also as, in respect of one particular Free Church, a stage from which it could move forward with heightened self-confidence,

[1] Holmes, I, p. 325, counts four definite privileges secured from Parliament, and these "were attended by other important consequences."

freed from harassing uncertainties, to whatever further tasks it might be called.

There was one interpretation of the significance of the 1749 Act which time has not substantiated, namely, Zinzendorf's own. We shall notice, later, how vehemently he dissented from the view which held that Recognition had gone far to turn the temporary tent into an abiding temple. All through the negotiations he had maintained in public and private that the *esse* of the Brüdergemeine was neither nationality nor a specific church-constitution but its quality of brotherhood, its family idea, with, for doctrinal standard, that most general formula of the Evangelical Churches, the Augsburg Confession. That was why " *Mährische Brüder* " must be struck out of the Act—" oder ich will die ganze Akte nicht haben " (14.5.1756). Membership is of men, not of nationality, and nothing must be allowed to obscure the *Brüderidee ;* they are a *Unitas Fratrum.*

> What might have appeared to have been conducive to the idea of a separate Moravian church, he saw how to turn in favour of Tropenkirche (Müller, p. 92).

Zinzendorf viewed the English Brethren not simply as the old Bohemian Unitas restored and transplanted to England, but rather as a community of eager and earnest English brothers and sisters fused into a spiritual fellowship, a social and religious brotherhood, by a longing for real and vital heart-religion ; the precious core, *die Tropenidee*, becomes thus the essence of the new community now enjoying the sanction of the State.

> *Unitas Fratrum* is not a church, nor an external identity of nature (Gemeinwesen) but a common quality of the moral-religious disposition and manner, which maintains itself in its external contacts, partly as a special Church-polity (Kirchentum), and partly by special organizations within the existing churches (Becker, quoted by Müller, p. 93, who adds, " Das ist gewiss Zinzendorf's Grundgedanke ").

It was the dissemination of these ideas, and not the mere removal of two legal disabilities, which formed the motive of Zinzendorf's long labours in England. " Recognition " once obtained he bent himself to the task of incorporating those ideas in appropriate organization, fortified by the conviction that *die Tropenidee* had become firmly embedded in the foundations of the renewed Brüder Kirche.

D. Constitutional and Administrative Foundations

(i) *Towards Devolution*, 1750–1755

The deepest and essential qualities of any religious association are certainly beyond the competence of a National Parliament to assess. Zinzendorf, his colleagues and their converts had now to justify themselves at the bar of public opinion. That evasive court of appeal is no more infallible than Parliament, but it is true that it is by its fruits that a religious society is ultimately sanctioned or condemned, prospers or declines. The Renewed Unitas had now to set itself to convince " the man of sense and candour," the more serious section of the nation, that it was in actual fact able to evoke and sustain those fruits of personal piety which would be the best proof of its spiritual descent from that ancient Brotherhood whose virtues had been given so large a place in the documents commending their cause to the sympathetic consideration of Parliament. Parallel, therefore, with the *theoretical* apology (" The Battle of the Books ") and long after its successful issue, there went on the *practical*, the work of evangelism, the gathering-in and building-up, the pastoral oversight, the philanthropic and moral crusades among the lowest classes of Society, the visitations of the city gaols and slums, the awakening of the rural areas, as well as the more intensive spiritual culture and discipline in the settlements, or among the choicer souls admitted to the fellowship of society or congregation. To neglect this side of the story would be to lapse into a very biassed and disproportionate presentation of the significance of the English Brethren in the religious revival. It would be an unfortunate effect of concentration upon Zinzendorf's "Church-ideas" if we allowed ourselves to lose sight of the access of spiritual illumination and moral vigour brought to those whom he and his disciples inspired and disciplined in Yorkshire, in London, in the Midlands and the West, in North Ireland and elsewhere. Even when that background has been sketched, there still remain to be recalled the contribution in those two great spheres of Christian service which are a peculiar glory of English Moravianism, their evangelistic missions overseas and their zeal in the cause of Christian education. In each of these departments success has far exceeded numerical increase within their own borders and has carried the influence of their gracious and cheerful piety beyond the bounds of their own Communion. It is positive achievements such as these which, after all, outweigh the importance of their peculiar constitutional position, and they ought therefore to be recalled as a preliminary to the attention we now bestow upon the general developments in national organization and local fortunes of the few years following 1749.

Nor is it pointless to add that what a German observer (Dibelius) of our national characteristics has recently remarked of "Anglicanism" is true of "Moravianism," namely, that its real character is to be apprehended not so much through study of its formal theology and controversial literature as through an understanding of the simple and homely aspects of English religious life which find their centre in the parish church. That observation is equally true in respect of the non-Anglican elements in the national religious life.

The successful conclusion of the appeal to Parliament, therefore, suggests an obvious point at which to notice the more prominent features of the provincial and local administration of the British Province of the Renewed Unity. Our special interest, no less than considerations of space, limit our survey to such features as illustrate the impact of the specific ideals and purposes of Count Zinzendorf upon those local circumstances and national characteristics which so seriously modified the application of those ideals to English conditions.

Spangenberg's summary of the post-Recognition period is

applicable to a longer duration than the few weeks of which he is speaking (*Life*, p. 390):

> After everything had been transacted with the parliament and the bishops . . . the Count devoted himself, for some weeks, more particularly to the church itself, and held several conferences with its teachers.

Spangenberg himself had pursued much the same course some seven or eight years before, when he had organized the Pilgrim House in London, with himself and his wife as house-father and mother, assisted by old friends and new recruits, Lieberkuhn, Schlicht, Töltschig, Piesch, Hutton, Viney and others (Benham, p. 88). But if the method was substantially the same, the agents had changed. In 1749, of the secondary figures, Peter Böhler had returned from Pennsylvania in 1746, and thence onwards devoted himself to evangelistic oversight of the work in England until 1752. With London as centre "he was to superintend the whole English work . . . and to keep up the connection with the Pilgrim congregation." These aims implied the introduction and guidance of the Choir-system and the pastoral care of the individual members (Benham, p. 221). John de Watteville was also active in visitation, Hutton was English Secretary. Gambold was assisting in the literary apologetic and in other kindred labours, Cennick and Töltschig were organizing their converts in Ireland. On the more official side there were Abraham de Gersdorf, Chancellor of the Advocate, David Nitschmann (3), Syndic of the Unity, and the indefatigable Henry Cossart as Agent for England. These three, with Hutton, Sigismund de Gersdorf and Fredk. de Marschall formed the *Commissariat Committee* appointed in 1752.[1]

The appointment of that Committee is important as one proof of the sincerity of the Count's dislike of, and attempts to escape from, the inevitable personal rule of the early years,

[1] Benham, p. 259, note: Cf. the grandiloquent letter to Archbishop Herring, pp. 237–40, for styles and status of the Prelates, Bishops and Primary Ministers, June 1749. Böhler, a "Rural Bishop," is "pastor of the Church of the Brethren in London, and Vicar throughout Great Britain and Ireland."

to avoid "a perpetual dictatorship during troublous times." The chief constitutional interest of the period following the turn of the century is, in point of fact, the transition from "a monarchical form of government to a collegiate board of direction." But this was a long process needing a period of years for its full accomplishment, and it is clear that the events of this period, both of good and evil fortune, served to accentuate the dependence of the English Brethren upon the Count and his intimates, the majority of whom were naturally of the same nationality as himself.

There are plenty of illustrations of this continued dependence. We may note that the "unhappy differences" brought about by the clash in 1744 between Spangenberg and Richard Viney "which threatened to dissever entirely the English from the German brethren" actually issued in the closer dependence of the English labourers on their German leaders and in an admission of their unwillingness and inability to "do anything without the Count." Such is the burden of the two letters of contrition sent, the one from Yorkshire, the other from London, to the Synod of July 1744. The English Brethren acknowledge their faults in no measured terms.

> Dear Brethren and Sisters, if you should leave us in this condition; you, who are nurses and the healthy parts of the body of Christ to which we belong; you would scarce leave anything but what is sick and faint. Be quite assured that all those thoughts of ours, of being independent and setting up for ourselves, came upon us as a punishment and plague for our pride, from which we wish to be delivered.

So London wrote, while Yorkshire asked forgiveness "desiring rather to be struck off the list of labourers than to be severed from the Count and the pilgrim-congregation." The Count's clap of thunder had certainly frightened the sheep back into the fold.[1]

[1] For *Viney's Rebellion*, see Benham, pp. 139–49; Wauer, pp. 92–5; also Herrnhut, R. 13, A. 5 (3) and R. 13. A. 7 (2)—a packet of many letters and testimonials from humble and unlearned English Brethren written after "the late confusions," saying how much they love the Saviour and His "dear disciple" or "the dear papa." See also R. 13, B. 1, No. 6, Report of London Provincial Conference, January 24, 25, 1747, opened by a speech from Böhler on this subject.

This was in 1744, but the letters represent the attitude of most, if not all, the English "labourers" to Zinzendorf's person and plans. Before the lease of Northampton House (1749) and after, events forced him to the centre of the stage, and his own protests against his immersion in "secular" affairs ring true. When the Lord Chief Justice asked Hutton whether the person called Count Zinzendorf was not "head of all the bishops," the Unity's Secretary replied, "The bishops among us are equal, and he acts, but unwillingly. We cannot get him to act enough" (Benham, p. 295). The Count seems to have become painfully conscious of this tendency to rely on him to do everything, to be at hand in every emergency. His own unsparing physical activity, the accessions to his personal authority and acceptance of his regulative ideas in various Synods (*e.g.* Hirschberg, 1743, and Herrnhaag, 1747), the enhanced freedom and dignity resulting from his reinstatement in his civil rights in Saxony, the growth of the Brethren's settlements from France to Russia and the favourable estimates of princes and nobles as to their moral health and economic value—these and other events give a certain symbolic significance to the migration from the hired lodgings in Bloomsbury to a set of three houses around Westminster Abbey (1751) and thence to Lindsey House in Chelsea, renovated at a cost of £11,000 (1753). Henceforth this was the Disciples' House and home of the collegiate Board of Direction. Here he gathered around him the closer circle of unofficial aides-de-camp who best knew his mind and were bound to him by memories of fights fought together, by personal affection, by reverence for his self-denying labours, and by identity of purpose. Sometime before 1749 James Hutton had sent a long despatch, running over the needs and the difficulties of the whole field in England and of each several locality. It was written with some forthcoming Synod in view, as we may gather from the following citation:

> The Tropus for the Church of England requires perhaps time or it may be in some lucky hour when the wind blows; even at this synod something may be thought of therein. I wish we had Brethren of ours, Communicants in the

> Church of England, who could upon occasion protest against Atheists or Deists being promoted to Bishopricks and who could if needful carry on a spiritual offensive *intra muros* against Satan and his clerks.

The writer goes on to suggest the creation of a "General Staff" for England: Gambold, Marschall and La Trobe would be a good triumvirate, sufficient for General Management—that is, supposing Böhler goes to America; he would be the best "Œconomus" for England.[1] As it happens, some such metaphor as that of a General Officer served by a staff of field officers is a fair enough analogy as applied to this period of Zinzendorf's last years in this country.

To add the melancholy truth that the Count was a commander-in-chief of an army on the defensive, if not in retreat, is to indicate a whole series of unfortunate events which underlined his own indispensability. The decade 1750–60 was not an easy period for one in his position. The "Sifting Time" had drawn to a close in the very year of the English parliamentary success, but the evil results of that unfortunate episode lasted for some years and provided fuel to the fires of scorn and vilification, the quenching of which tested to the uttermost the Count's moral authority, social prestige and literary talents. From 1750 much time and energy must have been absorbed in the task of arranging for the transportation of the Herrnhaag settlers to other settlements in the old and new worlds, the salving of the goods, archives and other material from the wreck, the transference of the educational establishments to Upper Lusatia and in the disciplinary measures entered on in the re-establishment of the general morale.

More necessary still it is to recall that it was within this period that those financial confusions befell the English Brethren from which, as was more than once acknowledged, they could hardly have escaped irremediable disaster without the assistance of Zinzendorf's credit and financial resources.[2]

[1] Herrnhut, R. 13, A. 9, No. 7. Themselves undated, the documents in this bundle have outside cover dated 1736–49.

[2] Benham, pp. 265–81; Spangenberg, pp. 400–1, on Zinzendorf as a financier; pp. 423–8, the mismanagements of 1753. Add Holmes, I, pp. 411–14.

Considered merely as a story, the narrative of the collapse of the English Diaconies is a most fascinating one. The *dramatis personæ*, in major or minor rôles, are numerous and varied—London lawyers, honourable women of wealth and devotion, business agents whose capacity for affairs is less obvious than their piety, James Charlesworth, the mystic turned business-manager, and, to add a touch of melodrama, the defaulting Jew, Jacob Gomez Serra. The total liabilities—in 1753 well over £130,000—were frightening enough for so small a community, and the contemporary lavish expenditure on the London headquarters may well " excite astonishment." Almost equally astonishing were the marvellous interpositions of Providence which from time to time rescued both Zinzendorf and his humbler friends from a debtor's prison. But for our special study the most significant feature is the clear proof afforded by these events that the " faithful ministers of the Unity " were thoroughly justified in their protests against the Count's verbal and written intimations of his intention to relinquish his offices in the autumn of 1751. They had then pointed out " that it would be impossible for him to withdraw without great injury, since the direction of the whole Unity had been hitherto confided to him."[1]

For it should not be forgotten that the official conduct of affairs from London was not the only or even the most formidable portion of Zinzendorf's labours. There were conferences with choir leaders, visits as pastor and teacher to the schools (at Mile End and elsewhere), there were the long and arduous

[1] Spangenberg, pp. 413 f.: "The Count afterwards perceived that he had been premature in his arrangements for retiring." Cf. Benham, p. 280. It was said after the Count's decease and was strictly true: "We ought always to bear in grateful remembrance the fact that from the year 1750, Zinzendorf and his family were alone the means of saving our Church from utter financial ruin." Zinzendorf made another effort to retire the next year. Apart from desire for quiet and theological study, he seems to have felt his incapacity for business management. This side of the Brethren's expansion may be estimated when it is remembered that in that year they negotiated the purchase of 100,000 acres in North Carolina, and that their budget for 1752 amounted to £200,000 (Benham, p. 279).

We shall later note effects of the financial crisis in certain constitutional changes—which in their turn issued in further crises in the next century.

journeys undertaken in the work of supervision. These last were not confined to England; during this period of six years we find him in Germany, negotiating with landowners, holding conferences, organizing theological teaching in the seminaries, then returning *via* Switzerland and France to do the like in England. The year 1754—" a calm liturgical year "—saw him in Wilts, Bristol, Bedford, Fulneck. And yet it was a year marked by an illness of six weeks, by negotiations in respect of the work overseas, by a conference in May, a Synod in November, by the publication of the *Plain Case*, of a new edition of *Liturgies and Litanies*, and by preparation of the new and official volume of Statutes. There was need indeed for a " General Staff." The manifold activities, literary, financial, secretarial, pastoral, pointed to the emergence of some sort of executive and administrative authority, and it is therefore not surprising that with the settlement at Lindsey House we come first upon a whole series of devolutions in the general management of the various branches. Some of these were spasmodic and temporary, the outcome of pressing necessities; others, like the Directory or Board of General Superintendence, had their offspring (or their counterparts) in the more permanent arrangements which survived until the middle of the next century.

(ii) *The Two English Synods of* 1754

Devolution of administration was therefore one mark of " the decline of the monarchical principle "; another indication of the simultaneous growth of " conferential government " during Zinzendorf's English residence was the increasing importance of the Synod, that characteristic feature of all subsequent Moravian history. The first Synod had been held as long ago as June 1739, and others, on the Continent or in London, have had some notice in earlier pages. But it seems possible to trace a growth of synodical independence as the scene and the time shift from Germany to England and from the earlier to the latter deliberations over which Zinzendorf presided. Lindsey House saw a goodly number of these assemblies and their place in the life of the Province and Unity vindicated and made permanent.[1]

The two Synods held in the last year of the Count's stay in this country (May and November 1754) deserve special notice. Bishop Hamilton interprets their work as marking a further stage towards "Denominationalism," and their deliberations as having "formally recognized the fact that the work had assumed such proportions that its distinct denominational character must be admitted" (Hamilton, p. 164). This, he adds, was effected by defining more clearly the line between "*societies*" on the circumference and the "*congregations*" enjoying full membership; the latter were henceforth to enjoy the administration of the sacraments while society-members must continue to go to their own ministers. It is an interpretation which can scarcely be justified.

As to the definite regulation on the administration of the Sacrament it will be sufficient to say that the change was no more than one of greater strictness in execution of a well-established regulation, since this rule had held from the beginning. A Provincial Conference in London, 1747, had made this quite clear:

> *Our Plan about the Administration of the Sacrament*, to such as do not belong to the Congregation is this: To direct everybody to their respective Constitutions without that thereby or therefore the Heartsfellowship which we have with one another should be broken off. About this we had a very large and blessed Discourse to the satisfaction of the whole Conference; several objections were made and resolved (R. 13, B. 1, No. 6).

And as to the general interpretation of the results of the two 1754 Synods, Bishop Hamilton's estimate seems a rather flagrant wresting of contemporary evidence to suit subsequent development. The extracts now to be given from the Acts of the November Synod *may* be made to bear some such interpretation as he suggests, but it will hardly be denied that their general bearing points in a direction quite other than that of the

[1] The Composition, Methods of Business and Power of the Synod, c. 1830, are described in Holmes, II, pp. 330–2.

attainment of a " distinct denominational character." If such phrasing is intended to bear its present-day signification it must be roundly asserted that neither Zinzendorf nor his colleagues, German or English, had any intention of leading the English Branch of the Unity towards such a goal. It may be conceded that the Synod marks a forward step towards " the conferential principle " as against " the monarchical principle," but so long as Zinzendorf's " ground-ideas " held the field, this advance could not spell " Denominationalism." To use such terminology is surely to antedate tendencies belonging to a considerably later era. There may have been, below the surface, in the minds of some of the subordinate leaders, a recognition that there were " two inherently contradictory purposes actuating the operations of the Unity," but so far as concerns the Synods of 1754, it can only be said that the contrasting policies were not in evidence.

Indeed the two great obstacles to subsequent expansion so lamented by the modern Moravian historians of the Anglo-Saxon Branches—the constitutional subordination to the Continental Directory and the Settlement System with its corollary, the discouragement of converts desiring full membership—were tendencies encouraged and fostered at this Synod. Zinzendorf's announcement of the intention to consecrate Gambold as a Bishop of the English Branch was accompanied by the comforting assurance that this action did not imply any withdrawal of German support and direction. The lines of future policy in relation to other churches and to internal development through Settlement and Diaspora work were discussed and decided, and so far as we can see, nothing was said or done, from either the German or the English members, to dissent from their leader's emphatic assertion that " the chief calling of the resuscitated Church (was) to be not self-propagation, but the infusion of a vital leaven into the Confessional Churches by the promotion of vital religion in the lives of individual members of those Churches who should not detach themselves from the fellowship of the ecclesiastical bodies in which they had been born, even though they became affiliated with the Brethren " (Hamilton, p. 112). That may serve as a fair summary of the Unity's policy so long as

Zinzendorf was alive—and its name is not "Denominationalism." Neither is it credible that the Count could have testified that the hand of Providence was manifest in this Synod (November) more than at any other similar assembly previously held in England, had that Synod shown any very lively symptoms of departing from principles he himself had so often and so earnestly inculcated.

It is for quite other reasons that the Synod which sat at Lindsey House, November 11–15, 1754, deserves serious attention. It had been preceded (June–August) by a tour of inspection, and within six months of its close Zinzendorf had left England for good. In all there were 87 delegates—63 Brethren and 24 Sisters. The "General Staff" fell into two groups, the one, "out of the Disciples' House," including Zinzendorf, John de Watteville, Hutton, the two Nitschmanns, Gersdorf, Cossart, La Trobe, Crantz, Metcalfe and several sisters; the other, from London and the North and West, including Gambold, Marschall, and West. Motived, probably, by the knowledge of his impending return to Germany, Zinzendorf addressed the Synod in a very long discourse, stressing his fundamental ideas and offering observations on the general situation then prevailing. Too long for transcription, the circumstances of its delivery and its value as illuminative of the speaker's mind warrant a few extracts.[1]

After noting the antiquity of the Bohemian Brethren's Church in Protestantism—"We are *primi inter pares*"—its bursting of the bonds of national constitutions and its possession of some peculiar treasure for he who is a true Brother-in-heart, the Count recalls his protest against "the Brethrens in London turning Moravian, and why I called the then reigning Primate to my help against them." He cannot narrate the whole history of the Brethren, but he will point out the difference between a Brother in England and one in Greenland or Morocco. It hinges on the presence or absence of religious toleration :

> When I find that the Liberty of conscience is fact in all England, except New England and, perhaps, part of Virginia,

[1] Herrnhut, R. 13, B. 2, 1*a*, 1*b*, 1*c*—three copies, of which the first contains Zinzendorf's own red pencil corrections in margin.

> for in all the rest I believe it is fact, then the chief reason for receiving people among us loses its force. . . .
> . . . We *cannot* reject people in Denmark, Sweden, Livonia because there there is no real safety for anyone who desires to be a Christian.

In these lands people join the Brethren at the cost of social ostracism or perhaps of loss of goods, but they gain full liberty of conscience for themselves and for their children . . . " that is pretty much the case in Holland too; the Menonists, Reformed and Lutherans, if they become true Christians have in many places no liberty of conscience without appealing to us, without being clothed with our ignominy; then they are scorned but safe." Since this argument does not apply to England, " I cannot say that there are no reasons at all in England for joining with us, but they are reasons absolutely different from those of all other countries." In England, as distinct from Germany (where " there are no such things as extraordinary pulpits ") the National Church being

> in extreme distress in spiritual matters and in expectation of losing more of her true foundation cannot but be glad that there is another Episcopal Church besides in the world intrusted with ye Treasury of a Church and the Christian faith itself, and the hearts and good wishes of all good clergy cannot but be with us . . . and this makes the *vox populi christiani* here in England to be always with us, tho' they will not venture always to say so publickly, yet they cannot help being so minded and occasionally showing it and promoting it *sotto mane*. The extravagant course of these two or three years will perhaps have its bad effects for a time but in two or three years all will be forgotten and our good fame be re-established by experience and the life and real nature of the thing as it is now related will thrill again in the veins of the old Christians in England, we will be restored again to be the object of the good wishes and hearty rememberance of all who expect consolation in Israel. The spiritual race of them will never forget or neglect us, will always wish well to us, and respect us;

be it a Peer, or a Bishop, a Dean or a Lawyer, or Curate, he will do so.

Such prognostications belong perhaps to the region of dreams and visions which were to fade in the light of common day. But they are important for the light they throw on Zinzendorf's mind at this juncture and their accents doubtless fell with grateful coolness on the ears of Gambold, Hutton and the other Anglicans present. Exactly similar is Par. 21 of the subjoined "*Recitatio*," a series of 179 short minutes registered by the Synod.

> 21. In all other countries except England it is hard for a child of God to come safe through this world without being united to the Brethren's Church, especially if he is not a Hero or a Genius. But that argument, to become a United Brother out of necessity, does not hold in England.

Another distinction between England and other countries is that in England a witness for Christ need never lack a pulpit, if not in the Church, there are the streets and fields where with very little courage and perhaps even to applause he may become a Trumpet of Grace. To which sociological observation Zinzendorf's red pencil adds with sardonic shrewdness,

> Here (in England) there is no occasion for Peter's denying his Master but only for Judas' selling him.

It was a pity there were not more itinerant preachers :

> for we have hitherto been too much for planting Congregations and making a wall or ditch round every class of Hearers, about every place where we dwell or preach, which is a thing not only quite different from the Apostleship, but in some measure a hindrance to it.

The *Recitatio* covers a very wide field, doctrinal, ecclesiastical and practical. Some few excerpts will be useful in estimating the Synod's view of the place of the Unity among the various "religions."

> Par. 5. A true English Churchman comes the nearest to our way of thinking.

7. We want such a true and noble Friend among the English Prelates for the good of the English Church; that the awakened souls might abide within the verge of the English Church.

17. Our Saviour's having been acknowledged the Sovereign Chief of our council was published and put in execution too soon. The Disciple going immediately after to America there happened in his absence, and against his Protestation, great confusion in the political and economical matters of our Church, so that our People became by degrees an Aristocracy and at last a Democracy.

31. *The London Congregation* was in the beginning a happy Democracy; and it is a pity this way of treating matters publicly with the Congregation was not kept up.

38. It is a Demonstration of the Sovereign Power of a People which can make laws to which they oblige themselves.

40. We should have a Bishop of this nation who could take the defence of our Church upon himself if a case should require it.

To this paragraph is added a notice of the election and consecration of Br. Gambold as a Bishop of the English Congregation, it being first explained that "we had no intention of forsaking the English Brethren."

Sections 41–89 are a reaffirmation of "*Principles out of the former Synod*"—presumably that held earlier in this year.

44. *The Congregation of Christ in general* hath as yet no house of her own "but is still looking for one." "The Bridegroom is still invisible, therefore the Bride must not covet more convenience." She appears under "a borrowed body," *i.e.* under the form or scheme of one "of the then best evangelic Religions and at another time of another."

45. The Brethren's Church is a Corporation (as the phrase is in England) and is likewise the Inn of all those children of God who cannot otherwise subsist and come through the world.

53. *The Tropuses* have no reference at all to the Heart. There is no difference in Christ Jesus: there is one Faith, one Saviour, one Merit, one Life and Happiness. The

difference consists only in that manner of communicating Ideas wherein a Person hath been brought up.

57. Our Communities are not only not commissioned to storm constitutions already settled, or even in a secret or subtle manner, to undermine them, but they ought to have in their mind a kind of veneration for every society that hath made a Regulation of its own matter, and where the Lord hath granted so far a continance that Doors could be fixed to the House, there it becomes them to use great Deference.

From Section 90 onwards are given "*The Principles of the Present Synod.*"

94. In England every Society has leave to form its own articles of agreement so they do not clash immediate (and we add, nor mediate) with the laws of the country.

110. Ideas rooted in the minds of people in their childhood and afterwards so often repeated to them, remain through the whole life the same, tho' explained to them in 20 different ways. The Tropuses are therefore among us in order to suppose an honest and innocent case of differing from one another in bye-parts and yet entirely to be joined in head matters.

132. It must be well considered if People who leave the Church wherein they are born and educated do it out of a certain spirit of novelty. A Brother must be forced to stay in his own Church as long as he can. If he can go to the Sacrament in the English Church then he enjoys the same there as he would enjoy in our Church ; he might there also embrace our Saviour who embraces us in the Sacrament.

Since the 170th Resolution enjoins the keeping of "an extraordinary Festival Day in all the English Congregations in order to publish the Maxims and Resolutions of this Synod" it may be inferred that both these and the other Resolutions (of a doctrinal, administrative and disciplinary character) were at any rate promulgated to all the faithful soon after, however much or little they were inwardly digested and fully comprehended. These Synodal *Acta* have been stressed as representing aptly and compactly and in its true historical perspective the high-water-mark of Zinzendorf's authority and influence on early English Moravianism. Not without significance in view of his approaching departure one of the final Resolutions appointed a German copyist for London for the quicker expedition and communication of congregation accounts. He was to work under the direction of Bishop Gambold, the new "Chor-episcopus," who, though lacking in certain qualities necessary to leadership, was, in virtue of social status, educational attainments and community of outlook, perhaps most suitable to act as liaison-officer between the English Brethren and the Unity's Directory at Bethelsdorf.[1]

(iii) *Settlements and the Brotherly Agreement*

In its survey of the Province the second Synod of 1754 included the regulation of what it calls the "Choir Ideas" (*Protocol*, or Report of *Sessio* 2, Nov. 11, 12). Some general principles and rules under this head (copiously amended by Zinzendorf's red pencil) did in fact provide that documentary basis of the settlement system, *the Brotherly Agreement*, by which the local Communities could cement their union with the whole body (cf. Hamilton, p. 164). Our account of these years would be most incomplete without some reference to that basic skeleton-document. The actual versions, embodying the appropriate local variations, were printed later, but, their general standpoint and substance being almost identical, the skeleton outline connects the later period of stabilization with

[1] The Reports of this Synod include a series of loose slips, 5 by 2½ inches, which may have been notes for the President's guidance. They are corrected in Zinzendorf's hand. One runs :—

"When there has been a solemn awakening among the Lutherans or Reformed then they have always had a certain man to whom they resorted and whose followers they were. The Pietists had Prof. Francke (inserted, Spener), the Anabaptists Bunian, the Presbyterians Baxter, the Religious People of the English Church, Beveridge. But our Church must have no other head of the family than our Saviour Himself. No spiritual economy that has any man living for its Head is a Congregation of our Rule, be it ever so wisely constructed. . . . Our Saviour is the (spiritual) Monarch of our Church" (R. 13, b. 4).

the earlier formative period now under review. There is no easier way to gain an accurate insight into the spirit and habits of the early English Brethren than through a perusal of one or more of the foundation documents of Fairfield, Fulneck or other Settlement.[1]

It is unnecessary to enquire how far the general framework of the Brotherly Agreement represents Zinzendorf's own conception of a *Gemeine Gottes* and how much was contributed in modification and supplement by the Directory, or by La Trobe, Hutton, and other English Brethren; in other words, how far German and English influences respectively were responsible for the final form. What is certain is that the Settlement was the distinctive feature of the Brethren's second stage of operations in this country, as on the Continent it continues to be today. It is to the Settlement that we must look to see the characteristic Moravian social and religious ideal in its purest expression. The diaspora-work, the little societies retaining a more or less close contact with the parish church, the educational establishments, the missions overseas, have no doubt been more fruitful in making the Moravians widely known and admired and in extending their quiet influence through the churches. These departments of their labours, however, reveal them fulfilling the rôle of leaven in the lump, while, to change the metaphor, it was the discipline of the Settlement, the intimate communal life, the elevation of Service to the Brotherhood as the mark of a true spiritual aristocracy, the careful nurture of souls through Choir and Band systems, which gave a backbone to the infant organism. The Brotherly Agreement was the official presentation of the

[1] The general draft was formally agreed upon at Barby (1775) and (after some misunderstanding had been removed) assented to by the London Congregation Council almost unanimously, 10.3.1776. It was then read to the new Helpers' Conference, printed and delivered to the several choirs and to every member (Benham, pp. 505–6). Our summary is based on those for Fulneck (1771), Grace Hill (1773)—both at Herrnhut, MSS. A. 39—and a printed copy of Fairfield, 1787, in Fetter Lane. As these dates show, we are here anticipating the formal documentary enunciation of principles of association operative for some thirty years. Cf. Hutton, II, X, and also pp. 442–5, 449, for stringent criticism of the Agreement as restricting expansion. A more objective description is in Holmes, II, X, pp. 320–43.

idea of a true Society of Brethren offered to the more earnest converts contemplating membership in the Unity. Our congregations, said the Synod responsible for the first outline of the successive local Agreements, should be

> cities set on a hill, whose inhabitants let their light shine before men, their walk and conversation proving that living faith in Jesus creates not merely true cheerfulness and happiness of mind, but also strict rectitude of conduct in its professors, who are zealously intent upon following after truth, faithfulness and charity towards their neighbours (Holmes, II, p. 63).

" Cities set on a hill " : the metaphor applies much more aptly to the *Settlement-villages* whose fame spread throughout the regions round about, than to the *Congregations*, whether " Town " or " Country," whose " members lived dispersed among other inhabitants," or to the *Societies* whose " members remain in religious communion with the established Church of the country where they reside, improving their connection with the Brethren for private edification " (*ibid.*, II, p. 325).

The Brotherly Agreement and Declaration concerning the Rules and Orders of the Brethren's Congregation at —— was much more than a bare enunciation of Terms of Membership. That for Fairfield extends to fifty-five printed pages, and, following six pages of introductory exhortation and historical references, presents sections on :

Pp. 7–12, I. The Relation of the Congregation to other Christian Denominations.
12–24, II. The Foundation and Rule of the Congregation-Constitution.
24–25, III. The Relation to the Magistrates.
25–28, IV. The Relation between the Congregation and its Servants.
28–38, V. The Relation of the Members of the Congregation to the Congregation itself.
39–44, VI. The Conduct of the Congregation-members individually, and towards each other.
45–53, VII. Rules and Orders of Trade.

The Compact is to be signed by all "labourers," servants of the congregation, house-fathers and masters, by other helpers, servants and curators, and "by whomsoever else it was thought necessary." Its concern ranges from the fundamental doctrinal basis of the Brotherhood to the care of orphans and apprentices. Considerable space is occupied by copious directions as to the choice and duties of the numerous "labourers," the congregation-helper, the minister of the congregation, the Choir helpers and their subordinates; the constitutional machinery, Elders' Conference, Choir Helpers' Conference, the College of Overseers, the Congregation Council; the regulation of domestic relationships, of parents and children, of masters and servants, of craftsmen and apprentices; care of the aged and orphans; debts and the provision of credit, new buildings, the preservation of public order, safeguards against fire, leave of absence and the assuagement of animosities. The details have on occasion a very human interest. Lord Westbury once genially observed that the Law "in its infinite wisdom has provided for the not improbable event of the imbecility of a bishop," and the Brotherly Agreement partakes of that embraciveness by a provision that mercy shall be shown to any who should be deprived of their reason "and if he should recover, what is past shall never be remembered to his prejudice" (VI, ii).

But the importance and attractiveness of the Compact does not lie in the specific regulations covering a wide variety of human relationships so much as in the unexpressed but obvious background of moral energy and spiritual fellowship. Here is another of mankind's oft-repeated attempts to build a City of God upon the earth, to found a Kingdom where the law of Christ might reign supreme over every personal habit and social relationship. It is an ideal, the service of which may well counterbalance its inutility in the cause of denominational expansion (cf. Hutton, *op. cit.*). If it be objected that the regulations were cramping and restrictive of individual initiative, the reply is forthcoming that it is an old lesson that the individual, fully to find himself, must be prepared to sacrifice something of his personal freedom. To the criticism that the system removed the zealous Brother from the dust and heat of the conflict in the world, the answers suggest themselves, first, that the settlement-village was not the only sphere in which the awakened soul could do battle with the Evil One, that entry was voluntary, that he could join a town or village congregation or, perchance, a mission settlement overseas; finally, that here again is an old problem admitting of no easy solution, and one which the followers of Christ in all ages have hardly solved, namely, how to influence the world without catching something of its stain. The Moravian Brother in his Choir-house, like the monk within his stone walls, was at least of that goodly company who have heard, and in part followed, the call to count all else but loss if only they might make their calling and election sure.[1]

The limitations of this essay preclude us from dwelling upon other developments in the life, worship, discipline and literature of the English Branch of the Renewed Unity during Zinzendorf's lifetime. We are driven regretfully to decline some notice of the provision of literature for the use of the societies and congregations—sermonic, devotional, liturgical, as distinct from the controversial pamphlets. That distinction, indeed, between those two species of literary production, is no rigid one. Zinzendorf's own preference and plan was, not to meet the literary attacks with counter controversial writing, but to go steadily on with the issue of suitable doctrinal and devotional literature for the awakened souls from which, too, any fair-minded enquirer could learn the real character of the new community. As Gambold, then engaged in translating the *London Discourses*, wrote to him, one effect should be to " cause the Lutheran Church and the Brethren to be looked upon partly together and with one and the same Eye which will be just and true and also put an end to many foolish suspicions

[1] Extract from document deposited under the foundation-stone of the chapel at Fairfield : " The earnest desire of many, to come together to be separated from the world and its seductions ; for their own sake and the sake of their children to enjoy true fellowship, as children of God, and to be prepared for the purpose of the Lord with them ; and the will of God, the only reason of every right act—is the cause of the erection of this house and of all the houses that shall be erected in this place . . ." (Herrnhut MSS., R. 13, A. 45, b.)

we unjustly labour under."[1] Much in the same way, there was a twofold purpose behind the decision of the Herrnhaag Synod of 1747 (attended by Gambold, Hutton, Ingham and Cennick) to put in hand the translation of various homiletic and liturgical compositions; to their devotional value would be added the happy result of a closer union of the German and English Branches and the clearer demarcation of the latter from the Methodists. Hutton and Gambold were especially indefatigable in this department, and from the break with Wesley onwards they translated or composed and printed a large number of Manuals, Tracts, Litanies and Hymns for the use of the faithful and the information of the outside public.[2]

[1] March 31, 1746, O.S. London; R. 13, A. 10, 8. The unjust suspicions, of course, are those arising from the untrue notion that Zinzendorf is founding a new sect.

[2] See Benham, pp. 75, 77, 84 and 222.

(I) *Early Moravian Hymnology* is a study with its own strong intrinsic interest as well as its historical value as "a mirror of Moravian life," Hutton, *Owen's College Essays*, and *History*, pp. 362–64. The hymns, too, were in effect part of the literary apology, though naturally less deliberately so. "The chief burden of the hymns was *Ecce Homo*." For Zinzendorf's enormous compilations, see Spangenberg, pp. 430, 439, 442. A Maxim of the second Synod of 1754 runs: "A necessary quality of a Church Hymn is, that there should be no shadow of Rhetoric or Poetry in it."

(II) *The Controversial Literature.*—I have not thought it necessary to do again what the Rev. J. E. Hutton has done so fully in his *History*, II, XIII. Lambeth Library holds a generous collection of pamphlets *pro* and *con* following the publicity of 1749. The ill-nature of the hostile elements is reproduced as late as 1873 in Tyerman's characterization of the *Acta Fratrum* as "full of repulsive jargon" (*Oxf. Meth.*, p. 135). Benham presents a summary, pp. 303–10, and see Appendix I; he prints the *Candid Declaration* (1768) in his Appendix II. *Theological Tracts*, 1751–2 (Lambeth, 113, E. 4), includes, *Some Observations on the Antiquity of the present United Brethren called Moravians*, 22 pp., Printed for W. Owen, 1751, which illustrates the charges of Popish superstitions: the Moravian sentiments on the Lord's Supper are so like Transubstantiation that Protestants cannot well distinguish one from the other. Yet the union at Herrnhut was an act of *Independency*, and the claim to antiquity is therefore baseless: the Brethren are not "so old as many congregations we have in London."

Rimius' *Solemn Call*, 1754, and Gambold's translation of the *Peremtorisches Bedencken*, 1753, are both in Lambeth, III, H. 13. See pp. 44–57, "Idea of the Present Ordinary of the Brethren," for a neat and homely piece of self-portraiture. Zinzendorf's personal character is further argued in *The Representation of the Committee of the English Congregations in union with the Moravian Church*, 1754 (Herrnhut, R. 13, A. 10, No. 11). See also Gambold's *Maxims*, etc., 1755 (Benham, p. 303). Gambold's *Modest Plea*, 1754, is in Lambeth, III, H. 13, 10, and *The Plain Case*, 112 f., 16, for which also see Benham, p. 310, note. This pamphlet carefully distinguishes " the case of our United Brethren in England " from " they of the Unitas "—a common line of defence. The following is a particularly clear enunciation thereof and may be worth transcription. It is from a series of twenty-eight questions and answers from Zinzendorf to Councillor T. White, July 1753, prefaced by a letter from Zinzendorf saying these answers are true and represent the principles on which he has acted for thirty years.

Question (4). " The Method in which the English Brethren are joined to the Foreign ? "

Answer. " The English Brethren have never been joined to the foreign: the Ordinary of the Brethren having constantly refused hitherto to join them to the Episcopal Branch of the Unitas, they formed a particular Branch for themselves, called the English Branch of the Unitas, different from the Lutheran or Reformed one. The Ordinary conferred a long time with the late Archbishop of Canterbury about having him or some other of the Bishops President of that Part of the Unitas ; the Archbishop liked it very much but believed that business must be carried on with the Chancellor ; these endeavours were prevented by the Archbishop's death and are now entirely spoiled by the unmannerliness (in Zinzendorf's red pencil, ' disobliging procedure ') of the present Archbishop " (Herrnhut, R. 13, A. 31).

Chapter IV

THE GROWTH OF PROVINCIAL INDEPENDENCE, 1760–1899

A. "Religionen als Nationalsachen"

IN concluding our account of Zinzendorf's personal activities, we noted that, for four years after his death, the direction of the Unity fell into the hands of a Provisional Board drawn together out of the more prominent leaders then resident at Herrnhut. It was the mid-point of the Seven Years' War and conditions in Central Europe were not conducive either to the convocation of representative assemblies or to the steady development of local life in settlement and congregation.[1] We noted also how, as soon as the political situation permitted, a Synod was convened at Marienborn, and the long process of evolving constitutional and administrative machinery for the Renewed Church of the Brethren was begun. Some particular phases of that evolution are now to be noted, though, even more than hitherto, our attention must be concentrated upon events relevant to our special purpose. Therefore, neglecting the parallel developments in Doctrine, Worship and Discipline, we now briefly review the progress of the English Branch of the *Unitas Fratrum* towards its present status of a Free Episcopal Church largely uninfluenced in its day-to-day activities either by the circumstances of its renewal within the circle of Zinzendorfian ideas or by its present loose attachment to the successors of the first Directory who succeeded to the control of affairs on Zinzendorf's decease.

Even in respect of the constitutional development it is not possible to clothe the outline with adequate detail. Nor is it

[1] A convenient summary of the political background and of the effects of the War upon Prussia and England will be found in Hassall, *Balance of Power*, pp. 283–94; and *Camb. Mod. History*, Vol. VI, Chap. ix.

necessary, since many of the phenomena to be met with invariably characterize any other of those historical transitions from " Society " to " Church " of which British Moravianism is one example. To compare small things with great, our present study recalls the task to which Edwin Hatch addressed himself in his Bampton Lectures; we are, in a vastly less momentous connection, engaged like him in what Fairbairn termed " a study in ecclesiastical biology " (*Catholicism, Roman and Anglican*, p. 417). And if, even in the domain of ecclesiastical history, Law and Evolution seem to afford an explanation of events preferable to those drawn from the region of the Supernatural and the Catastrophic, this is not to cast any shadow of doubt upon the institution whose origins and development are being explored.

> It (the Church) is as divine as the solar system is divine, because both are the expressions and results of those vast laws of the divine economy by which the physical and the moral world alike move and live (Hatch, *Organization of the Early Christian Church*, p. 20).

It will be further recalled how the great Anglican scholar, in his Hibbert Lectures, was able to move forward from this first position to show how the Early Church had assimilated, and, in turn, been transformed by, the moral, intellectual and political conditions of the time; how, in short, the Divine Society had developed within the framework of " secular " society. Just so, the evolution of the Brethren's Church cannot be dissociated from a consideration of those same creative influences of time and place and race. In particular, the fortunes of the modern Unity run parallel with those of the Primitive Church in reflecting on its constitutional side the diversity of racial membership—in the one case Jewish or Roman or Greek, in the other Teutonic or English or American. For certainly if " ecclesiastical biology " be the student's chief interest he will, in considering the later history of the Moravian Church, devote most serious attention to the tension between the German and Anglo-Saxon Branches—the one stressing the elements of order and authority, regimentation and submissiveness, the other those of freedom and elasticity, of personal and provincial independence.

Two qualifications of that broad delineation of the situation ought, perhaps, to be made. The first, by way of warning, is that it would be a false perspective if concentration of interest upon the constitutional aspect of the Brethren's progress should lead us to imagine a situation of incipient rebellion held in check by the strong hand of authority. Between the " constitutional crises " the work went forward at home and abroad, the Gospel was preached, mission-settlements were founded, lives were transformed, the schools grew in numbers and reputation. The very contrast between this quiet progress and the constitutional controversies during the same period may indeed be taken as proof that there is yet a wide and spacious future for an " ecclesiastical constitution " which survived the internal commotions and the external disturbances of that century during which the foundations of modern democratic nationalism were laid in both the Old World and in the New.

Secondly, it is to be noted that the lines of allegiance to the two complementary ideals of Order and Freedom were not dictated always by national *amour propre*. There was at least one of the foremost English Brethren in the post-Zinzendorfian period who took his stand stoutly on the side of Authority (*i.e.* of the Directing Board), while later decades present evidence of the existence of strong influences in Great Britain running counter to the American demand for provincial autonomy.[1]

B. The Constitutional Synods, 1764–1899

From the very first the Renewed Unity avoided the confusion from which the Salvation Army has only recently escaped.

[1] Bishop Hamilton is surely in error in including the names of James Hutton and B. La Trobe as opponents of the Unity's policy after 1769 (p. 248). As the two Appendices to this chapter show clearly, La Trobe was in entire accord with the authorities at Bethelsdorf; Hutton, while he expressed his own more liberal tendencies in ways which did not commend him to the U.E.C., was most submissive and acquiescent to their corrections. In the controversy of which the Bishop is writing, Centralization *v.* Denominationalism, neither La Trobe nor Hutton would have hesitated a moment in supporting the *former* policy.

If there was any danger of "an autocratic primacy" with John de Watteville in place of the Count, it was averted by the acceptation of "the principle of conferential government" implied by the admittedly provisional character of the interim arrangements preliminary to the calling of a representative Synod. That and the two following assemblies mark the first formative era (1764–1818) and fixed the lines upon which the Unity's polity was to fashion itself until well on into the next century. The Marienborn Synod of 1764 is rightly regarded as "the first General Representative Synod of the Renewed Church of the Brethren," and the situation resulting from its deliberations was indeed the governing factor for an even larger period. Some administrative modification resulted from the next and more widely attended Synod five years later, and the general tendency of both was intensified at the Barby Synod in 1775.

The temporary fixation of the constitution by these three Synods arises from the fact that they created and stabilized that Board of General Superintendence, known after 1769 as the Unity's Elders' Conference (the U.E.C.), which became the supreme executive authority. It consisted entirely of Germans, it had its seat in Germany (Barby, Gnadenfrei, Bethelsdorf, Herrnhut—once at Zeist in Holland), and was responsible only to the General Synod. Provincial Synods, it is true, might be held in each of the six "Provinces" (Upper Lusatia, Silesia, Holland, England, Ireland and America), but such assemblies were merely deliberative and their results must be laid before the General Synod or the U.E.C. The executive officers of the Provinces were appointed by the U.E.C. and were responsible to them, not to the Churches they governed. Moreover, in respect of congregational oversight, the U.E.C. appointed each local Elders' Conference, as also the managers of the Settlements who were to transmit to them yearly reports. At Barby, for instance, the minister was specifically declared to be the agent and representative of the U.E.C. They, too, controlled the selection of candidates for the ministry and of presbyters for the episcopate. No minister might marry without the consent of the U.E.C., which submitted the matter to the decision of the Lot. We have already referred to the restrictive effect of the Brotherly Agreement, fashioned and revised in Germany and presented for their acceptance to the Helpers' Conference in London at this date (1776, Benham, pp. 505–6).

No *serious* departure from the administrative principles of the first three Synods was admitted till well beyond the middle of the nineteenth century. At the close of the Napoleonic era an important General Synod met at Herrnhut (1818). Then, however, the counter-revolutionary and conservative movement educed by the revolutionary spirit of the preceding decades was not favourable to any large innovations. That Synod, in point of fact, came down heavily on the side of ultra-conservatism, under the direction of the more " elderly men who had participated in all the Synods since 1764 " (Hamilton, p. 297). It was a policy of conservatism in that its effect was the retention of the predominance of the Directory, of the clerical as against the lay element, of the German as against the Anglo-Saxon, and of those disciplinary customs (*e.g.* marriage by Lot) which seemed to the " progressives " ripe for relaxation. The German instinct for deference to constituted authority, civil and ecclesiastical, the desire for theological stability, the personal piety and prestige of the " elderly men " were able to withstand the demand for reform. As a contemporary observer prefers to state the situation,

> The Synod did not deem itself justified in making any material changes, even in the external constitution, lest, by altering, or abolishing, some regulations, hitherto deemed almost essential, the attempt which aimed at preventing the increase of tares, should injure the growth of the wheat, which still appeared in ripe abundance (Holmes, II, p. 164).

Whether or no this cautious leadership must bear the whole blame, it is not surprising that the first two decades of the century were marked by a decline both in numbers and quality. This, however, must be balanced by remembering that it was during this same period that the English Brethren, largely through their schools and missions, made distinct advance in the knowledge and esteem of the Christian public ; the London Association in aid of Moravian Missions was founded, on an "undenominational" basis and chiefly by English Churchmen, in 1817. Still, taking the Unity as a whole, it was evident that change must come, and in that very year the American Province had set its hand to the plough. But in 1818, and for some years, the reformists actually secured very little in the way of concession from the U.E.C. Even the death of Bishop Cunow (1823) and the changed outlook indicated by the theoretical abolition of the harmful distinction between the general membership and *der engerer Bund* in 1825 were more than counterbalanced by the conservative deliverance of an English Provincial Synod of the year between (1824), when the Choir-house regulations and the Diacony-system were defended as still necessary and indispensable. It was another British Synod which, ten years later, both reported a stationary membership and also rejected Archbishop Whately's offer to furnish land for a settlement in Wicklow under the impulse of "guarding against" the admission of "improper persons."[1]

For another twenty years premonitions of coming change were in evidence, but did not fructify until 1855, when an American Provincial Synod put forward proposals sufficiently radical as to justify the epithet "revolutionary." They included a scheme for complete provincial independence, the adoption of diocesan episcopacy, upper and lower houses of synodal assembly, and the change of name to "Moravian Episcopal Church in the United States of North America." The force of this tide of radicalism broke somewhat ere it reached European shores, and the agitation in England, both in preparatory Synods and—a new phenomenon—in two monthly periodicals, was of a more moderate character. Still, the years following the turn of the century are those to which the modern Moravian looks back upon as a time of transition full of the promise of liberalizing reform and reviving energies. Much of the success of the movement, as the British Moravian will readily acknowledge, was due to the impetus given from across the Atlantic.

In 1857 a General Synod promulgated what was, in effect,

[1] Hamilton, pp. 352, 356. Statistics of the membership of Congregations, Societies, etc., throughout the world c. 1830, so far as available, are in Holmes, II, pp. 353–62.

a new Constitution for the whole Unity. With the working out of that new order subsequent Synods, both General and Provincial, have been largely preoccupied, notably the General Synods of 1869 and 1879. The latter assented to the doctrine that the Provincial Elders' Conference is capable of powers of initiation and is more than a mere executive committee of the Provincial Synod. Satisfactory enough as a victory in the battle for Provincial independence this in itself was to lead later to protests against the irresponsible autocracy of the Provincial Board. The crusade for constitutionalism was evidently not ended by the achievement of provincial autonomy.[1]

Nevertheless, so much was clear gain, and from 1880 onwards, the Provinces have been able to give effect, with greater freedom, to their own characteristic expressions of their conceptions of the life of a Christian Society in polity, doctrine and worship. The British Provincial Synod of 1890 (Ockbrook) introduced the annual convocation of the provincial synod. The same assembly, by its courageous reaction to the spirit of reform as voiced by Maurice O'Connor, inaugurated a period of efficiency and energy, " a new and brighter era in the history of the Moravian Church in England " (Hutton, p. 495; Hamilton, Chap. 68).

Finally, a fresh recasting of the supreme authority of the Unity took place at the very end of the century. A General Synod, held at Herrnhut in 1899, reviewed the composition and defined the functions of the General Synod, and in Section XV of a new Constitution replaced the U.E.C. by " the Directing Board of the Unity " selected from the four Provincial Boards and the Mission Board, from the membership of which last the President of the Directing Board is drawn. The significance of this regulation is obvious. Through all the constitutional changes the missionary labours of the Unity

[1] See pamphlet, *A Plan for the Better Support of the ministry in the British Province of the Brethren's Church.* Private Circulation only. S. H. Reichel (Herrnhut, R. 13, A. 41, 18).

" The Congregational element is fast disappearing and what may be called the Episcopal element taking its place " (p. 9). The whole tone of the pamphlet marks it as an attack on the P.E.C.; the cure for the evils attending the present rule of a triumvirate is decentralization to District Conferences.

have acted as a cement in binding the Provinces together, and the Directing Board, as representing the whole body, was henceforth to retain control over the Mission Board in matters of major strategy.[1] The Directing Board was provided with an executive of three, and was to hold two or three meetings in the next decennial period.

Provincial independence once achieved, there remained the further task of the emancipation of district and local congregations from certain traditional restrictions without destroying the sense of fellowship with the larger unit. That reform was brought to successful issue at different dates in the three Provinces, and we can do no more than refer to it. It will be both pleasing and appropriate to end this slight sketch of the constitutional development in noting how, at the close of the last century, the composition of the supreme authority of the Unity bears witness to the central emphasis given by the Brethren's Church, then as in the days of Böhler and Spangenberg, to the work of Christian missions overseas.

C. In Defence of the Directory

(i) *Moral and Doctrinal*

It seemed best to give a brief outline of the constitutional development before seeing what there is to be said in explanation and, perhaps, in justification thereof, from an historical viewpoint. It may be admitted forthwith that even our hasty review of the story of the movement towards emancipation from the cramping bonds imposed by an absentee oligarchy does suggest some ground for caustic comment upon the Unity's policy before the reforms of the later nineteenth century (*e.g.* Hutton, p. 465, " senseless and suicidal "). The latent " possibilities of disharmony " are only too often apparent at many a juncture and the malignant effects of undue centralization of authority did in fact steadily militate against the easy development of the Unity as an independent and numerically important ecclesiastical organization. But is there

[1] Hamilton, p. 577. Cf. p. 453. " . . . the work of evangelization amongst the heathen remains one of the strongest bonds linking each division of the Brethren's Church to the Unity as such."

not something—in a due historical perspective, is there not much—to be said in defence of the policy of the Directing Board ?

First, neglecting for a moment the historical and geographical circumstances of the early decades of the Renewal of the Brethren's Church, it is worth while suggesting that behind the temperamental divergences due to national characteristics, there existed an even more fundamental cleavage of a moral and spiritual order. The " high churchman " of the Puritan stamp, who saw the Church as a redeemed Society within, but not of, the world, and heard the call to come out from among them and be separate, would have found many of his own special values stressed among the guiding ideas of the Unity in the late eighteenth and early nineteenth centuries. The constitutional struggle was, in some of its aspects, the reflection of the age-long diversity of ideal between those who prefer a Church small in numbers but pure in faith and zealous in obedience, and those who are prepared to stretch to its uttermost the principle of being all things to all men to gain some, between " a scrupulous endeavour to secure only an unquestionably regenerate membership " (Hamilton, p. 254), and a willingness to let both wheat and tares grow together to harvest. Certainly no member of the numerically greater Churches, Roman, Anglican or Free, will care to cast stones at those leaders of the Unity who chose the first alternative, and pinned their hopes on *das treue Teil der Gemeine*—the *teleioi*. It is, surely, rather dangerous to dissent from the general sentiment of the " fatal sentence " from the Pastoral of the 1800 Synod : " It will be better for us to decrease in numbers and increase in piety than to be a large multitude, like a body without a spirit " (Hutton, p. 428). Perhaps it was as well to have at least one Church in Christendom to which there might be applied words used (almost with an accent of regret) by the Moravian historian in respect of his spiritual ancestry in the early nineteenth century :

> As long as they were true to the (Brotherly) Agreement and the Bible, they do not appear to have cared very much whether they increased in numbers or not. For them the

only thing that mattered was the cultivation of personal holiness (Hutton, p. 449).

Theological orthodoxy, too, must be as jealously guarded as moral purity; hence a parallel conflict manifested itself between those whose first concern is with the preservation of the Faith once delivered and those who hold that nothing is so important as the current interpretation of the Faith in terms intelligible to serious-minded and thoughtful men. The Synod of 1801 in this conflict of temperament and doctrine, emphatically took its stand in the old paths.

Another consideration of the same general type is implicit in the particular quality of the heritage into which the Directory entered. The ardent denominationalist of our own day, thinking and writing for a Christian public which has almost completely lost the conception (assumed rather than argued by both the Primitive and the Mediæval Ages) of the Church as one undivided Body, is not in an easy position to appreciate at their true worth the ideals of the Renewer of the ancient Brethren's Church and of those on whom his mantle fell. The concentration of authority in a German Directory at Barby or Bethelsdorf was due neither to patriotic desires for predominance nor to a hunger for wielding the powers of a benevolent autocracy. It may have been a mistaken but it was a sincere attempt to preserve loyalty to the centre by men who regarded the Unity not so much as a distinct Church as a federation of members in societies and settlements auxiliary to the National Church, Lutheran or Anglican. The modern complacency—more obvious some twenty years ago than today—in face of the continual multiplication of ecclesiastical organizations may be one necessary disadvantage of the movement to substitute Freedom for Authority as the way to truth and certitude. If so, the price must be paid, but let it be confessed that that easy tolerance is at variance with the presuppositions of the Apostolic and post-Apostolic ages and with the creative minds of ecclesiastical history, whether Roman or Anglican, Lutheran or Calvinist. To such minds the right of private judgment in religion would have appeared at the best as an unproportioned and harmful overstatement of the individual element in a Christian sociology; a loose federation with occasional intercommunion as a remedy for "our unhappy divisions" they would have summarily rejected. In the eighteenth century certainly, both in politics and religion, individualism and federalism were plants of yet tender growth, and though it may be assumed that the Cyprianic anathema against those who set "altar against altar" had no terrors for the Directing Board, they yet had among them men of sufficient scholarship who knew that in the eyes of the Church, Roman or Reformed, it was one thing to hold preaching services or to organize religious societies, and another and far graver matter, to administer the Sacraments in those assemblies or societies. Thus when Bishop Reichel, during his official visitation to America in 1779, carefully explained why the Brethren had refrained from administering the Sacraments in "the societies of awakened persons affiliated as the fruit of former itinerations" he was not only echoing Zinzendorf's own accents but was witnessing to a point of ecclesiastical discipline with the most ancient and honourable lineage. The question, how far it was wise and right to apply that general principle to the particular circumstances, may be left to later remarks upon the situation in North America; at the moment we are merely suggesting that the Bishop's ruling is strictly in line with the general policy deliberately adopted and systematically pursued by the Unity's supreme authority at this stage.

(ii) *Influence of the "Lot"*

But before noting some features peculiar to each of the three main fields of labour one other consideration of a quite different character from the foregoing may be touched upon in extenuation of the Directory's policy: viz., their use of the "Lot." Here, again, the observation may be allowed that history is concerned, not with what men ought to have done, but what they actually did and why they did it.

The classic instance of the use of the Lot in the long history of the Unity is, of course, its employment at the Synod of Lhota in 1467 when, under Gregory the Patriarch, the first three ministers of the ancient Church were selected. Apostolic precedent might be, and then was, invoked in defence of a recourse to this substitute for the enlightened reason on such critical occasions of extraordinary difficulty and nicety, but its elevation into " a recognized principle of Church government " seems more difficult to reconcile with any wide study of the Scriptures—the practice of St Paul, for instance.[1]

Continual protests were made against the stifling effect of the use of the Lot upon projects for adaptation of the constitution and administration of the Church to meet new conditions. An early and apt illustration from the post-Zinzendorfian period is the curious case of the Rev. Laurentius Nyberg, minister of Haverfordwest, 1765–7. He is found complaining that the local deputies to the General Synod are not really freely elected by the congregations but have been nominated by the oligarchy at Herrnhut. (He adduces what he considers a suitable historical analogy: " I am just now reading the manner of convoking the Council of Trent.") Bishop Peter Böhler assures his irate correspondent that the local congregations could and should make free choice of their own deputies, save " That deputies so nominated . . . must also have the decisive vote of the only Head of our Church, namely, our Lord Jesus, who will be asked His vote by Lot. . . . For, *plurima vota*, yea even *unanima*, do not decide dubious matters in our congregations " (Benham, p. 436).

There were other English protests. The practice of settling marriages by Lot becomes susceptible of criticism all the weightier when it is remembered that marriage for ministers was compulsory. Under the conservative regime of Godfrey Cunow, " no man could be a member of a Conference, no election was valid, no important business step was taken, without the consent of the Lot " (Hutton, p. 430). Even pupils were admitted to the schools only with its sanction—with the mysterious exception of the school at Fulneck. A reforming Synod, long overdue and thoroughly necessitated by the moral and intellectual ferment of the age, was deferred

[1] See Holmes, I., pp. 50–1; I, pp. 288–92, where, quoting John Loretz's introduction to an edition of the *Ratio Disciplinæ*, he gives details as to the spirit governing the right use of the Lot and the restrictions to be observed in its employment.

repeatedly in deference to the decision of the Lot. When it at last met in 1818, one of its duties was to examine the continued usefulness of certain parts of the administrative machinery. One of the Resolutions emerging from this examination ran:

> The use of the Lot is not founded on any positive commandment in the writings of the New Testament, and therefore we cannot assert that the Lord must at all times govern the Brethren's Church by it (Holmes, I, p. 292).

That Resolution may be said to mark the beginning of the end. Yet only slowly did the compulsion of the Lot in settling marriages fade away (in 1836). As late as 1847 an English Provincial Synod reasserted the validity of deciding applications for membership by this ultimate authority. And as in England, so elsewhere, the official ban continued to fall upon all attempts at adaptation to a new social and intellectual environment, on the principle that "what God called good in Germany must be equally good in America." The implied deduction that what the Lot sanctioned or forbade had the force of a direct Divine interposition in human affairs is an example of those strong simplicities, by which the course of events has been so often swayed for good or ill. Both as to the persons, and as to the particular decisions, of the members of the governing Conference the sanction of the Lot gave a quality of peculiar force and dignity. Every election, both to the general and to the provincial Conferences must be so sanctioned. It is easy to see how, this confirmation once achieved, the official elected conceived himself invested with a sort of Divine right to a loyal and submissive obedience, and how the very consciousness of his own insufficiency might be subtly transferred into unconscious authoritarian austerity.

(iii) *Regional: Europe, Great Britain, America*

That body of doctrine, teaching and discipline which, in book, manuscript or actual organization, "the late Ordinary" had left behind him becomes, as we have seen, most readily apparent through its incorporation in the Brotherly Agreement.

Much of the point of later Moravian criticism of the Unity's policy following Zinzendorf's death really amounts to an unwillingness to recognize that that policy inevitably reflected the moral exclusivism, " the heroic for earth too hard," which inspired the conception and controlled the structure of that " ground-document." If, that is to say, the policy pursued was " senseless and suicidal " the responsibility must be attached elsewhere than to those leaders of the Unity who could undoubtedly fall back upon the principles of the Brotherly Agreement in justification of their line of action. The Brotherly Agreement, the Settlement System, the Diaspora Plan and much else distinctive of Moravian history, is open to easy and obvious criticism—given only a viewpoint which rejects both Zinzendorf's own most cherished ideals and, be it added, much of the distinctive character of the old Brüder Kirche. What may be, and with greater fairness, equally easily admitted, is that the mechanical application of these directive principles grows less and less defensible, even from the Count's own idealistic purpose, as the Unity spread from Europe to England and from England to America. A few brief notes on the situation in each may lend point to this plea for discrimination in condemnation.

(*a*) *On the Continent*, both in the years preceding the French Revolution, when unenlightened despotism and grinding vassalage were still unchallenged, and after that cataclysm had, by its excesses, driven the National Churches outside France into equating dissent and progress with impiety and subversive propaganda, there was much to be said on the score of practicability and diplomacy for the humbler religious communities like the Unity adopting a policy based upon conservation rather than expansion. As they rightly interpreted their times, their duty was to hold fast to those things they had already attained lest by " a forward policy " involving propaganda within the parochial systems of the various National Protestant Churches, they should bring down upon them the hostility of the authorities in Church and State and suffer expulsion. Circumstances in Sweden afford a typical illustration of this position. There, where the members in their societies were increasing (c. 1780), they had obtained licence to build chapels in Stockholm and Gothenburg but with the proviso that the "members of their Societies did not absent themselves from public worship and the sacraments in the established (Lutheran) Church." The National Church, strict in upholding pure Lutheranism must be propitiated and the Brethren would have been driven, *nolens volens*, to prove

> that a sound Lutheran might conscientiously conform to the Lutheran ritual, and be a faithful attendant at his parish church and at the same time improve his connection with the Brethren for his spiritual benefit (Holmes, II, pp. 125–6).

The situation in Sweden, that is to say, was precisely the same as in the various German States where equally the principles of the Peace of Westphalia held the field. The precarious tenure of any non-national religious organization and the paramount need under which it laboured of avoiding any appearance of proselytism might be further fully illustrated from the fortunes of the Brethren elsewhere on the Continent, *e.g.* in Norway, Denmark, and various settlements within the Russian Empire. Only limitations of space preclude illustrations of what is, after all, a very familiar platitude.

Concern, therefore, for the preservation of their own peculiar pastoral discipline among such as would voluntarily submit to it, and a practical sense of the limits of the possible and the permissible—the wisdom of the Gospel and the wisdom of this world—marched hand in hand. The policy of the leaven working secretly was the only possible one in the continental fields of the Brethren's labours where they were working within a national Church system; there, at least, the Zinzendorfian teaching on "Tropos" and "Diaspora" and "vital leaven" can claim easy and ample justification through a survey of the religious and political environment amid which the expansion of the Unity had necessarily to be regulated.

(*b*) *Great Britain*.—Thus it is not in relation to continental affairs that the Unity's Elders' Conference falls easiest under criticism. Their error was in not seeing that what was right (because necessary) in Germany, Sweden, Livonia and other fields of Diaspora-work and settlement-foundations, might not be either inevitable or wise elsewhere.

> What was in accordance with the mode and spirit of the Settlement congregations in European lands, that lacked absolute liberty of religion, was taken to be in and of itself the supreme object of all efforts under any and every set of conditions (Hamilton, p. 254).

This policy, of course, was clean contrary to Zinzendorf's teaching on the accommodation of " religions " to the climate, atmosphere, even the food and drink, of each nationality (see Uttendörfer, *op. cit.*, p. 83). The clearest call for greater elasticity in the application of fundamental principles arose in the striking contrast presented by the situations in, say, Germany and Russia on the one hand and the new democracy rapidly rising to a sense of nationhood across the Atlantic, where there was no State Church, where the tide had run strongest towards representative government in Church and State, where " home rule, from the town meeting up, was seen to be fundamental." There the situation was surely one which presented problems of administration and government plainly impossible of solution by means of the periodic visitations of a few members of a Board resident in Germany.

To take first the failure in the British Province. The " great strategic blunder " of the U.E.C. in discouraging the developments of " congregations " and in enforcing the strict Moravian discipline in the settlements, was at least more explicable, if no less disastrous, than the application of the same minimizing policy in America. These islands were, after all, not so very far from Zeist or Herrnhut, there was a long tradition of helpful intercourse between ourselves and the Protestant forces of North Europe, above all, Spangenberg, the Wattevilles and other of the leading personalities felt themselves conversant with the British environment. So that on the major matters of general strategy and in minor matters of administration and altogether apart from the supposedly providential enforcement of their authority through the Lot, the authorities may well have felt they had reason in these early years for exercising a benevolent despotism. Nor should it be forgotten that the most influential personality among the English Brethren, Benjamin La Trobe, 1765–86 (see our Appendix E, and Hutton, pp. 438 f.) had been appointed by the U.E.C. and was a strong protagonist of the "German" policy. So long as he and James Hutton (d. 1795) were the official representatives of that policy there was no likelihood of serious strain between the two groups of leaders.[1]

The restrictive regulations were therefore accepted as regulative for this country. Crantz, even while detailing the progress of new awakenings, "even as far as Cornwall," in the years 1764–9, has to add:

> But no new Congregation-regulations were made, except in the City of Bath in the year 1766, as since the synod (of 1764) the method of settling societies which remain wholly in their religion, was adopted rather than the regulating new congregations, according to the constitution of the Brethren (p. 570).

La Trobe himself, present at that Synod, has told how the delegates "were encouraged to attend to and pursue the (Diaspora) plan (in England) and to be more strict with respect to those who should be proposed for reception into the Congregation." At the Provincial Synod held at Lindsey House following the General Synod, these principles were accepted as directive for England (see Appendix: La Trobe

[1] Both the firm control, extending to unimportant details, of the U.E.C., and Hutton's own acquiescent attitude appear in the circumstances of the origin of the famous *Periodical Accounts of the Missions*. It was proposed in a meeting of the S.F.G. in 1769 that a periodical report be printed instead of being circulated in MSS. But there was a synodal rule that "nothing be printed without the previous approbation of the Directory for the time being," and Br. Hutton "was not for innovation." The project therefore hung fire for twenty years; even then permission to print was made conditional on the submission of the manuscript to the Directory before printing (Benham, p. 547).

Among many other possible examples of the same dislike of provincial initiative was the refusal to countenance a proposal of John Hartley, Director at Fulneck, to provide there some preliminary preparation for future ministers: "the entire project received official condemnation as 'impracticable,' 'unausfuhrbar'" (Hamilton, p. 287).

to Loretz, 6.1.1786). Hence "the British Collapse," 1760–1801. Hence the long list of Diaspora-centres which never developed into permanent congregations. Hence the failure to develop, as at one time there seemed good prospects of doing, a strong evangelistic "connection" with, as in the case of Primitive Methodism, special strength in the English countryside. There was a strong body of preachers endued with admirable zeal and brave devotion, but "their exertions did not materially increase the number of persons belonging to their own congregations" (Holmes, II, p. 112). The names of John Cennick, "the Apostle of Wiltshire," and of his spiritual son, John Caldwell, who began the abortive work in Ayr in 1765, would be better known in the West of England, in North Ireland and in South-West Scotland had other Brethren entered into their labours and built upon their foundations.[1]

The conversion of Woodford in Northamptonshire from a Society to a Congregation is one of few exceptions to the normal policy of the Moravian authorities in this era, and the story of that transition is illuminative. The first request of the "little religious society" gathered around Farmer William Hunt to be joined to the Brethren's Church, was rejected in favour of its organization "on the plan of a society," since the authorities were "unwilling to see them separate themselves from the national Establishment." Four years more had to pass ere their request was granted and a Provincial Synod ratified their union as a "Country Congregation" (Holmes,

[1] Some idea of the failure "to take the tide" may be given by noting that the Synod of 1747 estimates the Wiltshire membership at 1000 persons. The name of *John Cennick* should not be passed over without some notice of his heroic labours in this county and in North Ireland. His career resembles that of Benj. Ingham: both began in the Church, engaged in field-preaching with marked success and passed on *via* "Methodism" to join the Brethren, to whom they handed over the Societies they had gathered. There is an excellent short biography of Cennick (J. E. Hutton, Fetter Lane, 78 pp.) and large portions of his diary were printed in the Baptist Magazine, Jan.–May 1865. The Moravian Hymn-Book contains forty-four of his hymns: he is the author of the well-known "Children of the Heavenly King," and of the familiar "Grace," "Be present at our table, Lord." In the Herrnhut Library is James Hutton's copy of Cennick's *Hymns for the Use of the Religious Societies*.

II, pp. 108–9). More welcome to the authorities, no doubt, was the procession of events in the case of a similar Society at Kirby Lonsdale, originally organized by the parish clergyman. This group came into conflict with a new incumbent, fell into separatism, but was induced by the Brethren's minister at Mirfield " again to frequent the parish Church." Thereafter, of course, they continued their own corporate devotions of prayer, Bible-reading and other spiritual exercises.[1]

(*c*) *North America.*—The difficulties of the Brethren in the new Republic across the Atlantic must have been in any case sufficiently serious in and after the period of the American Revolution. An attitude of aloofness in the political crisis was in itself regarded as treason to the new nationhood, while the aversion to taking the oath required by the Federal General Assembly might easily be misinterpreted as positive disaffection to the new regime. To these disabilities should be added the serious practical difficulty in the way of maintaining contact with their leaders in Europe; no American deputies, for instance, were able to appear at the 1782 Synod. The delegation from the U.E.C., headed by Bishop J. F. Reichel and armed with the Resolutions of the 1775 Synod, spent six months between London and New York in the winter of 1778–9. That important delegation was followed, on the conclusion of the War, by another (1784), of which the head was Bishop John de Watteville. Of his labours in propaganda and organization there should at least be mentioned the consecration of the devoted Bishop John Etwein, one of the heroes of American Moravian history. That history in its early stages provides

[1] Holmes, II, p. 110. Cf. also the explanation of the declension of the work around Doncaster: " It must, however, be remarked here, that the Brethren in visiting these places, did not aim at establishing Societies, in connection with their Church. . . . Their simple object was to promote the spiritual welfare of those who sought their aid, and instead of alienating them from that denomination of Christians with which they were previously connected, to cultivate the Unity of spirit with all the true followers of Christ, with whom they became acquainted, in every division of his fold " (II, p. 112). It is instructive, incidentally, to contrast Holmes' dispassionate accent with the tone employed by the twentieth-century historian of the Brethren's Church in discussing the Diaspora and Society work.

a recurrent succession of key-words similar to those met with in the Old World : the same insistence on a pure membership, the same reluctance to entertain proposals of indiscriminate admission, the same centralization of the work in a few areas around the more prominent settlements, the same rigid adherence to the principles of the Brotherly Agreement as incorporated in the settlement discipline.

One phase of the problem was naturally peculiar to America : the absence of any national religious Establishment. This striking contrast to those countries in which hitherto the Brethren had worked, compelled the visiting agents of the Directing Board to consider how far it implied modification in the methods employed in Europe. How would the " Society " idea fare in a land where there was no State Church with which Society members could remain in communion, and no parish churches whither they could go to make their communion ? Motioned by a jealous concern for the purity of doctrine and morals among those belonging to the inner circle of the Brotherhood, and resolute to maintain its standards of obedience and discipline, neither Reichel nor de Watteville could contemplate an indiscriminate admission of Society-members into their Church. But, on the other hand, neither could they lightly leave these little groups of baptized Christians without the possibility of ever participating in the Sacramental Meal of Christian Fellowship. Where there was no *ecclesia*, what were the *ecclesiolæ* to do, and where there are no great national confessional Churches, what becomes of *das Tropen-prinzip* ? Characteristically, the policy to be followed was settled, not in America, but in a General Synod of 1782, to which, presumably, Bishop Reichel had reported the results of his visitation. The members of the North American Societies were divided into two classes : those who seemed worthy were to be admitted to full membership ; the others were to be advised to join some other religious community where they might hear the word preached, but be under no necessity of submitting to an ecclesiastical discipline for which they were unprepared. The children of Society members, having a moral claim upon the Brethren, were to be instructed and trained—at least so far as that was possible in a vast and thinly-populated territory. The unsuitability of such a policy (if numerical increase was held to be a desirable end) is obvious. It practically prohibited the turning of casual acquaintanceship into a permanent relationship. Most colonists, it may be assumed, desired some minimum of religious ministrations—if only at baptisms, weddings and funerals. Others, possibly, as in the sparsely settled areas of Canada and Australia today, would probably have welcomed an occasional "preaching-service." This class of religious ministrations was, in fact, often performed by the Brethren's ministers, but unless such colonists were prepared to accept the full Moravian discipline, those ministers were precluded from attempting to organize a permanent congregation. Hence the American parallels to the abandoned preaching-places in England. The same policy of centralization in settlements produced an identical result. Thus in the Wajomick district on the Susquehanna, a group of colonists, mainly English, were visited by the minister of Gnadenhuetten for some years, "but serious obstacles rendered it impracticable to grant their wish of being admitted into regular connection with the Brethren's Church."[1]

Many another instance of similar failure in the new townships and rural areas could be readily provided. But so much must suffice in explanation and, to some extent, in defence of the Unity's policy up to the successful issue of the reform movement in the second half of the nineteenth century. The Unity's Directing Board was not the first nor the last "oligarchy of elected persons" to fail through a too enthusiastic tenacity and inelastic loyalty to a great name and a splendid ideal. At least we may say that these are failings which posterity, remembering how difficult is the task of leadership amid the storms of revolutionary transformations of the conditions of human society, may find it easiest to pardon.

[1] Holmes, II, p. 143; cf. also Hutton's statistics, p. 465: it is the American policy which this historian condemns as "senseless and suicidal." The contrary plan, as adopted by the Methodists under J. Wesley's formal authorization, may be studied in Stoughton, VI, pp. 275 f.

Chapter V

THE UNITAS FRATRUM AND THE CHURCH OF ENGLAND

A. The Ancient Unitas and the Reformed Church of England

ADEQUATELY to discuss the principles, as well as to narrate the facts, relating to the present negotiations between the Anglican Communion and the Moravian Church of Great Britain, would be to open up the whole vast subjects of Christian Unity and Church Reunion. That task, it may be said, would not be unwelcome to any student who has acquired some knowledge of, and interest in, the early ideals of Count Zinzendorf, of his later efforts to realize those ideals through his connection with the Renewed Unity, and of the history of that little community set amid the larger confessional Churches of the post-Reformation era.[1] That task, however, is clearly too large and, for this essay, equally so is the more restricted one of narrating the points of contact, in spirit and in conference and in practical sympathy, between the Brethren's Church before its Renewal and the Reformed Church of England. From the very dawn of Bohemian Protestantism reciprocal influences with England were real and fruitful and

[1] Recalling, for instance, Zinzendorf's dream of one Holy and Catholic Church and his use of the metaphor of the "temporary tent" to describe the transitory character of the renewed Unity, it is most interesting to find the Bishops at Lambeth speaking of the Anglican Communion "as in some sense an incident in the history of the Church Universal," as "in its present character . . . transitional," and forecasting "the day when the racial and historical connections which at present characterize it will be transcended, and the life of our Communion will be merged in a larger fellowship in the Catholic Church" (Lambeth, 1930 Report, No. IV, 1, 2). The two paragraphs following are strikingly reminiscent of Zinzendorf's ideas on the place of the Brüdergemeine in the future ideal great Society of all Christian people.

whatever the exact quantity and quality of the influence of Lollardy upon the Hussite Movement may have been, there is at least no doubt of the fact of Wycliffite influence upon Huss and the Bohemian Reformation, and, therefore, upon the beginnings of the *Unitas Fratrum*; "the Brethren's Church could in its origin be traced back to the effect of English influence" (Wauer, p. 11). Nor did that intercourse end with the initial impulse. The general character of the early Brethren's Church made for easy adaptation to, and close co-operation with, the other evangelical continental Churches of the sixteenth century. Wauer stresses its "unionist character," a quality which, if no more than the result of an instinct for self-preservation against Rome, did lead the Brethren to desire "to enter into the most intimate relations possible with other Churches" (p. 12). In respect of England it is possible to detect four separate phases of the character and fortunes of the continental Brethren conducive to friendship with the Churches of the English Reformation :

(i) The influence of Wycliffe and Oxford upon Huss and Prague implied the likelihood of co-operation and goodwill between the two nations in the storms of the century following.

(ii) The Brethren's retention of Episcopacy commended them to the Church of England.

(iii) On the other hand, the Presbyterian elements in its constitution and its ability to unite with Lutherans and Calvinists (*e.g.* in the Union of Sendomir, 1570) commended them to the Puritan-Presbyterian elements in this country.

(iv) The disasters and persecutions which befell the Brethren evoked the sympathy of English Churchmen of both wings.

The mere enumeration of these lines of early contact will at least serve to underline the fact of English responsibility for the preservation of the very existence of the early Unitas—a fact marked, of course, most pathetically on that day when J. A. Comenius ("*inter ultimos ultimus antistes*") commended the remnant of the Brethren to the care of the Church of England. The previous pages have noted some of the effects on later history of this original *rapprochement des cœurs* between the ancient Brethren and the Anglican Church ; and now in considering what hopes the future may hold of even closer union, it would be eminently suitable to enter into some examination of that intervening period of lively contact between the two Churches, *the seventeenth century*, when the non-Papal Churches were undergoing a process of continually shifting alignment.[1]

One interesting circumstance at least, seems to justify some few remarks on this phase of interrelation. Then, as now, there were the two complementary attitudes within the Church of England, the one emphasizing her heritage of Catholic tradition and order, the other turning with more kindliness towards Geneva and with more bitterness away from Rome. The striking circumstance to which we would call attention is that the Church of the Brethren was regarded with favour by *both* these schools, since, like the larger body itself, the Brethren were seen to be both Catholic and Reformed. In

[1] For the connection of the *old* Unitas with the Church of England (mainly in reference to acknowledgment of its Episcopate) see :—

(i) Hutton, pp. 56, 57. Note on Origin, Maintenance and Validity of Moravian Episcopal Orders.

(ii) *Ibid.*, pp. 172–4, Supplementary Note, the Bohemian Brethren and the Church of England.

(iii) Wauer, Chap. I, pp. 11–27.

(iv) Mason : *Church of England and Episcopacy* ; see under Index, *Unitas Fratrum*, for the more stringent Anglican view of various cases of ministerial recognition.

(v) In greater detail and critical incisiveness, Archbishops' Committee's Report, 1907, Section III.

One might add, *An Enquiry into the Episcopacy of the Moravians*, occasioned by a letter from a Presbyter of that Community to the Rev. Dr Hook (Lambeth, 114, H. 8 (8)) ; a small pamphlet from *The Christian's Miscellany*, 1841, by A. P. P. (=Arthur Philip Perceval), giving the Tractarian view and with inadequate knowledge of the Brethren, who are descended from the " original Taborites." " A greater mass of imposition was never palmed upon the public " than the *Acta Fratrum*, and the English prelates who have recognized the Moravian Episcopal succession erred from lack of full knowledge.

that age, the spectacle of a foreign Protestant Church which both Oliver Cromwell and Prince Rupert wished to protect and encourage is at least as noteworthy as Innocent XI's secret countenance of the designs of the Calvinistic Prince of Orange against the last Romanist King of England (Ranke, *History of the Popes*, Vol. II, Bk. IX, I). On the one hand those in the Church of England who affirmed her Protestant or Reformed character, found it easy to stretch out hands of help to their fellow-Protestants on the Continent, not least to the scattered congregations of the Unitas, now no longer strictly "Bohemian" either in locality or in membership. Churchmen of this school manifested in such ways as the troublous state of the times required or permitted—by political support, financial aid, educational facilities—their interest "in a Church which, like that of the Brethren, was engaged in conflict with Roman Catholicism. . . . English self-consciousness and liberality were not appealed to in vain" (Wauer, p. 13). On the other hand, those English Churchmen who did not think that the true end of a reformation of the Catholic Church was to get away as far as possible from all that Rome supported, and were seeking to distinguish between the Papalism of the Council of Trent and a primitive or conciliar Catholicism, were attracted to a continental Church, sprung from an anti-Papal movement prior to Luther's and enjoying an episcopal succession and ministerial orders whose authenticity was then not questioned. Here was another Church, which like the Anglican, claimed to be Catholic while rejecting the unconstitutional assumptions of Rome. Herbert Thorndike, for instance, died in the same year as Comenius (1672). He was so unyielding in his assertion of the Catholic character of his Church as to draw from the author of the Preface to the Book of Common Prayer a warning about children of the Church who had "overrun their mother." To Thorndike Presbyterian ordinations are "mere nullities." Yet, when countering the suggestion that the "abolition of Episcopacy would assimilate the Church of England to the other reformed Churches," Thorndike propounds the position that there have been three forms of reformation beside the way of the Church of England: those of Luther, of Calvin and of the Unity of Bohemia; and of the three he prefers the last as consonant with Catholic principles and with the Vincentian canon.[1]

Other instances of the same fraternal attitude of the English Church of the seventeenth century to the "episcopal and reformed Churches formerly in Bohemia and now in Poland and Polish Russia" could be easily provided. Enough has perhaps been said to prove the case that throughout there was a peculiar fitness, due to the twofold stream of influence within the Church of England, in the practical and moral support she was able to afford the Church of the Brethren. Each Church might be expected to claim the sisterly affection of the other since the precise and unique quality of each lay in its eirenical attitude towards the ecclesiastical controversies of the time. Comenius' impartial reproofs to Presbyterians and Episcopalians alike for their exaggerated stress upon their distinctive tenets was quite in character with the later, Zinzendorfian, standpoint. It was also an instance of the highest unconscious wisdom, for when, subsequently, the Brethren fell on evil times, "then it was that the above-mentioned characteristics of their Church stood them in good stead; for by virtue of those characteristics they were assured of gaining ready compliance with their petitions from many an Englishman, were he Episcopalian or Presbyterian" (Wauer, p. 19). Even from considerations of worldly wisdom, it was not for nothing that the *Ratio Disciplinæ* had been dedicated to the Church of England, or that the English translation thereof was asserted to be motived by requests *from both parties* in the English Church to be given more information on the constitution of the Unitas.

Finally, even this cursory survey of the spiritual and practical bonds forged between the two Communions anterior to the Renewal, must not omit the important name of Daniel Ernest Jablonsky, grandson of Comenius, Court Chaplain to Frederick of Prussia and (1699) Bishop of the Unitas. Educated at Oxford, he sent other younger men of the persecuted Polish Branch to enjoy that same advantage. Through his efforts,

[1] Quotations by Mason, pp. 194, 195. Concise summary of Thorndike's position in Bishop Dowden's Paddock Lectures, *Theological Literature of the Church of England*, pp. 146–8.

collections were made in the English parish churches for the now dwindling remnant of the Unitas. For what it was worth, he secured from Archbishop Wake an acknowledgment of the validity of the Brethren's Episcopate.[1] There was also a memorable correspondence between Jablonsky and the Northern Primate, Sharpe, having in view the introduction of the English liturgy and episcopate into Prussia.[2] That project was found impossible of achievement and neither was Jablonsky able to save the Unitas, of which he was the sole surviving bishop, from practical extinction in the fires of persecution. When, however, the exiles at Herrnhut entered into their heritage from the ancient Bohemian Unity and thence moved on as a Branch of the Renewed Unity to this country, it meant a great deal that they were able to point to a long series of friendly contacts between their own spiritual ancestors and the English Church during the sixteenth and seventeenth centuries.

The subsequent history of the British Branch of the Renewed Episcopal Church of the Brethren, the passion for unity and the punctilious deference of its chief patron towards the national Church-constitution, the slow fading of the impress of his spirit and aims on his removal from the scene, the steady growth towards a denominational self-consciousness, have formed the subject of these pages.

At last, after some three centuries, preserved largely by the friendly countenance of the English Church, and rescued from the unhappy fate forced upon it by the fierce intolerance of the Counter-Reformation in the seventeenth century—" a persecuted and moribund Church," driven to accept " the rôle of an unfortunate petitioner "—the Ancient Church of the Brethren, in its later history, finds itself, not indeed numerically imposing, but firm and self-reliant, occupying an honoured place among the Free Churches of the modern Anglo-Saxon world.

[1] The facts relating to D. E. Jablonsky's consecration are most simply put by Hassé, E.R.E., p. 838. Daniel's father, Peter, was consecrated by Bishop Bythner of Milenezyn; Daniel himself consecrated Nitschmann in 1735.

[2] Wilson, *Episcopacy and Unity*, Chap. XIII; Mason, *The Church of England and Episcopacy*, pp. 349–51.

B. The Renewed Unitas as a Via Media

In view of the facts thus briefly touched upon, it was not surprising that even before the Reunion Movement among the non-Papalist Churches had attained its present momentum, the project should have been entertained of a corporate reunion of the Church of England and the Renewed Moravian Church in Great Britain. A consideration of past historical contacts would seem to lend point to the observation since suggested by the representatives of the latter Communion that if these two Churches cannot agree upon a common platform, what other Churches are likely to do so? Even apart from the intimate relations in past centuries, there were, at the beginning of the present century, other factors, at least as important as the controversial question of "valid" Orders, in the situation as between the two churches, which seemed to indicate the probability of a speedy success in the negotiation already inaugurated.

"It is now held by some Moravians that their Church offers a *via media* between Anglicanism and Dissent" (*Ency. Brit.*, 14th Edn., Vol. 15, p. 791). If this opinion be accurate, then it will be worth considering some few of those qualities in the general spirit, traditions and customs of the Moravian Church which should conduce to the closer union of that Church with Anglicanism. Moravian fellowship with "Dissent" is not in doubt; one of their representatives, the Rev. Bishop Mumford, sat with other distinguished Nonconformists on the Committee appointed by the Federal Council of the Evangelical Free Churches after the Lambeth Appeal of 1920, and indeed perhaps the most obvious practical difficulty under which the Anglican and Moravian negotiators have laboured has been the plainly expressed unwillingness of the latter to commit their Church to any concession in respect of Catholic order which would hinder their present fellowship and intercommunion with the Free Churches of this country. What, on the other hand, are the elements in Moravianism which suggest the naturalness of union with Anglicanism? Is there anything else, beyond the above-mentioned historical events common to the history of both Communions, which accounts for the fact that definite negotiations between these two Churches antedate those between Anglicanism and the general body of British Nonconformity by some forty years ?

In *Christian Doctrine*, that first and fundamental matter, there seems no likelihood of divergences incapable of reconciliation. Differences of emphases there no doubt are—but not within one of the two Communions only. Moravian theology, though it has not, in some personal interpretations, altogether escaped the extreme Liberalism so often associated with an eager interest in continental scholarship, has never surrendered its hold on the fundamental verities of the Christian Revelation or dethroned the supremacy of Holy Scripture as the norm of faith and worship. Formally, too, the authority of the Church has been allotted a due reverence in respect of defining the limits beyond which enquiry may not trespass in seeking to accommodate Catholic doctrine to the changing concepts of Biblical criticism and philosophical speculation. On the other hand, had the Moravian Church desired equivalent assurances from the Anglican Church, either in respect of its steadfast hold on the Faith once delivered, or of its tolerance of the place of Reason in the correlation of the Faith with the intellectual atmosphere of the age, the Anglican representatives had, of course, only to point to the official creeds and formulæ of their Prayer Book and to underline that well-known and complementary quality of the Church of England, that love of sound learning, which enables her to find a welcome for whatever light science and philosophy and historical criticism may have to throw upon the implications of Christian dogma.[1]

Again, in the important spheres of *Public Worship*, of the

[1] This paragraph obviously opens large considerations. Anglican fear of "doctrinal disintegration" among Protestant Churches drawing water from German wells is illustrated by Mason's footnote, p. 451, quoting a dictum of Professor Loofs', who "does not know a single learned man in Germany who holds the belief in the person of our Lord which is defined in the decrees of the four great ecumenical councils" (1914). No reference is made to the source whence the quotation is drawn and the utterance as it stands is plainly in need of further elucidation. As far as the Moravian Church is concerned, it can point to what is still, one understands, its formal, doctrinal standard, viz. : *An Exposition of Christian Doctrine as taught in the Protestant Church of the United Brethren, or, Unitas Fratrum,* by August Gottlieb Spangenberg, Preface by Benj. La Trobe, London,

Church's seasonal observance of *Fast and Festival*, and of the colouring thus given to usages of *Private Devotional Exercises*, the minds of the two Communions are not so alien one from the other as is the case with Anglican and Nonconformist. Though perhaps of recent years the tendency of English Moravians has been to approximate more closely to the non-liturgical, extempore and freer forms characteristic of most of the British Free Churches, still in its Litanies, its Festival Services, its generous employment of Christian symbolism, the Moravian Church was already in possession of a devotional background, honoured by its ancient origin, intelligible to and affectionately regarded by, its adherents. It is a background which might be thought likely to dispose the majority of the Church membership, ministerial and lay, to welcome contacts with that fuller and richer provision of Catholic devotion to which the Anglican Churchman would premise he, from his position, has readier access.

Deeper still, and certainly of more concrete value, in preparing the way for the obliteration of constitutional barriers, are the effects of that warmth of fellowship resulting from past and present co-operation in the *Mission Field*. Here Moravian zeal has consistently evoked the admiration of all, and the financial aid of some, Anglican Churchmen. That admiration and co-operation have been something more than merely the indirect consequence of the common pursuit of a noble aim.

The preaching of the Gospel and the propagation of a definite Church-System have ever been hard to dissociate ; it will be remembered how Dr Jonathan Mayhew, the Boston Congregationalist, objected against the S.P.G. that that Society was attempting to foist Episcopacy upon the Colonies instead of confining itself to its avowed object : the propagation of the Christian religion in its bare simplicity.[1] However adequate the answer to that particular complaint may have been, and however impossible it is to " preach the Gospel " without

1784. This compendious volume of some 550 pages covers in 24 sections a wide range of Christian Theology, Ethics and Eschatology. Its characteristic marks are a deep and simple piety and an unquestioned acceptance of the authority of the Biblical records.

[1] A. L. Cross: *The Anglican Episcopate and the American Colonies*, Harvard, 1902, pp. 147–9.

commending, consciously or unconsciously, an ecclesiastical discipline of one sort or another, it is significant that at the revival of the Moravian counterpart of the S.P.G.—the Society for the Furtherance of the Gospel—Spangenberg issued a manifesto in which this very difficulty was countered in what is perhaps the only way so long as Christendom is divided into a multiplicity of Churches. The "*Candid Declaration* of the Church known by the name of the *Unitas Fratrum* relative to their Labour among the Heathen" was issued from Lindsey House, 22nd September 1768. Opposition had arisen to the Brethren's evangelistic labours overseas, especially on the part of some "Protestant divines." These well-meaning friends advised the Brethren to surrender their episcopal constitution. But, says Spangenberg, the Brethren had been warned against this surrender by their late Ordinary and by "some eminent divines not of our pale." Resolute, therefore, in their determination to retain their episcopal orders, the *Unitas Fratrum* nevertheless desire to discourage the suspicion that their adherence to episcopacy renders them incapable of working amicably with other missionaries or leads them to encourage disaffection to the civil power.

> We confess and preach to the Heathen, "Jesus Christ and Him crucified" as the Saviour of the world . . . and we seek, as far as in us lies, to keep them ignorant of the many divisions in Christendom: But if they happen to have been informed thereof by others, we endeavour with great precaution to approve ourselves impartial, speak of the several divisions with much tenderness, and to extenuate and not exaggerate the differences, that thus the knowledge of the mystery of Christ may be increased and misapprehensions diminished (Herrnhut, R. 13, A. 38; cf. Crantz, par. 281).

These sentences have been quoted, not only for their own intrinsic excellence, but as relevant to any discussion of the spiritual *preparatio* which must precede any practical proposals for reunion. Equally apposite is the citation from another Missionary Manifesto, this time from the Anglican side, of half a century later. In commending the Moravian Church and its Missions to the Church and People of England, the London Association in Aid of the Moravian Missions, in July 1839, after a recital of the past happy relations between the two Bodies, adds :

> It will be evident, therefore, that a Church of such antiquity, acknowledged through successive centuries as a Sister Church and acting so long and to the present day in friendly intercourse with the Church and Government of England . . . cannot be viewed as a body of Dissenters who have separated from her Communion or as standing on a similar footing to the Dissenters of this country in relation to the Church of England (Pamphlet in Herrnhut, R. 13, A. 44, 3, p. 3).

The London Association in aid of Moravian Missions is still in active existence with several Anglican bishops among its vice-presidents, and with, doubtless, some modification of phraseology, its standpoint might still be similarly expressed, while from the other side, it is a Moravian bishop quite recently deceased who re-echoes the eighteenth-century ideal of co-operation in " labour among the Heathen." The Unitas does not, he says, exist for the sake of self-propagation ; national differences and sectarian customs must be welded into the framework of the one Body of Christ ; the Unitas, as its name implies, " is above all else a missionary and a union Church."

> Had there been more denominationalism, no doubt a larger numerical increase would have resulted, but it would have meant the loss of that kindliness of mutual feeling which has marked the Church's relationship to other Christian communities (Bishop E. R. Hassé, Art. in E.R.E., pp. 839, 841).

When two Christian Churches, therefore, animated, as to a considerable proportion of their membership, by such warm sentiments and fraternal feeling, find themselves already closely knit in the task of founding and establishing infant Churches overseas, it would indeed be surprising had not, sooner or later, the project of a closer corporate reunion at home suggested itself. It was, in fact, the situation in one

Mission Field (the West Indies) which gave the initial impulse to the present negotiations; a circumstance patient of wider application (*e.g.* to South India) but here operating with especial force in the case of two Churches, each an historic, episcopal and evangelical Branch of the Universal Church, each with the open Bible in one hand and the Catholic Faith and Orders in the other.[1]

Such, then, are some of the features of the situation: a long tale of sympathetic assistance in the past; and, in the present, a parallel appreciation of a reverent mingling of credal orthodoxy with freedom of theological enquiry, a not negligible approximation in forms of worship and devotion; above all, a practical co-operation in the labours of the Gospel overseas. Such advantages might have seemed sufficient to ensure that the pathway to corporate Reunion would be both easy and speedy. In particular, the importance each Communion attached to the possession of an episcopal succession running back to the undivided Primitive Church seemed to imply the absence of difficulties attending similar conferences with non-episcopal Churches, and to afford a firm foundation upon which might be stabilized a machinery of easy adjustment in respect of the lesser differences of jurisdiction and pastoral discipline. Those hopes have been frustrated and if disappointment is proportionate to the original optimism, some comfort is at least to be gained in reflecting that the conversations have been fruitful in an increase of mutual understanding and that they are not yet at an end.

C. The Present Negotiations

The actual course of the Reunion Conferences may be briefly told; with brevity since the last two Lambeth Reports provide a convenient summary. The fuller summary of the

[1] The congruence of Anglican and Moravian traditions and character was stressed in the speeches of Bishops of both Communions at the Moravian Synod of 1908, Bishop Hassé presiding. See Verbatim Report, Moravian Church House, London.

first of those Reports (1920) has been supplemented, in the writing of these paragraphs, by :

(*a*) *The Report of the Committee* appointed by the Archbishop of Canterbury to consider the Orders of the *Unitas Fratrum* or Moravians.

(*b*) *The Confidential Documents*, Memoranda, Correspondence, etc., pertaining to the later stage, 1920–23, during which the late Bishop of Gloucester (Dr. E. C. S. Gibson) was Chairman of the Anglican Committee.

The story opens as far back as 1878 when Bishop Mitchinson of Barbados raised the subject at Lambeth. (The 1930 Report places the inception of the negotiations ten years earlier.) Nothing was done, however, until 1888 when Bishop Mitchinson was appointed Secretary of a Committee which included the great names of Browne of Winchester and Stubbs of Oxford; Creighton of London was also consulted. Nothing beyond a draft report to, and two non-committal Resolutions by, the 1897 Conference resulted, and matters hung fire until the appointment in 1906 of the Archbishop's Committee which, with Bishop Mitchinson as Convener, included scholars of the eminence of Bishops Wordsworth, Gore, Gibson, Collins, Canon A. J. Mason and Professor Knowling. The last three formed a sub-committee and were mainly responsible for the Committee's Report. Dr Mason's study of the Bohemian tongue proves at least one member bent himself to the enquiry with zest. On its historical side, the main task of the Committee was an examination of the Moravian claim to the possession of an episcopal ministry.

Narrowing down that crucial problem to a " question of fact " the Committee's Report (published 1907) surveyed the intricate details attending the institution of the Moravian Episcopate in the fifteenth century and its subsequent transmission. It should be noted that the Anglican Committee relied for much of their material upon a Moravian scholar, the learned Dr Joseph Müller, Archivar at Herrnhut, including his specialist study, *Das Bischoftum der Brüder Unität*, Herrnhut, 1899, and a letter from him (1.7.1907), printed in the Appendix to the Report, embodying his latest researches.

The *Historical Enquiry* is in three sections.

(*a*) The first discusses the *Origin* of the episcopal ministry at the Synod of Lhota, 1467. From much detail there emerges the first important question, that of the identity of Stephen the Elder who consecrated Michael of Zamberk (Seftenberg), who in turn consecrated Matthias of Kunwald. That identity, the Committee decided, must remain uncertain. Even if Michael's consecrator were Stephen the Waldensian Elder (burned at Vienna, 1469), there remains the further uncertainty as to the source of his episcopal orders; what, too, was his "intention" in consecrating and with what purpose had the ancient Brethren sought him out? "The Brethren applied to him, not so much because they thought him a bishop, which was a matter of indifference, but because they believed his Orders to be independent of Rome." "Bishop," "Elder," "Priest," were terms used quite independently by these Brethren, and Stephen's aid was invoked, not because he was a Bishop, but because he was not a Roman. But "this is the presbyterian theory of the ministry, not the episcopal: and it is the theory according to which the succession among the Brethren seems to have been both given and received" (p. 33).[1]

(*b*) The second critical stage in the transmission arrived in 1500 when Thomas and Elias (whom Matthias had ordained in 1467) consecrated Luke and Ambrose, an event accepted by the Community, as proving that "Their ordination to the priesthood, in the opinion of the Brethren, carried with it the power to ordain . . ." (p. 38) Dr Müller's pamphlet is thereupon quoted with approval in summary of both these stages:

> The result of our statement which is grounded upon the original documents, is that even if Matthias, by means of the Waldensians had received an episcopate with apostolical succession, this became extinct again with him, because it

[1] The evidence relating to Stephen, Michael and Matthias is discussed in *Episcopacy, Ancient and Modern*, pp. 370–4; *The Origins of Episcopacy in the Unitas Fratrum*, where is noted the emphasis laid by the first Brethren on the *ethical and spiritual* criteria of a "valid" ministry. Hence their rejection of both Roman and Utraquist successions. Stephen's death is dated 1467 and the date of Synod of Lhota (p. 370) needs correction.

is proved that he never consecrated any bishop (*Das Bischoftum usw.*, p. 21).

(*c*) Thirdly, there were various critical dates in the sixteenth century, especially in connection with Bishop Augusta (d. 1572). The opinion is maintained that the consecrations of 1553, 1557 and 1571 were performed by persons insufficiently qualified and were not supplemented later. Orders so received, in fact, are comparable to those of the Danish Church or of the American Methodist Church " which began from the presbyter Wesley."

The *Second Section* of the Report narrates the manner of ordaining and consecrating employed by the Brethren of various eras, beginning with the evidence of the views of Stephen the Waldensian Elder (p. 45), including the practice enjoined by the *Ratio Disciplinæ* (pp. 47–9), and concluding with a notice of the ideas underlying the present Moravian Liturgy and Church Book (pp. 49–50). Since, however, this section is prefaced by a remark to the effect that " after what has been said " (in the historical enquiry), " it may seem superfluous to enquire into the forms used by the Brethren in conferring their respective orders," the question of " form " seems to have been regarded, from the Anglican viewpoint, as one of theoretical rather than of practical interest, and need not delay us. The *final section*, too, that on previous relations between the two Churches, though of great interest, has been already touched upon. All we can here find space to mention are the valuable remarks (pp. 55–60) on the events recorded in the third Chapter of this essay.

Subjecting Zinzendorf's contacts with the English prelates and the events connected with the Parliamentary Recognition of 1749 to a detailed criticism, the Report concludes : (*a*) an Act of Parliament is not an Act of the Church of England ; (*b*) (Moravian) " orders have never been officially recognized by the Church of England. The management of Moravian missionaries in the eighteenth century by the S.P.G. and other Societies, although under the sanction of English Bishops, was not the action of the Church in its corporate capacity. It stands on the same footing as the employment, by the same Societies, of Lutheran missionaries from Denmark and Germany in India" (p. 60). Finally, after remarking that much fresh light has been obtained on the historical facts since the days of Wake and Potter, the Committee refer to Lightfoot's investigation of Moravian Orders in the case of a Moravian minister who had applied to him for ordination. The applicant indeed "assumed he would have to be reordained" and the Bishop followed Bramhall, who, in the case of presbyters during the Commonwealth added to their Letters of Orders: "non annihilantes priores ordines (si quos habuit) nec invaliditatem eorundem determinantes." The conclusion is reached: "No instance has been brought to the knowledge of the Committee in which a Moravian bishop or presbyter has been admitted as such to the same office either in the Church of England or in any other similarly constituted Church."

So much attention to this document seemed justified, since, on the historical side, it left nothing more to be said—and it is unlikely that any further historical data remain yet undiscovered. But the strictly historical criterion has its limits, and when the Lambeth Conference of 1908 was called upon to deal with the question, the problem was deflected by them from historical analysis to the present ordering of the Unitas in relation to the Ministry, and it was on this basis that subsequent discussion has rested. Rightly or wrongly that Conference proposed certain conditions under which joint recognition of Anglican and Moravian Orders might be achieved.

Paragraph 70, ii. which has bulked so large in later discussion may be noted. The Unity was asked to do four things:

(*a*) To give due assurance of doctrinal orthodoxy.

(*b*) "To explain its position as that of a religious community or missionary body in close alliance with the Anglican Communion."

(*c*) To "accord due recognition to the position" of Anglican Bishops in their dioceses.

(*d*) To approach the Anglican custom in respect of the rite of Confirmation.

As to these assurances or conditions, happily 1930 is not 1908; the present Bishop of Gloucester's adverse opinion on this strategy was frankly expressed in his Bampton Lectures, 1920 (p. 293). A new series of conferences was nevertheless inaugurated, with the Bishop of Durham (Dr Moule) as Chairman, but to quote Dr Headlam, we "are not surprised that no action has resulted." Conditions (*c*) and (*d*) seem reasonable enough; as to (*b*), that could hardly have been accepted by the Moravian Church without surrendering all pretence of negotiating as a Church and denying just those values and that status towards which it had striven since Zinzendorf's death. But in point of fact the acceptance or rejection of that condition had little more than academic interest; it was the failure to give on the one side, and to secure on the other, assurances in regard to the restriction of the celebration of the Holy Communion and the administration of the rite of Confirmation to presbyters (and bishops) only, which brought the negotiations to a temporary suspension.[1]

By 1920 the position was, that (*a*) offered no difficulty; (*b*) and (*c*) were "uncertain"; (*d*), and also the problem presented by the Moravian custom of permitting deacons to celebrate the Holy Communion, still remained a stumbling-block on the road to the resumption of negotiations. It is to be observed, as a deduction from the concluding passages of the 1920 Lambeth Report, that the question of the possession of the historical Episcopate by the Moravian Church seems to have

[1] It is perhaps only just to the Lambeth Conference of 1908 to remark that the Bishop of Gloucester is himself an instance of the effects of the growth of mutual understanding resulting from the discussions of the last twenty years. In 1920 he is "not surprised that no action has resulted. No action ever will result from such one-sided proposals" (Bampton Lectures, p. 293). Yet in 1909 he notes that these same proposals have been received by the Moravian General Synod and discussed at great length in an "attitude of friendship towards the Church of England and gratitude for its overtures. These very proposals and their reception "definitely bring the two Churches nearer to each other." *Church Quarterly Review*, Oct. 1909, Art., "The Moravian Church and the Proposals of the Lambeth Conference," by the Rev. W. N. Schwarze, Editor's Note. In point of fact, the American contributor's examination of the Proposals reflects more accurately the characteristic Moravian attitude to these and to subsequent Anglican approaches than did the official and synodal welcome at Herrnhut.

been tacitly dropped, though the condition (*b*) is still regarded as essential.

The Anglican Committee was reappointed with Bishop Gibson of Gloucester as Chairman. Its hope was that the Unitas would be able to change its rule as to the powers of the Diaconate and, further, remove the uncertainty as to conditions (*b*) and (*c*). Brief notices from the Correspondence may be given as presenting both sides of the discussion on these three points.

Condition (*b*).—The conception of the Unitas as a Religious Order is rejected. " We regard our position as that of an independent branch of the Church Catholic " (General Synod, 1909).

> There may be certain features in the origin and tendency of our earliest work in this country which suggest the parallel (with the Franciscan Order in the Middle Ages). Since that time, however, we have become settled in this country as a branch of an international Church, with its organized congregations and system of Church government. Throughout the world we are known, not as a religious " order," but as a *Church*, in the same sense as the term is used in reference to other Churches (Moravian Committee (undated), Memorandum on certain points raised by Lambeth Resolutions, 1920).

The importance of the Anglican reply is self-evident :

> English theologians have not been accustomed to speak of a plurality of Churches except in the only sense which has the sanction of the New Testament, viz., of the local branches of a single and undivided society. It is only in this sense that the Church of England itself claims to be a Church. It was presumably unwillingness to recognize two or more Churches in any other than the local sense that led the Conference of 1908 to use a form of words which might seem to do less than justice to the history and significance of the Moravian Church. . . . The Church of England has no desire to lower the status of the Moravian Church, or to take away its autonomy. We

believe that it would be a loss to Christendom if union were to be effected on terms which would hinder the free development of the *Unitas* on its own God-given lines. But we think this development could go forward even more favourably within the larger Unity, consisting (it must be remembered) not of the existing Church of England alone, but of the existing Church of England with the addition of the Moravian Church itself, to be joined eventually, as we hope, by others now in separation, as honoured and self-governing factors in the composition of the whole. Such is the meaning which we would attach to the phrase of 1908, " a religious community . . . in close alliance with the Anglican Communion " (Reply of Archbishop's Committee to the Moravian Committee, May 2nd, 1921, sgd. E. C. S. Gloucester).

Condition (*c*).—The Unitas cannot admit the position that Moravian Ministers should be under the jurisdiction of Anglican Bishops: their Church might suffer in some areas where perhaps such Bishops were unfavourable to them. To this the Anglican reply is that Bishops, as leaders of the Christian Community at large and also responsible for all the souls in a given area, are already concerned for the spiritual welfare of many who do not explicitly acknowledge their jurisdiction. Due recognition does not mean interference by the Bishops. " Those (Moravian) Communities would remain responsible to the Moravian Bishops alone. Their manner of Divine Service, their discipline, their finance, their missionary activities would be independent of the Diocesan." Nor would the Bishops wish to weaken the British Moravian connection with Herrnhut and the foreign Provinces of the Unity. On the other hand, after Reunion, the Moravians would not, naturally, enter into new relations with other Christian bodies without conferring with their Anglican brethren.

Condition (*d*). *Confirmation*.—The Moravian Committee offered to " recommend to our Provincial Synod that authority to confirm be given to presbyters at their ordination." Administration of the rite by presbyters is, they claim, no innovation in either East or West. The Anglican reply, naturally, affirms the claim to scriptural precedent in regarding Confirmation as proper to the highest order of the ministry. The Lambeth Conference of 1920 had spoken of a direct and special *delegation* by the Bishop, meaning an authority renewable from time to time and conferred only on particular presbyters. Later (12.12.1922) the Anglican representatives point out that presbyteral Confirmation in the West was an exceptional innovation, and in the East, the chrism must be consecrated by the Bishop. As to the *Holy Communion* the Moravians are prepared, without denying the principle on which they have hitherto acted, to forbid deacons to preside at that Sacrament.

These three problems, then, cover much of the ground in the subsequent conversations and correspondence to 1924; our limitations prevent more detailed notice. A bare reference may be made to one further issue which perhaps accounts for the underlying reluctance or inability of the Moravian Church to regularize their position in respect of what, for brevity's sake, may be termed Catholic custom. This was the fear that by so doing they would " disturb " their existing relations with other Christian Communities with which they are already in intercommunion, *e.g.* " the position of communicant members of other Churches which do not observe the rite of Confirmation " (Moravian Committee Reply, June 1922). The Anglican reply was obvious: Relationships based on Reunion (not on an " alliance ") " cannot but affect to some extent the freedom of the two bodies united." And if, as now appears, the assurances given by Bishop Hassé in 1909 are no longer correct, and non-episcopally ordained ministers of other denominations have been permitted to celebrate the Holy Communion, then a regard " for the security of our Common Sacraments," compels the Archbishop's Committee to secure further assurances that the careful practices asserted in 1909 and 1911 will be maintained. To these requirements the Moravian Committee was, to some extent, able to agree (pars. 3 and 4 of their Reply; no date). As a general rule only their own ministers (? presbyters) celebrate; and ministers coming to them from non-episcopal Churches rank as deacons—save that the Provincial Board can decide otherwise in extraordinary cases.

But the Anglican wish for assurance on these points of

Church order had brought to a head the fundamental issue: Were the representatives of the Unitas prepared to enter into a corporate union on a basis of Catholic order with a Church which, like the Anglican, is Reformed yet Catholic, and, if so, were they prepared to sacrifice, for the sake of ultimate and wider Christian Reunion, something of their liberty in respect of other Christian Communities to which such considerations do not appeal? Faced with this issue they are impelled to answer in the negative: they cannot encourage their members to cease sharing the joys of fellowship in worship and sacrament in other Churches: to do so would be to depreciate other Ministries and would not be conducive to the cause of Christian union. That decision the Archbishop's Committee accepted with sorrow (26th November 1923). It is the problem which has arisen elsewhere: Should intercommunion precede or follow Corporate Reunion? The only course is to await the result of other discussions now in process with the various Evangelical Free Churches.

Lambeth Conference 1930

The Sub-Committee of the Third Committee ("The Unity of the Church") discussed with five representatives of the Moravian Church the question of the reappointment of a joint Committee to continue negotiations. This it was decided to recommend the Archbishop of Canterbury to do, with the hope that a final decision may be made at the next Lambeth Conference.

SUPPLEMENTARY NOTE TO (5) *C*

Plainly, the subject-matter of our concluding paragraphs might be elaborated at such length as to destroy any symmetry our historical survey might claim to possess. The discussion of any one scheme of Christian Reunion necessarily both involves some acquaintance with the larger movement in all its ramifications and implies some understanding of the great issues presented by the varying interpretations of the Church's Constitution, Worship, Dogma. There is no need to remark on the enormous body of literature on each of those three aspects of the Reunion Problem. This note, confining itself mainly to the first, suggests only such topics and books as the writer himself has been impelled to consider and able to consult in the preparation of his account of the Anglican-Moravian negotiations.

Out of the multitude of books on Reunion and " the several Church-constitutions," an objective, compact and wide survey will be found in C. A. Briggs, *Church Unity* (Longmans, 1910) as also and in more contemporary accent, *The Doctrine of the Church and Christian Reunion*, Headlam (Murray, 1921). A previous set of Bampton Lectures, *Dissent in its Relation to the Church of England*, G. H. Curteis, 1871, is old but significant of the beginnings of a more friendly attitude between the two great camps of British Christianity. Its object is to advocate a closing of the ranks " in front of the deep and serried phalanx of Rome." For the contemporary situation the *corpus* of Memoranda, etc., in the two series of *Documents on Christian Unity*, Bell (O.U.P., 1924 and 1930) are invaluable. A general survey of a popular character is *The Reunion of Christendom*, edited by J. Marchant (Cassell, 1929). The last essay in *Essays in Christian Philosophy*, L. Hodgson (Longmans, 1929), on " The Reunion of Christendom," is a plea for Reunion based upon the suggestion that the Church was prior to the Ministry. The significance, for the future, of events in South India is obvious : the Joint Committee of the three negotiating Churches have published their proposals, *The Proposed Scheme of Union* (S.P.C.K., 1930).

Turning to the particular issues of Orders and Episcopacy raised by the Moravian claim, the analysis of the situation is complicated by the presence of the twofold attitude, liberal or catholic, within the Church of England, an attitude reflected in the diversity of view held in either school on the problems of the origin and status of the Episcopate in the Early Church. The groundwork might be covered through Lightfoot, *Philippians* (7th edition, 1883, " The Christian Ministry," pp. 181–269) ; Hort, *The Christian Ecclesia*, 1888–9 (cheap edition, Macmillan, 1914), and Hatch, *Organization of the Early Christian Churches*, Bampton Lectures, 1881 ; add Harnack, *The Constitution and Law of the Church in the First Two*

Centuries (Crown Theol. Library, Williams & Norgate, 1910). For criticism of Hatch and Harnack by a Presbyterian scholar, see Rainy, *The Ancient Catholic Church* (Clark, 1913 edition, pp. 40–42), and by an Anglican Catholic in Mason, *The Church of England and Episcopacy* (C.U.P., 1914, pp. 452–63); there also an explication of Lightfoot's dissertation (pp. 463–82). Add as important, H. B. Swete and others, *Essays on the Early History of the Church and the Ministry* (Macmillan, 1918). The *Didache*, now increasingly important in these discussions, is available in a cheap translation (Texts for Students, No. 13A, S.P.C.K., 1921). See discussion of date and origin in Streeter, *The Primitive Church* (Macmillan, 1929); a most stimulating discussion of the Origins of the Christian Ministry, stressing the importance of the Charismatic ministry revealed in the *Didache*, and the variety of first-century rule and discipline. Also on the "liberal" side is the Bishop of Gloucester's little book, *Apostolic Succession* (S.C.M., 1930). An Anglican "Modernist" presents his view in *The Evolution of the Christian Ministry*, J. R. Cohu (Murray, 1918). Mason, as above, is most valuable; his standpoint is, however, controverted by Hunkin, *Episcopal Ordination and Confirmation in Relation to Intercommunion and Reunion* (Heffer, 1929), which, by a series of citations from Anglican authorities seeks to show, if we may so say, the congruence of Canon Streeter's hypothesis with Anglican precedent. The same purpose underlies *Episcopacy and Unity*, H. A. Wilson (Longmans, 1912). "It seems that today there is a marked tendency to plant in the Church a narrower and more exclusive view upon both these questions (Episcopal Ordination and Intercommunion) than is either justified by the Church's formularies or is in accordance with the practice and teaching of most of our best accredited divines since the Reformation" (p. vii). Wilson and Hunkin both decline to recognize the conclusions of Denny, *The English Church and the Ministry of the Reformed Churches*, Ch. Hist. Soc., XVII (S.P.C.K., 1900), on the supposed acceptance by the Church of Presbyteral ordination: apart, at any rate, from the "plea of necessity" in the case of foreign Protestants; Mason follows Denny, see his Appendix A.

Against these set Bishop Gore's well-known *Orders and*

Unity (Murray, 1909), and *The Case for Episcopacy*, K. D. Mackenzie (S.P.C.K., 1929); which, holding the stricter view of episcopal Orders, yet suggests that Presbyterianism and Methodism, if not Independency, are not incompatible with that view. Mr Mackenzie has recently collaborated with Canon Jenkins in editing an important survey: *Episcopacy: Ancient and Modern* (S.P.C.K., 1930), which, while not without attention to the problem of origins, is mainly concerned "to supply an exposition of the practical working of episcopacy at different times and in different parts of the Church." There emerges an impression of the variety of governmental systems obtaining among the Episcopal Churches, not least those of the Anglican communion. In *Calvin et l'Épiscopat*, Pannier (Strasbourg, Faculté de Théologie Protestante, 1927), a French Reformed scholar makes an interesting attempt to show that Calvinism is not necessarily anti-episcopal, but is, in fact, not only not contrary to but is actually favourable to the institution of episcopal government; French Protestantism would gain in efficiency and fellowship by the recognition that there are other bishops than Roman Catholic bishops. On the allied topic of the administration of the rite of *Confirmation*, the reply of the Anglican Committee to the Moravians, seems to summarize accurately the normal Catholic practice in East and West. *The Prayer Book Dictionary*, Harford and Stevenson (pp. 236–239), represents the central Anglican position; in much greater fullness, *Confirmation*, *Vol. I*, *Historical and Doctrinal*, K. D. Mackenzie (S.P.C.K.). See also under Index in Mackenzie and Jenkins, *op. cit.*, for modern modifications. On the admission to the *Holy Communion* of Lutherans or Presbyterians, and others "who for a time wish to use the Church Services without joining her," Hunkin (Pt. II, pp. 111–12), adduces on the side of "Christian courtesy" the great names of Benson, Tait, Stubbs, Creighton, Temple, Maclagan, C. Wordsworth. Creighton's opinion is emphatic: Archbishops Temple and Benson frequently discussed the matter. "They agreed—and so do I—that the Church of England may allow its services to be used by members of other communions at their own responsibility, as a matter of Christian courtesy, not of right. There is no principle involved in this, except the principle of Christian charity " (20.5.1899). *Kikuyu* (Macmillan, 1915), by the late Archbishop Davidson, gave official endorsement of the view that this concession (and also the regulation of interchange of pulpits) are matters for the discretion of the diocesan bishop.

APPENDICES

APPENDIX A

THE RELIGIOUS SOCIETIES: WOODWARD'S "ACCOUNT"

The copy at Herrnhut (A. 33, 6A) preserves testimonials to the influence of this book in Germany.

1. The pious and learned *Dr Frank*, Professor of Divinity in *Hall* in Saxony writes thus concerning this matter to *some gentlemen in London*:

Jan. 21st, 1700.

"The eminent success of your pious undertakings has been made known to us in Germany by the Reverend Doctor Jablonski Chaplain to the newly crowned King of Prussia, who hath translated the account of your Societys out of the English into the German language nor has this Gentleman's pains proved unuseful, for besides the good it has done to many Particular Persons who have been thereby awakened to a greater concern for their spiritual edification, a great number of the citizens of Nuremberg who had a little before begun to meet at each others Houses in order to their mutual improvement in the Knowledge of the Truth, are by this Book mightily encouraged and Envigorated in good things, as a very Pious Minister (who with two other Divines is wont to preside at these meetings) has in the name of them all informed me from the place. And indeed the field of our Lord waxes more and more white unto harvest and the true Savour of the Gospel daily increases among Persons of various Ranks and Conditions both men and women with a general desire of living suitably thereto."

2. A very worthy Gentleman from Schaffhausen in Switzerland.

Jan. 12th, 1700.

"Dr W——'s full account of the Religious Societys in London is translated and printed at Berlin and is dedicated by the Translator to the Princess of Brandenburg who is lately married to the Young Prince of Hesse-Cassell. We have here some examples of the same sort of societies and it rejoices many among us to hear of the great piety and zeal that reigns in England."

3. Undated.

"A very learned and pious Foreigner who is pleased to favour me with his correspondence, in a letter of his (March 14, 1700) informs me that not only at Nuremberg but also at Augesburg and Ratisbone they find great benefit by their Religious Societys. That Dr Lange at Altorf had begun to use Religious Exercises with his scholars in imitation of those at Hall as Dr Spener had long since done at Frankfort."

APPENDIX B

A PROTESTATION OF LOYALTY, 1745

(The Name: Licence necessary through popular hostility: Herrnhut MSS., R. 13, A. 5 (4).)

To his Grace the Lord Archbishop of York. May it please your Grace.

We have related to our Brethren what we have done and the humane treatment we met with from your Grace and this is the result of what they and we have to observe concerning what we desired and what passed between your Grace and us.

1st. As to the Name, we are informed, that the Act of Toleration does not say or imply that any name distinguishing us from others should be made use of by us when we would have a License; the name *Protestant Dissenters* being sufficient; and others chusing to distinguish their sort when they take a License will not oblige your Lordship's Court to insist on it, that we should distinguish ourselves by any other name than Protestant Dissenters.

It is with the utmost unwillingness that we at any Rate call ourselves Dissenters at all from the english Church for we love her, and respect her as an episcopal Church, and we willingly would be as your Lordship says in Union with her, as far as it is possible.

Yet as divers Rumors are spread about us already and some of our Preachers ill treated, more disturbances may yet arise against our Meetings which those will venture to disturb, while unlicensed, who would not venture it if our places were licens'd. Disturbances are at all times odious to us, and much more in these unhappy times: and if our Places remain unlicensed the Blaim of all these disturbances would be laid at our Door, tho' we should only be the Persons who were *disturbed*.

We and our Brethren ev'ry where, have a respect for the Laws as for the Commands of Parents under God; and our Hearts are subjected to the Magistrates willingly; and tho' if it had been left to our choice, we had still continued unlicensed (because to the taking out of the License it is required, that we give ourselves the name of Dissenters) yet rather than not to act according to the Laws, or be even innocently the occasion of Disturbances, we chuse to be licensed.

And the Imprisonment of the Reverend Mr Ockertshousen, an episcopally ordained minister of ours (who has been treated as a Spy and an unworthy Person, without the least ground) alarms us so, that we cannot but make haste to do every thing which may shelter us from forced Constructions which ill-meaning Persons may put on the Law to our Prejudice, and can no longer continue unlicensed, being liable to daily vexations on that Account. And we had licensed our places long ago, if we had not been unwilling to declare ourselves Dissenters, a Name, which we like not: But we must either discontinue our meetings, which we can not, or be licensed as Dissenters which we like not: but which cannot be avoided. A Dilemma as disagreeable to us as to your Grace.

2. On the news of the Pretender's intention to invade us last year from Dunkirk, all of us in England agreed to present an Address to his Majesty (which accordingly was presented), wherein we told his Majesty with a sincere heart, that we were glad that it had pleased God to place Him and his Family upon the Throne; as Your Grace may easily conceive, we could expect no protection, no Liberty, no Toleration, under the Pretender. If we were at all mindful of our own Benefit, we could not be but hearty friends at the bottom, to the now reigning illustrious family, and we were, and are, truly sensible of the Blessings we enjoy under His Majesty King George and we pray for Him by Name in our Meetings every where.

In the Beginning of these present Troubles we considered if we should present an other Address to his Majesty, but upon mature and sincere Declaration:

That we have with the utmost sincerity taken the Oaths and are true and hearty and faithful subjects to His Majesty the King George; that we abhor and detest the Pretender and the Rebellion and that we are so truly sensible of the invaluable Blessings we enjoy as a Protestant people under his sacred Majesty King George that we are very thankful to God Almighty for his being on the throne and that though we are but few in Number yet we are all as one man hearty in this matter and we can and do assure your Grace, that we have not amongst us one Person, that is either *disaffected* to His Majesty's Person, Family or Government or at all *indifferent* how matters go, and that we believe it impossible for any Protestant who is in his Senses to have the least good wishes for the success of this unnatural and ungrateful rebellion. And we tho' in very moderate circumstances, have, do and will contribute all what is in our Power to the Support of his Majesty's Person, Family and Government and we desire your Grace as we think ourselves too mean to appear again at court to transmit this our honest and hearty Declaration which we chuse should go through your Grace's hands to His Majesty or the Secretaries of State.

Before the throne of God we shall remember your Grace and wish you all Blessing from Him, who died for us and is alive for evermore, Amen Who hath the Keys of hell and death. We desire to be remembered also by your Grace and are

May it please your Grace

Your Grace's oblig'd Servants,

W. H. (William Holland)

J. C. (James Charlesworth).

Pudsey, 15th Dec: 1745.

APPENDIX C

The Tropus Scheme:

Zinzendorf and the English Bishops: 1740–1752

The following series of letters which passed between the Count or his Agent and several of the English prelates are transcribed from copies in the Herrnhut Archives. Some are printed in Benham and are here merely noted. They illuminate certain aspects of " the Ordinary's plan " as well as the mixture of idealism and egotism, of worldly sagacity and childish simplicity in his conduct of affairs. An interesting comparison for the psychologist lies in recalling the somewhat similar correspondence of the adolescent Zinzendorf with Cardinal Noailles. Obvious resemblances in the two sets of correspondence show the child as father to the man.

I

Zinzendorf and Archbishop Potter

(*a*)

R. 13, A. 11, No. 3. *The Archbishop's letter of congratulation*, 4th August 1737 (see Benham, pp. 26, 27).

(*b*)

No. 7. *Zinzendorf to the Archbishop*, 31st December 1744.

The Count is sorry to trouble his " dear Father and Brother " but is distressed about the poor Brethren " persecuted by the Presbyterian People in York as hot and popish-like that it passes imagination." " My dear Antecessor Jablonsky who is gone home two years ago in an age of eighty years reckoned allways of the Archbishops of Canterbury in the Quality of Fathers to our constitution."

(*c*)

No. 8. In Double Column.

(i) *Zinzendorf to Archbishop*

I have two cases wherein I pray your Grace to inform in particular the Bearer of these, one of my Chaplains, a worthy man, who has been the former year visiting the Vallees of the Waldenses :

1. If one of our Ministers is to (be) consecrated in England by one of our Bishops, if he may be assisted by one of the Bishops of the Church of England.

2. If in that case the English Bishop may conform himself with the Liturgy of the Bohemian Church.

(Sgd) Lewis,
Cossart.

Red Lion Square,
12.9.1746.

(ii) Second Column.

The Answer of His Grace

1. Though the English Church will not say that the Moravian Church *is not* an Episcopal Church, yet out of want of a mutual correspondence she never acknowledged the Bohemian Church to be Episcopal and therefore (perhaps) an English bishop will not assist to any consecration of the Bohemians.

2. And in the Case anyone should do it, he never could part with his own Liturgy.

(*d*)

No. 9. 17 Sep. 1746.

Zinzendorf sends his son with papers " on matters of great importance." The youth does not speak English but has a German Baron as interpreter. These two only expect the Archbishop's blessing : a chaplain will come in some days for the answer.

(*e*)

No. 10. 6 Oct. 1746.

Zinzendorf sends Gambold who will be able to make the Archbishop understand the Count's purpose: viz., to restore strayed members to the Church of England, to show the Moravian Episcopal Church as a sister Protestant constitution, and to secure Harmony with the English among the heathen-missions. "Finally he will offer to your Grace's consideration the simplest and easiest way for restoring a good correspondence, establishing a perfect harmony and, if possible, curing the Church-Disease I spoke of."

(*f*)

No. 11. Copies (or drafts) of three letters from *Zinzendorf to the Archbishop*, the last dated from Red Lion Square, 6th October 1746.

i. Finally, my Lord, if things happened so, that I am inabled to do any good to your Church, pray let me be excused with all the Inconvenience the Bishop of London and others are used to lay to the charge of the Moravian Brethren; from which *Nodus Gorgius* I know a solution, but by no other way than a free and open transaction between your Grace and me, in the beginning merely private and without settling anything but Preliminaries which afterward may be laid before the whole world. I have no time to wait for Ecclesiastical Convocations. . . .

[Note: "Of the answer of his Grace no copy taken."]

ii. There is a clergyman, a learned man, one of the Oxford Scholars, *not* unable to continue this business after Zinzendorf goes home.

I shall send him to your Grace with the first plan of my proposal; Had I thought on him from the beginning I would have had less difficulty in acquainting your Grace with a matter so weighty to me and at the same time so important to be well managed and kept private.

iii. My Lord, I send to your Grace dear Mr N., a clergyman I know more acquainted with my way of thinking in ecclesiastical matters than any.

He will be able, I hope, to give your Grace a better preliminary account of my aim in the Business I began to lay before your Grace than all my writings. He will make your Grace understand what Real Good shall necessarily become of my Endeavours altho' its Principal View should be so intricate that all my first thoughts may prove to fall too short :

1. for putting the more effectual stop to all the motions already made and to be made *pro futuro*, in order to deprive the Church of England of her best members.

2. for reuniting thereunto all those who have hitherto been persuaded to separate themselves from the constitution of the same.

3. for giving a Solemn Testimony that the Moravian Church not only opposes directly such Persuasions and Misleadings, but on the Contrary proves herself a peaceable edifying and useful Sister to all Protestant Constitutions.

4. for clearing *in facts* our Brethren in the most *incontestable* manner from all the aspersions to the contrary *etiam circa prœteritum*.

5. for procuring to the Brethren who live among the Heathen a Christian Harmony with the English and at least as friendly a treatment as the Lutheran missionaries in East India have met with hitherto.

Finally. He will offer to your Grace's consideration the simplest and easiest way for restoring a good correspondence establishing a perfect Harmony and, if possible, curing the Church-Disease I spoke of.

The Plan I am about writing, in order to leave it to the Disposition of your Grace, is only a fuller explanation of the same matter and therefore will serve only to your Grace's Private Use.

I am with all my heart
Your Grace's faithful, most
obedient servant.

Red Lion Sq.,
6 Oct. 1746.

(*g*)

No. 12. Various drafts or copies: *Zinzendorf to the Archbishop.*

i. Sept: 1746.

My Lord,

I venture to write to your Grace these lines in a language which I have on the one side the good Fortune to understand enough for to perceive the full thoughts of my friends; but on the other Hand, prove myself not indifferently acquainted with speaking or writing it.

The Reason, for which I prefer running the hazard of rather explaining myself but in broken words, than in giving the satisfaction to your Grace to read a more elegant letter, is that you might have an upright confession from my own heart in a matter very weighty to me and to all true Believers within Doors and avoiding all witnesses which will be the more necessary in beginning when matters are yet indigested. I shall write in the most simple way, yet I shall keep myself from consulting any Dictionary, or other Book which might furnish me with terms and phrases so strange to me that it would be impossible for you to have my first thoughts in that childlike and native manner I endeavour to preserve, and which I am the most acquainted with.

The matter of my letter is to that purpose, your Grace may see very plain in the papers I have had the honour to communicate to you yesterday, that my Thoughts, in reuniting the Brethren of the Moravian Constitution with such of the many Protestant Religions the particular principles of which were most according to their spiritual judgment, have shown themselves now lately as successful in the so-called Reformed Religion, as hitherto in the so-called Lutheran.

But, my Lord, as the Spirit of Peace which rose in my heart soon after I was awakened near 40 years ago, is Universal I can't see Dissensions and Schisms arise in any part of the Protestant particular Churches without becoming very much concerned about it, and above all in the English Episcopal, the constitution of which I love and consider so particularly as none of the others.

The endeavours of the Methodists having had always somewhat that shocked me, their methods in preserving themselves within the pale of their former constitution being such as must necessarily become abortive *in fine*, that matter becomes the more serious to me. When many of that pious People in England who left their Way, appealed to me and the Brethren, I not only protested against receiving them among us, but endeavoured in the same time to recall them *home:* But alas all my repeated Contestations with both sides proved to be to no purpose.

Nevertheless I have persisted in protesting against the little congregation in London which stiled itself The Brethren in Union with the Moravian Church: and I have approved of the Idea of the Arch-Bishop of York, who desired the Brethren (asking for some licensed Places) to stile themselves Brethren in Union with the English Church; tho' the Counsels of his Grace were not followed, and then he gave the Licenses according to their Request.

I wrote to my Lord Bishop of London who was said to be the Author of a Pamphlet against the Methodists, wherein were some aspersions against our Brethren plainly showing the intire Unacquaintance of that Author with them.

Your Grace has seen, I believe, the mentioned Letter; but his Lordship objected in an Answer he gave to a Committee of the Brethren, which waited on his Lordship in order to receive his Commands, that it was not kind of a good sister to deprive her fellow-Sister of her best Souls.

This answer confirmed me in the Opinion I had before, that it would be a Blessing for me, to effect the Re-union of many thousand good souls with their former Constitution; so that the Question of AN is plainly decided in my heart. I ask only for that necessary part of things QUOMODO by what means?

I beseech your Grace to let me know your Intentions and to join your Experience with my Goodwill.

If the following points may be settled to the satisfaction of pious men, I believe, the Reunion is not impossible.

1st. That the administrator of this constitution is to be elected.

2nd. That your Grace might be pleased to take on yourself the Burden of the first Episcopal Administration ; Your Grace being in the same time the only Prelate, and the only Minister of the Church of England whom I durst nominate to the thousands awakened and almost separated Men in England for a Director of them ; for I am under a deep concern, that the most of your Church-men will be reputed *by them* as Deserters of the primitive Doctrine of the Church and Restorers of Platonism and Deism ; whose contestations I would rather see avoided than ventured.

3 ly. That seasonable reflections may be made upon the Proposals of such pious persons ; the more as the same involve by no means the Constitution of a whole Nation or Religion ; but afford a *Remedium* in behalf of a desperate cause and make the cure of it a possible thing.

It is true, my Lord, that the event of Things in the present state of the world and the Church being extremely uncertain, all my endeavours may fail or meet with such unsurmountable difficulties that the whole must be laid aside.

But even the very Motion which will be made on that Account can't fail of producing many good Effects, part in the Minds of People who have already separated themselves from the English Church Constitution without dissenting from its Foundation ; part in the thoughts of those, who still remaining with their old Liturgy, should meet with any Temptations for the future to leave it.

I am with all my Heart

Your Grace's faithful servant and assured Friend

LEWIS.

ii. 18th Sep. 1746. Another long letter, the substance of which lies in the final paragraph :

" Out of all which your Grace can plainly see that we might treat so weighty a matter between us without the least apprehension of sending ourselves responsible to any body for our private transactions thereupon."

The need of secrecy is stressed. When the right time comes Zinzendorf will be very pleased to lay the plan before the King, Chancellor and perhaps the Privy Council. Meanwhile, he supposes the Archbishop to be "in such circumstances which make it necessary for your Grace to be cautious in corresponding with foreigners." He himself had sent his son "in order to avoid the interfering of my Brethren and Fellow Labourers, in that kind of matter in which I confess our thoughts are hitherto somewhat distant from each other; and I believe it a Providence that I am impowered to act in such like matters without communicating the first steps I go to any body of my Colleagues."

This Claim is expanded through two pages: he shows how free he is, having no master in Prince or King, being a citizen of the *Libre Empire*, subject to none but the Empire itself. As for spiritual matters, his *Advocatia* of the Moravian Church "is as sovereign as any cause in Christendom"; no religious body "without doors" has any jurisdiction. In social life, too, he has preserved his independence. "I live in a Royal City whole months without paying visit to any Courtier or Statesman; seldom I repaid those I received from Lords whose business brings them to me." No one, therefore, expects him to pay social calls; "so that what your Grace treats with me, nobody shall try to get out of me."

Then follows the last paragraph already quoted.

iii. 21 Sep. 1746. Red Lion Square. "In the very moment of my departure for the country."

My Lord,

My intention was not to bring the English Church to the Moravian Constitution, but the Moravian Church which dwells in England, in America, and the English People which have given themselves over to them out of all sorts of Constitutions, to the plain English constitution. If it is needful to consult the King and his Council on account of the Preliminaries, before matters can be brought to any maturity, I chuse rather to hold my Peace, than to proceed any further; for I am no Avanturier, or such a maker of Projects who are used to bring their first proposals before Princes. I consult your Grace, not as Archbishop, but as a Theologus, who is the only one of that kind I am acquainted with in the whole Kingdom, being a man of a simple way, and intirely indifferent for making new Acquaintances. In short, if the matter I proposed is not intelligible enough for your Grace, it will be a Nonsense for the rest of your learned men ; and therefore it will be impossible for me to go on in my Plan, unless your Grace may, and may with Freedom, prepare Matters with me without committing any of our mutual Friends for to give up the whole, if we find it situated so, that it can by no means be brought safely into execution ; or if we find any Probability to go throughout with it, to lay it before the clergy of the English Church with the King's approbation in due time.

Yours entirely,

LEWIS.

iv. By the same copyist, there are other copies of certain letters already given, *e.g.* that relating to the Oxford scholar (no doubt, Gambold) the wording is almost, though not quite, identical.

Under 7th October 1746, is a letter presenting Zinzendorf's son-in-law, Frederic, Baron of Watteville's only son, about 30 years of age, a Bishop of the Moravian Church, a President of the General Synod, and Vicar-General of the Prime See.

Follows : I intend to deliver my own Speculations about Reuniting your Separated Members with the constitution they belong to.

The paper itself will show my simplicity and if not any good to the intended Aims, it will certainly be a private Memorandum to your Grace of the Character Mind and Personal Love of Order and Christian humility joint with universal and impartial Duty to all protestant and particularly the Divinely provided national constitutions

of Your Graces faithful and most humble

Servant.

II

Henry Cossart to the Archbishop of Canterbury—now Herring (Potter had died in 1747). Two copies: each is dated at the beginning July 12, 1748, and at the end July 21, 1748.

MY LORD,

I take the liberty before I go out of town to beg of your Grace the favour of (not) communicating the letters his Lordship Bishop Count Zinzendorf wrote to your Grace's predecessor. I hope your Grace will readily grant me this my Petition considering that my instrument is not further but to let your Grace alone have the perusal of the said letters of which a good part doth not seem to have that degree of Maturity which is requisite for being made more public.

I have also a remark to add to the conversation Mr Boeler and I had the honour to have this morning with your Grace. Your Grace seem'd at a loss what Bish. Count Zinzendorf meant with the word *Administrator* and I am afraid our being foreigners hindered us to give Your Grace a full satisfaction, nor do I know if I am able to do it in writing, nevertheless it is my duty to doe towards it what layeth in my Power.

Christian Union and good Order have at all times been fundamental rules of God's people and so weighty to us that in the year 1570 our forefathers of the Bohemian Confession formed with the Reformed and Lutheran Protestants of the Augustan and Helvetic Confess: that famed Synod called the *Consensus Sendomiriensis*, the history of which has been so elegantly writ by our old Bishop Jablonsky and dedicated by him to his assured friend, the late Archbishop Wake, in which Synod it was agreed on all sides that the doctrine of these three different Protestant Churches being the like in Substance they would bear with one another not only in the arbitrary Points of Doctrine but also in the different Liturgies and Ceremonies of each of the said Churches, and in this fraternal Union they went on till the spirit of persecution in the year 1628 routed our Clergy in Bohemia and Moravia and at sundry times expelled almost all Professors of the Consensus out of great and lesser Poland.

[Cossart then refers to the histories of Comenius, Camerarius and John à Lasco, as well as to MSS. relating to the Moravian Church in Lambeth Library.]

But when it pleased God to Gather the remnants of the said Churches in the territories of Count Zinzendorf in Lusatia under the Protection of the Liberties the Country enjoieth since it is in the hands of the Electors of Saxony, He raised also by his infinite mercy the same spirit of Union, Order and Love which had been the soul of the Consensus of Sendomir. Therefore the Brethren renewed their ancient systeme; to give to the different branches, according to the different Protestant schemes their Members under Persecution had followed in the different countries of their exile. Branches were called TROPOI, viz., *The Moravian Church* KAT' EXOCHEN of which Bishop David Nitschmann and after him Bishop Count Zinzendorf were elected Presidents: the *Lutheran* whose President and Administrator are Polycarpus Muller who formerly had a Professor's chair at the University of Leipsic, now lately deceased, and the now elect and lately first Chaplain of his Majesty the King of Dennemarc, Mr N. Gerner; and the *Reformed Tropus* of which the last President was the old Bishop Baron of Watteville and the present Administrator is Mr Christian John Cochius who is at the same time first Chaplain of the King of Prussia; of which Administrator's office I shall give your Grace in the following lines the true idea:

> When a presiding bishop of a Tropus dyeth, resigneth or is abroad in the Visitations, one of our Coadjutors of that Branch or any other worthy Protestant divine known to have the increase of the Kingdom of Jesus at heart, whatever station he may be in his respective church, is elected *per suffragia* to be the representative of the Presiding Bishop of the Tropus who wanteth him, and the person who is invested with this office we call an *Administrator;* he is to the clergy of the Tropus over which he presides the same what a Bishop is to his inferiour clergy: his office is to appoint ecclesiastical conferences and to enquire if the decrees of the precedent conferences or synods of his Branch

have been executed ; and to look into it that Union and order may reign among those committed to his care and the intercourse of love with other Branches may be maintained.

[Annotation in margin : " *Voicy le point en question.*"]

It was under such a scheme that Bishop Count Zinzendorf endeavoured to reconcile to the Church of England those of her members tired of Methodism after having followed it a considerable time and who insisted for several years that the Brethren might receive them under their care—which was constantly denied on our side ; but to give them some satisfaction and to prevent more evil the Count writ to Your Grace's predecessor the 'fore mentioned letters and would have been glad to find an English Tropus a practicable matter which he thought of great consequence for bringing many wandering souls who had applied to us, into the Pale of their own Church, provided one could grant them such modifications as should be found necessary to satisfy them in matters they might think to have some reason to complain of.

All these matters might have been set in a clearer light if the preliminaries could have been settled with the late Archbishop but Count Zinzendorf, understanding by his Grace's answer that the English Church did admit of no modification and that its members must either comply in every thing, yea in every syllable of the Common Prayer, or be Dissenters and turn to what party they liked best and enjoy the effect of the Toleration Act ; He saw clearly that matters standing so, his endeavours were not like to answer, and comforted himself with having done the best that lay in his power towards a Reconciliation, Union, and Order in the Church of England. Now he hath thought fit to have these letters communicated to your Grace that your Lordship may be the more able to judge of his pacific intentions and of his great regards to the Church of which God hath been pleased to make your Grace the Angel and first Guardian.

I have but two words more to say. Our regard to the established Church of these Realms is well grounded and sincere ; for though we have a different Liturgy, other Rites and Ceremonies and might differ, too, in some less essential

Points of Doctrine, or in case the 39 Articles should not imply the full sense of which the Words are susceptible we should explain ourselves with other words, as in that of Predestination whose opposite, viz. Reprobation we do not at all admit ; and in that of taking an oath which many of us scruple. Yet far from persuading any of the members of the Church of England to leave their Constitution we would rather for Union and Order bring to her again her strayed sheep, though we must own on the other side that the nature of our Call cannot well suffer us, to leave those souls to themselves who will not be persuaded to go back to their mother-Church but insist upon our taking care of them, yea we are of opinion that it is the interest of the Church of England that such people may rather be gathered in the Pale of an Episcopal Protestant Constitution who (which) makes much of the Church of England, than to fall into the hands of sectaries which find their interest in keeping their flocks at a distance (not to say something worse) from all well-regulated Protestant Church Schemes.

[He is off to Ireland : hence the address, Parkgate in Chester, where the ship has been obliged to put in. He begs pardon for his freedom of expression, for length and for any verbal awkwardnesses.]

Most obedient and most humble
Servant

H. COSSART.

Barkgate, July 21, 1748.

III

No. 12. (1) *The Moravian Bishops to the Bishop of London* (Edmund Gibson). A copy of the Latin original, of which the translation is given by Benham, p. 164.

No. 12. (2) *Gibson to Hutton*, on Neisser's visit ; Benham, pp. 159–60.

No. 12. (3) *Hutton's reply* thereto ; Benham, pp. 160–3.

No. 12. (5) *Zinzendorf to Gibson ;* observations on the previous two letters. 29 Sep. 1744. Benham pp. 164–7.

IV

Zinzendorf to Bishop of London, Thomas Sherlock, 6th Feb. 1752.

MY LORD,

When I wrote to your Lordship now almost a year ago I desired you to do something to get a true knowledge of our Expressions ; and very well knowing the great difference of one language from another, and satisfied that none of the translations would do, not ours because we are not masters of your phraseology, not that of the English men because they are not of ours : the Harmony of your Church and ours, and the serious endeavour to prevent the eloping of your people to our Church in these Realms where everybody is inclined to make the best of his liberty, on that account is really to be backed by the following principles :

1. That a hearty Intercourse of the worthiest prelates of your Church be maintained with our Foreman which will keep our mutual Pastors in awe.

2. That if Necessity requires to erect here and there a Chapel (the number of which compared with other Denominations will always be of no consideration when placed in its utmost Height, viz., at London, where the French, the Baptists, yea the Methodists have at least 50 Chapels, three will be sufficient for our Church and two Tropus's) the Licence must be carefully ask'd for from the Ordinary in order to pay *per Indirectum* the due Respects to him and to appear a Christian Family in Union with his See.

3. The system of Divinity must be maintained on both sides to be almost the same and therefore the obscurities must be cleared and the mutual misrepresentations, viz.

Of the *Brethren*, as if they turn'd metaphorical sayings into Plain truths which must needs cause an Erroneous Theory and an Enthusiastical Practice ;

Of the *English* as if they spiritualized too much a Creator who by his Supreme Wisdom chose to become flesh and bone and as if in order to honour a Divine Person who must be honoured in *Him* they neglected the main point of all Christianity, which is Christ Crucified, God over All, which of course will make a religion of Deists and a conversation agreable to such a Theory :—should cease on both sides.

As for the first two points, they are chiefly the duty of our clergy, so during my lifetime I hope to keep them carefully a-standing.

As for the third, as we are in a full view of your Church and your old Books are pretty conformable with our Theory, if we hear you should preach Christ crucified, and as the necessity of assisting the Laws of the Realm by your Morals is not to be denied, so on the other hand, if the great Apocalipps of the Mystery of Beatitude is served in its turn with as much fervour and assiduity, we may be satisfied at a very little Expence.

[The Count then requests the Bishop of London " to make 100 questions in writing." If this makes the Bishop apprehensive, let him reflect it is Zinzendorf who ought to fear " such a collation in writing." From it might flow three blessings : charity between " the only two Episcopal Churches in the Evangelical Body," increased understanding of the Brethren among Churchmen, assistance for the Church in building up Christians and converting heathen.]

Your most humble servant and Brother,

LOUIS.

The Bishop of London's replies are uniformly courteous and patient. On two occasions he is unable to use his hand for writing (15th February 1752 and 4th March 1754). On the latter occasion he encloses a volume of his sermons. On 30th May 1752 he sent a letter of condolence on the death of Zinzendorf's son, Renatus.

The *Bishop of Worcester* also wrote in June 1752, a letter of condolence. There are also in the same packet two friendly letters from the *Bishop of Lincoln* (30.10.1749 and 8.8.1752).

MSS. A. 14, *No.* 13, encloses several letters of friendly encouragement from Wilson of Sodor and Man. He, too, is sometimes shaky through gout. He addresses Cossart as " Archdeacon of the Unitas Fratrum." Letters referring to the aged Bishop's acceptance of the office of *Administrator of the Reformed Tropus* will be found in Benham, pp. 246–8.

APPENDIX D

The name of *James Hutton* is associated with the story of the Unitas in England from the very beginning: his character, as revealed in Benham's *Memoirs*, is certainly unsurpassed in its appeal among all the English Brethren thence onwards. The intrinsic biographical interest, therefore, furnishes an additional incentive to some slight notice of the attitude adopted by the Central Authority of the Unitas to their official English Secretary. There is something typical of the contrast between the freer spirit of the English—one might say, the Cockney—temperament and the more austere Teutonic preciseness revealed in the constant objections on the part of the Directory to their London brother's free and easy contact with all sorts and conditions of men, to his jovial companionship and his readiness to converse on all manner of subjects, including politics, wars and revolutions. As his biographer puts it, "he felt himself at perfect liberty to appear cheerfully before the public, and cultivate a free intercourse with all classes of society" (p. 371). During a sojourn in Switzerland, 1756–63, his conduct in this respect had received a good deal of unfavourable comment. In a lengthy and self-revealing letter to the Board, the offender defends himself, partly on the ground that he was made to be "social friendly and without affectation. Any one with a human face was welcome with me; for such a being needs but to be seen to be saluted, yea, loved, by his fellow-creatures. This I have found to be the case everywhere." It was indeed a principle on which he seems to have acted unabashed in the presence of explorers, scholars, ministers of state, even Majesty itself. (See pp. 477, 503, 540. The amusing report of the King's new favourite, "the old deaf Moravian, James Hutton," should be read (p. 507). For other meetings of Hutton and George III, see pp. 498, 509, 526, 529.) Moreover, by such friendly intercourse and innocent, though non-religious, conversations, he had gained many to have a better understanding of and affection for, the Brethren. "Providence everywhere (in Switzerland) brought me into contact with people who took delight in a social friendly intercourse with a Herrnhuter. . . . But even should little or no good result it is at any rate a great pleasure to myself to love others and have intercourse with those who will converse with me. *Nihil humani a me alienum puto*" . . . (Hutton to the Directing Board, 28th September 1768, pp. 453–6).

"Jemmy's" creaturely fellow-feeling certainly accounts for his removal from Switzerland, where he had been very active and happy, to London where it was evident the Directory hoped he would remain quiet, and be content to do little (see pp. 372, 414, 419; his English colleague, Br. Charles Metcalfe, was also under a cloud of depression "arising out of an apprehension of being severed from the affection of the Brethren of the Directing Board," p. 415). In 1767 Hutton is provoked to write a long letter to the Board, detailing the causes of estrangement, of unavailing efforts to evoke friendly confidence in John Nitschmann (to whom he is supposed to report), and the resulting alienation of the Board from himself.

> I was found fault with, and misunderstood again and again. . . . In short, I might fill a whole sheet with weighty reasons for my dissatisfaction. But discontent, although human, is at all times wrong, and often becomes more or less a sin, according to circumstances (pp. 428–31).

Two years later the Directory rather churlishly objected to paying his expenses to the Marienborn Synod, and surprisingly suggested there was no need for the presence of the Unity's Secretary there (pp. 478–9). The worthy Secretary was evidently labouring under a sea of suspicion: numerous other instances could be given. One will point the relevance of these interesting *biographia* to our more serious study. In 1767 the Directory applied to Hutton to transfer property in North America, and also Lindsey House (both vested in his name as Unity's Secretary), to Br. F. W. Marschall. The exact legal advantage seemed dubious; Hutton, however, acquiesced as to the American property, and as to Lindsey House "left the matter in the Saviour's hands." That this affair was "a further evidence of distrust towards him in the minds of the Directory" seems a reasonable deduction—and doubtless also the Chronicler's further observation: "This may have been induced by a fear of the independent spirit of the English Brethren" (pp. 442–3).

APPENDIX E

THE LA TROBE–LORETZ CORRESPONDENCE

(*Herrnhut MSS., R.* 13, *A.* 43)

Benjamin La Trobe first enters the Brethren's history c. 1745, when a Religious Society, which he, a young Baptist student, had organized in Dublin, invited Cennick thither. He served the Brethren in Ireland, at Fulneck, and finally as General Superintendent of the whole work in England. An eloquent preacher and a copious apologist for the Unitas, he was the protagonist of the minimizing policy of the "United Flocks." He appears in Benham's pages chiefly as, for several successive years, President of the S.F.G. "His influence was entirely German in character" (Hutton, p. 439).

Johannes Loretz, b. 1727 in Switzerland, became a close confidant of Zinzendorf, whose *Berliner Reden* had brought him to an assured faith. He served the Brethren at Neuwied, at Herrnhut, and after Zinzendorf's death, became their chief agent in negotiations for state concessions, *e.g.* that with the Empress Catherine relating to the Settlement in Russia (1763). In 1770 he undertook a visitation of North America and the Danish West Indies. His official status was the important one of "Senior civilis." He died in 1798. He has left an autobiography which has been printed in the *Zeitschrift Der Brüderbote*, 1897, 1898 (available at Fetter Lane). He has been conjectured to be the original of Major L., in *Wilhelm Meister's Apprenticeship*.

The *Correspondence* illustrates the two opposing attitudes among the English Branch subsequent to the formation of the Central Executive. The one policy would have led to greater freedom and independence; the other was based on "the original plan," "the Diaspora plan," "the plan of the late Ordinary," "for which only our Church polity exists," on which the Brethren aimed definitely at being primarily a "vital leaven" among the other English "religions." The first alternative has been, in the view of a devout and loyal Brother, "a real detriment to the Congregation" and must be withstood. Both writers say, "We must return to our first principles."

Further, Methodist proposals for the amalgamation of the two groups of Societies must not lead the U.E.C. to deny the real and essential quality of the Unity as leaven within the national Churches. Hence occur certain illuminative sidelights on the divergent attitudes of John and Charles Wesley and of Dr Coke.

Lastly, it is repeatedly stressed, that in the direction of the Unity, the Elders' Conference is central ; it is a constitutionally elected executive and there must be no suspicion of a personal autocracy, as seems to be the case with the Methodist societies now being organized into a church-constitution.

[The translation of the Loretz letters is largely the work of the Rev. Dr Henri Roy, Ex-Principal of the Theological Seminary, Herrnhut. The MSS. are very lengthy and the less valuable portions have been summarized.]

No. 1.

La Trobe to Loretz (for U.E.C.). London, 25.10.1785

Dearest Brethren,

[Some preliminary remarks]

I need not give you a description of Mr John Wesley. Brother Joseph knows him of old. You know that his societies are very numerous and exceed in the three kingdoms more than can well be imagined. His chapels are to be met with everywhere and he has many hundred local and itinerant preachers. His Br. Charles has been attached to him in a manner that has made him unsteady in all his connections with other persons, being his implicit follower in all things. Though it is very doubtful whether John ever knew himself as a sinner or our Lord as his Saviour, yet it is beyond a doubt that many of his people are sincere followers of our Saviour and have experienced the power of his grace and love to hear the pure Gospel. He has taken up some of our regulations and established them in his Societies. He set out as an avowed partisan of the Church of England and his people have kept to it. To prevent schism he published 20 years ago his reasons *for not separating from the Church of England*.

Several were proposed for his successors when he should depart this life (he was and is absolute head of his Societies), Mr Fletcher, a Swiss but Rector or Vicar of the parish of Madley in Gloucestershire but he died lately. However, before his death—*Coke* LL.D. a young clergyman who is very fiery lately got an ascendancy over him and has been his chief counsellor. This young man has at length persuaded him that he is as truly an apostolic bishop as any now living and he should use his authority. There was now a fair opening. America was separated from England and it would not be acting against either the law of God or man to *establish a new Episcopal Church* among the *Methodists* and whoever would join them there. To this end they formed out of the Common Prayer Book a new Common Prayer book for the use of their new congregation. It is, however, that of the Church of England with some alterations which are so far as I can judge for the worse. They have added the form of consecration of *Superintendents* in the room of Bishops, of *Elders* for Presbyters and I think Deacons. *Dr Coke went to America to establish this church. Before his departure, Mr Wesley ordained or consecrated him superintendent of the American Church* with a commission to him to consecrate a Mr *Asbury* superintendent in America and to them both power to ordain Elders &c. Dr Coke went and has executed his plan: and a sermon has been published at Baltimore before the Conference of the Methodist Episcopal Church at the ordination of the Revd Francis Asbury to be superintendent of the said church by Thos. Coke, LL.D., Superintendent. *Dr Coke is returned and will not rest until he has formed a Methodist Episcopal Church in England.*

Mr Charles Wesley having soon shown his dislike to the first movement of this new plan was no further consulted; and since it has been made known, he has opposed it. He has long sought my acquaintance and lately requested a couple of hours with me. He has communicated a correspondence between him and his Brother wherein he is plain and severe, though kind, and John says we must agree to disagree. Charles will not publicly oppose but he declares he will oppose this new schism, which will end in a number of new sects ; and now he wishes that *the Brethren might be of the use* they were originally intended for, *to nurse these souls* who are truly awakened and who adhere to the *Church of England.* John says he does not intend *to establish his church in England* but, says Charles, Dr Coke &c *will*, and this seems indeed probable. Hitherto I have advised him to let his Brother know clearly his mind but not to make an open opposition. He is really hurt in his health by it, and remembers what the Count told him when he sent for him with a message to the Archbishop of Canterbury, viz. that his Brethren did not intend to take the people out of the Church of England but to edify them. He thought afterwards that the Brethren forsook their plan and on this account he was against them. But he always felt that they had the true doctrine in essentials and the most reality.

Now many of Mr Wesley's people, preachers as well as laity, show an affection for the Brethren and attend our Chapel and it has appeared that the testimony in the country I have delivered has been acceptable to them.

When I consider the present state of things in the religious world around us it confirms me in the idea I have long had, that there is a great field for our Saviour in England in which he will use the Brethren much more than he has hitherto done.

Lady Huntingdon has appointed two Presbyters of the Church of England to act as *Bishops* in ordaining her students. Mr Wesley has followed her, only he takes the episcopal character. Mr Whitefield's successors have some connexion, but no regular constitutional connexion. The zealous clergy in the Church of England are in connexion with none but all these parties think more favourably of the Brethren than they have done and some in each look on us with affection and prize our connection. Our Lord has some aim in all this ; may his aim be obtained. After many pressing invitations I preached last Wednesday night in a chapel in Mr *Whitfield's connexion*.

Before I close I will mention something of America. There is now a Bishop there consecrated last June by three non-Juring Bishops in Scotland. The Bishop of Chester told me that they could not deny their regular succession. I have got an account of it which I transmit to you as it belongs to Church History and may have some influence in America. Bishop Seabury is in Connecticut. You have here a copy of his Certificate. You may be surprised that one is stated "*Episcopum Rossensem et Moraviensem*" but the cause is this, that part of Scotland called Murray was in old maps called Moravia. There a question might arise: Did any emigrants from Moravia *go at any time to Scotland?*

Be tenderly saluted by

Your troublesome but affectionate

Br. B. La Trobe.

No. 2.

Loretz to La Trobe. Herrnhut, 27.11.1785

Loretz wishes blessing to La Trobe's preaching and to that of the Methodists. It must be our care to preach the Cross in every church and denomination, in the Church of England, in Whitefield's or Wesley's Connexions, the Presbyterians. God has given success to the Brethren in all Protestant Churches—witness the number who have joined and have been blessed in living with the Brethren. If the Lord would give us the same blessing in England we would be thankful to be his colleagues. Perhaps the time is not distant when many of the Wesleyans may join in receiving blessings along with the Brethren. The Wesleyan scheme comes from the Brethren, from Zinzendorf himself, viz., that we would not take people from the Church of England but build them up wtihin the Church. So we work in our Diaspora work. It must be said, however, that we have abandoned this idea in England and attempted to build up a church of our own and have taken members from the other churches—except that we did not take those who went to the Holy Communion in the Church of England. But now we do not say that—but we say that a man can do both. Wesley on the contrary maintains the principle of not separating from the Church and has been blessed in his work. We remain small in England because of our fault. Now it seems Wesley has made the same fault and has abandoned his first plan and is degenerating into a sect.

Wesley's pretensions to ordain cannot be maintained according to Canon Law (Ecclesiastical Right) and therefore the Methodist ordinations and ministerial acts cannot be valid. For although church constitutions do not touch the inner essence of Christianity—which is a religion of Spirit and Truth—nevertheless the lack of true qualifications will lead to trouble in the Methodist church because all right thinking men hold good order as healthy and necessary. As Charles Wesley said to you, there are many people who are friendly to the Brethren and seek their help. We must therefore consider whether it is now the time to become busy and adopt plans for God's work among this favourable party, or remain quiet for them to make their way to us. Our inclination and circumstances recommend the first but we must wait to see what is God's will—perhaps the way of private visits and conversations with individuals, not propaganda in Methodist chapels, by those who have experienced salvation and who understand our plan and are hungry for souls. Men must seek communion with God and with the Brethren and thence human fellowship will spring. Charles Wesley is right in saying that if the Brethren, according to their original plan, will help the awakened in the Church and nourish them, and not allow members of the Church to join our church, then the clergy will not have reason to be jealous of the Brethren.

No one can reproach us with making schisms and sects or with proselytizing. That is not a matter of indifference, but the chief thing is that we do all we can to make the work of the Lord to increase.

I have to ask you in the name of the Unity's Elders' Conference to consider the matter and all the circumstances with your colleagues, and to give us an opinion whether now is the time to get busy and what measures are requisite to bring the matter to a good end. Another confidential conversation with Charles Wesley may help—yea, he himself might assist the Brethren to enter into the circle of the awakened.

No. 3.

La Trobe to Loretz. 6th January 1786

[This is a reply to No. 2, the latter letter having raised La Trobe's hopes (which had grown dim) that the original plan will be adhered to.]

Certain I am that our departure from the original plan in England has not only been a means of preventing our general usefulness in this country but has been a real detriment to the congregations which our Lord intended to establish here. . . .

[He had almost ceased to struggle against the tide.]

The beginning of the present awakening was in the Established Church, the few orthodox dissenting congregations were at that time sunk into mere systematic laodicean religion and were the greatest opposers of the simple truth as it is in Jesus and of the practical profession of it. The Wesleys and their adherents and other clergy of the Established Church at Oxford were awakened and Brother Boehler when he went there found a preparation for the Gospel.

[The sojourn of the two Wesley brothers in Georgia strengthened the bond, and]

Georgia was also a means of the connexion with Mr Ingham who was minister of the established Church in which the awakening began in Yorkshire. Societies established under the direction or patronage of the Bishop of London held in the Vestries of several churches were also a preparation for the Gospel. To these, Hutton, West, Edmonds, &c belonged. During the connexion with Messrs Wesley the late Ordinary began his connexion with the Archbishop of Canterbury and he then declared by Charles Wesley who was sent to Archbishop Potter with a message from him that the Brethren would not draw the good souls from the Church, but labour to keep them in it and preserve a good seed in it.

After the Wesleys separated from the Brethren and it was found well to form a congregation the general plan was not immediately altered nor have we ever theoretically and synodically altered our plan, but we have altered it practically. The first Congregation settled in England was a Pilgrim Congregation : it was that of Yorkshire (I pass over the German and Sea Congregations). This congregation was settled in London and the members removed to Yorkshire from whence the Yorkshire congregation sprung, the members of the Society going until that time to the Communion in the Church of England. The London Congregation was soon after settled and that upon a pilgrim footing and indeed the greatest part of the first members became pilgrims and labourers.

[Thereupon many applied for membership.]

But, a rule was made, That no person should be proposed for reception into the congregation who had been within two years at the Holy Communion in the Established Church. This arose from a supposition that no one who could with a good conscience go in the established church would stay from the Communion two years, in hopes of being received in that time into the Congregation and therefore it would be a means of keeping the awakened people in it and this was the ground of the Societies being formed. The reason here assigned for the above rule of two years abstaining from the holy Communion I have learned repeated from the late Ordinary and other Brethren who were then active. It is confirmed by the *Form of a Testimonial &c* laid before Parliament, to be found in *Acta Fratrum Un. in Anglia*, No. LXXIV in the Appendix of Vouchers. This must have been before my time discontinued as I never saw or knew anything of the kind. Here it appears that not only the persons received were to have a time of trial of two years that their call to the Congregation might be clear, but that after reception, if it was found that their consciences would allow them to communicate in their former church, they should be sent back to it, though they had been received. . . . I know these were the principles of the late Ordinary to the end of his days, as I have heard him declare his sentiments upon this head very frequently, roundly and warmly both in conference and in private conversation with me. . . .

After the happy departure of the late Ordinary our late Br. Johann Nitchmann came to England as Oeconomous; He saw into the use and blessing of the Diaspora plan as it was called at that time and I will beg to make use of that word yet, as I know none more convenient. At the Synod in 1764 we were encouraged to attend to and pursue that plan and to be more strict with respect to those who should be proposed for reception into the Congregation—to keep the members of the Societies in their respective churches. At a Provincial Synod held after the General Synod of 1764 in Lindsey House, the encouraging and re-establishing the Diaspora plan in England was a subject of much deliberation and it was the unanimous opinion of all the labourers present that we should begin it in the name of the Lord with zeal. I never remember a synod where more of our Lord's presence was felt and the members more unanimous. We separated with a resolution to undertake this business for which preparation seemed to have been made. The protocalist wrote in strong terms and the minutes were not conferentially revised. The protocol was taken to the Directory by a Brother who at the Conference was zealous for the Diaspora. Some of the members of the Directory were alarmed that the plan was to destroy the City and Country congregations and being Church-men were apprehensive of the consequence and immediately set themselves against the plan. 100 members of the Society in Yorkshire entered heartily and with blessing into the plan as did a company in Bristol. A proposal was sent to the Directory from the Conference of Fulneck for the furtherance of the Diaspora plan. A letter was sent from the Directory disapproving the resolutions of the Conference at Lindsey House and the proposals from Fulneck. Br Johannes was called to Sarepta from England and Br Petrus Boehler sent to England as Visitator. Our late dear Brother Boehler was a church-man and came determined to make an end of the Diaspora. A provincial synod was convened at Fulneck at which the whole of the plan was begun in blessing, though mistakes were made through the zeal of some for it; and some of the labourers who had been most zealous in making all to Diaspora and had been checked in their proceedings (under such influence) became opposers of it. I mention this period with sorrow: as it almost shook my confidence at that time in the direction of the Unity. I was told that if I would give up the Diaspora plan, I should become Oeconomous of England. I could not but reply with warmth that if Bribes were used in the Unity there was an end of our life and blessing. It was said publickly that the poorest member of the Society who wished to be in the congregation was better than the best Communicant in the United Flocks or Diaspora, and yet it was owned that those who had been formed into United Flocks had grown thereby in grace, and many of them were spoken to, upon which they desired to be received into the Congregation. . . .

It hurts me to write of this period but it seems necessary that we may see by what means at different periods this important part of the Brethrens' call has been prevented or frustrated. Through the want of this plan there has been a kind of necessity of receiving persons into the congregation who had no immediate call to it and consequently not the genuine congregation-principles. The late Ordinary, apprehensive of this, proposed seriously to establish a Brethren's religion distinct from the true congregation of the Brethren particularly in some parts of England and the North of Ireland. Our dr. Brethren will know that at every synod this subject has been on the carpet, both with a view to receive none into the Congregation but such whom the Lord hath called and formed for it and to keep souls in the religions by forming United Flocks. Principles were established in 1775 &c, but in 1782 I was afraid that both the Congregation and Diaspora would fall together, by setting up congregations who should be regulated according to the genius and circumstances of the people. After every synod the principles have been renewed in the several Conferences in England, but the labourers in general have been, since 1786, not attentive with open ears or active in the affair. The attention, so far as it has gone, of not proposing improper persons into the Congregation, has kept back many from our connection, as we had no other mansion for them and by this means, too, many are Congregation members who have not Congregation principles, and many keep aloof and only attend our preaching. Had we had from the beginning more attention to the Diaspora plan, and to place-congregations, I doubt not but that where we are now useful to one soul in caring for them we should be useful to one hundred. Wesleys took the plan from us and they have increased to 50,000 at least in England and Ireland. John Wesley is now turning about and I have not a doubt that if they begin their own church in England they will in a few years be broke into a great number of dissenting parties.

So much for the time past. I will now proceed to the present movements. B. La Trobe.

[*The Postscript* covers eight long pages and bears the title:

" *Of the Movements relating to the Methodists.*"]

La Trobe remarks that before Br. Loretz' letter came, he had had " several solid conversations with Charles Wesley " who is in deep affliction of mind and sickness of body through the methodists setting up a new religion ; John is being led away by young Coke.

I visited him in his sickness and he continually repeated that he hoped and believed that the Brethren must be the means of preserving the true seed in the established church and of keeping the living souls among the methodists together. The way how was difficult, he told me his brother would be pope and was already envious of my entrance among the methodists.

The account goes on to say that La Trobe had met Dr Coke two or three years ago when Coke was thinking of going to the East Indies. To La Trobe's surprise he now had received a letter from Coke, dated 23rd December 1785, asking why cannot the United Brethren and the Methodists unite, in view of the similarity of their doctrine and discipline ? Dr Coke says he is willing to meet La Trobe at breakfast in Fetter Lane any time next week. This letter La Trobe took to Charles Wesley.

He (C. W.) having a very unpleasing notion of Dr C's views and proceedings, begged me to take care that the sender (viz.

John Wesley) and sent (Dr Coke) did not mean to spy out our liberty.

However, Coke came to breakfast on Wednesday, 4th January 1786, and the conversation ran as follows :

COKE hopes the time has come for uniting, as the two bodies seem to agree in doctrine and discipline.

LA T.: Yes, it was a pity we separated. As a preliminary, let us open up the present state and constitutions of both parties and of their intentions in forming a new church. Let us be frank and simple.

COKE thereupon showed how the numbers in the connexion have grown beyond expectation—and there are several hundred local preachers. The problem is how to care for them properly. In general members were exhorted to attend the ordinances of the church, but some were Dissenters by birth and would not—their own religions would not admit them to the Communion if they kept to the Methodists. Some had applied to Bishops for ordination but were refused. Proposals had been made to Mr John Wesley to ordain but he had resolutely declined. Then their people in America applied to him and he asked the Bishop of London to ordain a worthy and qualified man. The Bishop refusing, John Wesley resolved to form a church-constitution as near that of the Church of England as possible and to ordain Superintendents, Elders and Deacons to correspond to the three orders of Bishops, Priests and Deacons. But only for America. The Book of Common Prayer with alterations was sent over with Dr Coke for the use of the church to be formed in America. He went in 1784, ordained several, met with no opposition and there were now some 18,000 members.

LA T. asked whether there was not a danger that the newly ordained ministers might become independent and set up for themselves ?

COKE : Yes, there were such symptoms. But then, in England, the lay preachers had already sought ordination from the Independents. In Scotland, Coke had administered the Sacrament in the Presbyterian way—and J. W. had reproved him for it.

La T.: You will shut the door of the national churches against you, for you take people from the different churches.

Coke: But what about your Tropuses?

La Trobe: I showed him that he misunderstood our meaning quite. We did not form new churches from the national churches, but sought to preserve a good seed in the national churches themselves. And he owned that all the dissenting congregations formed from among the Methodists in the present times had in general sunk into a laodicean state, and that this would probably be the case of the new Churches proposed to be formed by them.

Coke remarked that in America there was no national church, and Mr John Wesley had not yet made up his mind about forming the Methodist Episcopal Church in England.

The two discussed National Churches, which Mr Coke is persuaded are all the invention of Satan and not of God.

At 12.30, Coke "put the question, Whether I believed there could be a Union?"

La T. replied that the preliminaries were not yet settled—neither as yet knows enough of the others' constitution.

Coke begged another meeting and they parted very friendly.

Following the interview, Coke sends La Trobe a sermon on the Godhead of Christ and La Trobe sends Coke a copy of Dr Franklin's Abstract of the Book of Common Prayer, a work showing the undesirability of making alterations in that Book.

On the same sheet there is *a further postscript*, dated 11th January.

La T. has visited Charles Wesley who wishes him to have an interview with John.

I told him candidly that I could not seek an interview with his brother, as I had never done it, for his Brother's method of publishing the conversations he had with anyone, and giving the other parties' words such a turn as suited his purpose, made it dangerous to converse with him.

Charles, however, thinks the danger might be risked, since both he and John are of great age and probably near their end.

La T.: I told him I would think of it.

From Charles Wesley, La Trobe went to see Dr Lort, a

more numerous or to have a more extended plan than is quite conformable to His heart or mind and make us as useful in all respects as he has intended.

I am, dear Brethren,

Yours affectionately,

B. LA TROBE.

No. 5.

La Trobe to Loretz. 17th January 1786

My dearest Bro Loretz,

Have you got a large packet in answer to yours of the 27th of November ? I was not made short, and am therefore not only long in stature but in everything ; bear with me.

[La Trobe has been prosecuting enquiries about *Moravia in Scotland*, but has gained no information about an emigration from Moravia to Scotland. " Moravia " is the Latin name for the district or shire of Murray—so much is certain.]

It is also certain by what I am informed that there has been an emigration from the *Sclavonian provinces* to *Scotland :* from Hungry many settled there.

He will continue his enquiries.

No. 6.

Loretz to La Trobe. 17th February 1786

[We give a translation of Loretz's original letter, which seems to have been returned to Herrnhut. It is the reply to No. 3, that of the month before, 6th January 1786.]

We must return to our first principles and to the task which our Lord has given us and we see by your letter that you are in accord with us. We have wandered from the plan of the Ordinary. We have given a promise to the Parliament and to the Archbishop to retain the awakened within the Anglican Church. We have not done that but we have closed the door for us to the Church of England by our mistakes. We have nothing else to do than preach the Word of the Cross. That was the original idea of our work in England. We cannot deny that it was a principle that a member of the Church of England should not enter into the Moravian Church before he had left the Church of England. . . . Our colleagues in England had not the courage (*Muth*) to work upon the Diaspora plan—for which we can only ask the Lord's forgiveness. He can bring good from our mistakes.

Herrnhut thinks (with Charles Wesley) that John Wesley and Coke are not walking in the right way.

In your last letter, you say that Dr Coke is the mouthpiece of John Wesley, and Coke has made to you an unexpected proposition of the union of the Brethren with the Methodists, a proposition which has given us more fear than joy. If John Wesley and Coke are sincere, we have many doubts (hesitations —*Bedenken*). They are chiefs of a party and move in the interests of a party (*handeln im Geiste derselben*). We cannot suppose they are concerned merely with a spiritual fellowship (*Gemeinschaft*), since all the children of God in this world should hold communion with one another, whatever their church-constitution. That is not what J. Wesley is after. If they wish for a union in work, we must be very prudent how we act.

i. That we are agreed concerning the Diaspora plan.

ii. That we are at liberty to form little societies for those who are fitted for them.

iii. That we can maintain our principles and customs among those brought under our care and exclude from our communion those who do not abide by our customs.

iv. That we must be able to convey reports from our communion to those who join and so maintain communications with the Brethren.

v. According to our constitution and the rule of our Lord we cannot permit to them (the Methodists) any participation (*Mitdirection*) in the training of our ministers.

vi. Our plan in the work of the souls we cannot permit to be upset.

vii. We cannot supply methodist chapels with ministers, still less administer the sacraments in them.

If Coke wishes for a more intimate union still, we shall have further considerations to put forward. We are not meant for a great company ; only men whom the Lord has chosen are our members, therefore we cannot walk with every party. Our relationship (*Verbindung*) is and must remain individual in character and is based on the gracious call of every individual member of the community.

[John Wesley and Coke have brought up the idea of a Union—and the U.E.C. are anxious, not wanting to engage in ecclesiastical politics.]

It seems to us likely that their real purpose is an ecclesiastical union with us, and a wish that we should share with them our Church-Right (*Kirchenrecht*) and help them thereby to a legitimate and legal ordination and constitution. Their own lack in this respect cannot be hidden and already your first conversation with Mr Coke contains traces that they are convinced of that, and have a presentiment of the consequences which will arise for themselves and for their sect.

[All reasons are against such a Union ; it would lead to the overthrow of the Diaspora plan—for which alone our *ministerium ecclesiasticum* exists.]

Our *Kirchenrecht* is from the Lord for a shield for the Brüder Gemeine and its Missions, but we have no vocation to erect a new religious edifice in Christendom. That would be contrary to the universality of our call to serve in the Kingdom of Grace and we would close the door to the English Church, in creating a new church-constitution. We are, essentially, propagandists.

We will wait upon your conversation with Mr Coke. We wonder how he will persuade Methodists who still belong to the Church of England why they should give up their own rights. Others of them will return to their own church-constitution and the most will split up into small sects. If they will remain by their constitution as at present and will have a brotherly connection with us, we will gladly give our hands, and according to our knowledge, build them up in the Lord.

No. 7.

La Trobe to the U.E.C. 22nd April 1786

[Extracts are given from a very long rambling epistle, telling of the progress of the conversations with Dr Coke.]

i. Breakfast with Dr C. and discussion on the spiritual state of members of national churches.

LA. T.: Will not your newly ordained pastors think they have a right to ordain and so in a few years the methodists will evaporate into broken sections.

COKE: It may be; we hope not. Mr Wesley had done right in founding a church in America, and had not yet made up his mind about England and Scotland.

Coke then brought forward his proposal of a union with the Brethren—and is told the time is not yet ripe to speak upon this subject.

ii. The two had another breakfast after Coke has returned from the Channel Islands.

Coke relates the circumstances of the new ordinations in America, how that Asbury himself was at first unwilling but consented when Coke showed his credentials. Discussion on National Churches and Apostolical Succession; the latter cannot be proved, says Coke.

LA T.: No use in taking up time in discussing that subject. J. W. has gone the wrong way to work. If he had wanted to found a new church, he should have called an Assembly of the whole body who might then have set apart as many of their own number as they thought fit to ordain in virtue of the power given them from the Church. Wesley's method is neither episcopal nor independent and is likely to end in every man ordaining whom he will—of which they have already had one example in America.

COKE answers that Mr Wesley did not come to a congregation but they all came to him; he did not join a ministry already formed but he from time to time formed a ministry—and naturally the government of the preachers and the societies was from the beginning in his hands.

La T.: I showed the difference between the conduct of Count Zinzendorf and John Wesley; the Brethren came to him not he to them. He was in truth at their formation their spiritual Guide and their temporal Lord but he was chosen their Antistes and took no office upon him but what was given to him by the Congregation and for which an instrument was executed.

La T. promises another conference and bade Coke read the history of the Brethren and an account of their constitution.

[There follows a long account of the Wesley Conference of the previous year, with remarks on the Deed J. W. has executed relative to the formation of the Legal Hundred.]

iii. Another breakfast and colloquy with Dr Coke, this time in New Chapel House. Coke presses that it is right to establish a new church in England: "he said Mr W. had not yet resolved to form such a church though the Doctor thought it might come to that either before or after Mr W.'s death, and I remained firm in declaring that such a regulation would be the ruin of the Methodists."

La T. explains the Moravian constitution and how a Union would be impossible between us and their Societies.

"Coke saw into it, but he was much pleased with the Tropus and Diaspora plan; he thought that upon that ground there might be a Coalition, we had here a large field for conversation and he spoke with admiration of our constitution and the use of the Lot."

iv. After this interview La T. visited Mr Atley, a Book Steward in the Wesley Societies, a preacher and well affected to the Brethren. "He is quite against their new scheme and thinks that Dr Coke, through inexperience and zeal without knowledge, if not stopped, will be the means of pulling down all that has been reared and built up by our Saviour among them."

v. Another visit of Coke to La Trobe.

" After breakfast the Doctor and I retired to my room and he immediately began the business by producing a writing with proposals for preliminaries of a junction in a certain point of view." Coke proposed that Mr Wesley and the U.E.C. should appoint delegates to a mutually agreed place—probably London—who should discuss proposals for a union or alliance, " that this Union should be upon the plan of the Tropuses (which he had studied) or the Diaspora " . . . " that it might be perhaps laid down as a principle in setting out that in case of a junction a Conference should be established of Brethren of both Tropuses who should have the direction of the labour in the societies."

La T. made answer on the following lines :

i. The difference of Mr W. as sole autocrat and the U.E.C. as responsible to the Synods.

ii. We ought to know more of Mr W.'s mind, *e.g.* has he resolved to form a new church in England ?

iii. The Diaspora plan needs fuller explanation—its great object being to keep awakened souls in the established national church——

" But how could we act with them if they separated from the established church. If the Doctor thought we should help them to a regular ministry he was mistaken. As that our ministers would administer the Sacraments to them, it could not be. Our Church and Congregation Constitution must not counteract the purpose of God with the national churches."

" The upshot was I returned to him his writing."

Coke urges La T. to have a conference with Mr J. Wesley, to which La T. professes to have no objection—but J. W. must agree not to publish the conversation.

vi. Conversation with the Bishop of Chester about the Methodists, and the increase of Dissent. The Bishops ask, " What can we do ? " La T.: One great stumbling-block was that the Bishops made no difficulty about ordaining frivolous or even immoral young men from college, but refused ordination to even learned young men known to be methodists or to have exhorted fellow sinners to turn to Christ for salvation. The Bishop answers (*a*) they cannot know the personal character of all who ask for ordination ; they must take the testimonials of the university or college. (*b*) Methodists as such are not refused but only some who have attacked the clergy or cannot get testimonials.

There followed a discussion on Enthusiasm and they parted friendly.

vii. " Last Saturday Mr C. Wesley called upon me, told me that by some letters he had hope from his brother, he had reason to hope that he was coming round and would not begin a new church-system in England and he wished that I might see and converse with his brother John when he came to town."

La Trobe agreed, but again stipulates that there must be no publication of the conversation.

Thus far we are come, which is all preliminary.

Your affectionate Brother,

B. La Trobe.

No. 8.

La Trobe to Br. Loretz, for the U.E.C. London, 7th July 1786

[The purpose of this report is to enclose copies of letters which have passed between La Trobe and Dr Coke.]

Upon my return (from Fairfield) Mr Charles Wesley called upon me and urges much that I should have an interview with his brother John as he believes he partly sees into the impropriety of their forming a new church-constitution and he hopes that I would be made a means of preventing it ; but he wishes that I may settle the preliminary, that he shall not print, without my concurrence, anything that passes between us. This I also think necessary. Mr Charles Wesley has owned to me that he was formerly very inimical to the Brethren, and his chief reason was that he apprehended the Brethren were undermining the Established Church by drawing the good souls out of it. To confirm this he showed me several MSS. poems which he had written against us—very clever, but as I told him, they were very malign and his observations founded upon untruth. He said he was convinced I was right and he now showed them to me as a proof of his sorrow that he had been in such a spirit. He had had a zeal but not according to knowledge and he was thankful that these poems had never been printed and he would consign them to the flames that they might never offend others. He is gone to Bristol where they are to have a conference this month and he has left these poems in my hands. He is fully persuaded that our Lord aims to make the Brethren useful in bringing souls to Himself and being a blessing to the remnant of the sincere methodists and of being a salt in the Church of England.

. . . at Fairfield, I received the following letter from Dr Coke, though his statement of our conversation in his letter to Mr Wesley was rather as he could wish it than as it really was: I was very glad that he was so explicit as I could by that opportunity give him a written explanation of what had passed and what was my mind, by which means Mr Wesley would not be misled.

ENCLOSURES (Copies)

Dr Coke to La Trobe. Dublin, 8th May 1786

My very dear and much respected Brother,

I have had the pleasure of seeing your Oeconomy at Fairfield and was highly satisfied with it, and almost tempted to wish that the methodists had institutions upon the same plan.

When I met with Mr Wesley though I was with him two days, I had but one mornings conversation with him in private and though our Union was one of the most uppermost things in my thoughts and indeed in my affections, I thought myself obliged to settle with him some very important matters concerning our connection in Ireland and America in the first place, which engrossed so much of our time that I was obliged to inform him that another very important matter which I was desirous of laying before him I must defer and inform him of at large by letter. Some company had joined us when I mentioned the above which induced me to conceal the business.

A few days after I mentioned the nature of the business which I intended to lay before him in a letter on another subject. I had no time to draw up my thoughts on the matter till last Saturday when I wrote Mr Wesley a letter, a copy whereof (as you and I have proceeded in simplicity and Christian sincerity) I send you underneath.

Dublin, May 6th, 1786.

[*Coke to John Wesley*]

Honoured and very dear Sir,

I have had the pleasure of spending four mornings with Mr La Trobe on the practicability of an Union between the Methodists and the Unitas Fratrum. The results of our conversations was the following proposal :

That a Conference be formed of an equal number of both Societies who shall meet at specified times to consult in what degree and by what methods a further union may be brought about, as far as it may appear to be for the Glory of God, the good of his Church, and the prosperity of both the Societies. The Report of this Conference to be laid from time to time, on the one hand before you and our General Conference (when it sits) and on the other hand, before the Elders' Conference of the Brethren through Mr La Trobe ; and in consequence steps be taken for a further Union as to the two Governors of the two Societies respectively may be seen necessary. Also, if it be thought expedient, there may be more than one conference composed as above of Delegates out of both Societies, one for instance in England, another in Ireland and another in America for the same purpose.

This is all it appears to Mr La Trobe and me that can be done at present, and such is the influence of Christian Fellowship and Converse that these Conferences will *of themselves* have a Tendency to promote union and love between the two Societies.

Our first intention was that I should immediately lay the proposals before you, and Mr La Trobe immediately write on the same subject and in the same manner to the Elders' Conference. But at our last meeting Mr La Trobe expressed a desire of having, first of all, a private conversation with you yourself. I ventured to assure him that I had no doubt but you would willingly grant him one, as soon as an opportunity offered. But he expressed in a delicate manner his fears lest you would afterwards publish the whole or part of the conversation in your Journals supposing you could not come to an agreement. I wish you would be pleased to enable me by your answer, to assure him that you will grant him a private conference on this important business and also that you will not take any advantage by publishing anything that passes, supposing you do not agree in sentiment.

As to the condition [La T. inserts " I shall explain that presently "] *implicitly believe and implicitly obey*, I do not think, whatever might formerly have been the case, that any such condition is now even thought of by Mr La Trobe or will be proposed by him or any of the Brethren. The point which took up our conversation for two whole mornings, either directly or indirectly, viz., the Validity, Expediency and Admissibility of our Ordination, is so far given up by Mr La Trobe that it shall not be (as far as his influence goes, which is not small) an hindrance to our union.

Indeed, my dear sir, I know not a desire in my soul that is stronger than that of uniting all religious Societies in love and in the closest union that the Circumstances of things will admit of. I think the desire of my own salvation is not superior. To use our utmost endeavour to gain this most favourable point as far as the grace and providence of God enables us, is only to do our part to hasten the fulfilment of that blessed prayer which is even now presented before the Throne by our great Intercessor.

> I pray that they also, who shall believe in me . . . that they may all be one . . . that the world may believe that thou hast sent me.

The great Prop of Infidelity would then be thrown down—the divisions among the professors of *vital* piety and the antient wonder again be expressed in, See how these Christians love one another. And the bigots of every party would gnash their teeth and melt away like snow.

I am, &c, T. C.

In answer to my former letter in which I informed Mr Wesley of the nature of the business on which I intended to write to him, he observes,

> About 20 years ago I talked with Mr ——, largely on joining with the Moravians which I had long desired. I asked him, on what terms they will unite with us ? He said on one condition alone, You must be *implicit :* implicitly believe and implicitly obey.
>
> Then, said I, we must remain as we are.

From this I judge that Mr Wesley will have no objection to a proper union. He will receive my letter, God willing, at Edinburgh on the 17th inst. So soon as he answers it, I intend to write to you again. But in the meantime favour me with a few lines. I trust I have not at least materially, mistated the business, but if I have, inform me of it, and I will endeavour to rectify it. Give my affectionate Christian love to Mrs La T. and remember me in your prayers, and believe me to be what I really am through divine grace in simplicity and godly sincerity

Your very affectionate Brother & Friend,

THOMAS COKE.

La Trobe to Coke. Fairfield, 24th May 1786

My dear and reverend Brother,

[Acknowledges receipt of Coke's letter of the 8th inst., and his praise of this Settlement.]

I am obliged to you for your communication of your letter to Mr Wesley and as we began our correspondence with a determination to act simply and sincerely with each other, I will tell you a few points in which I would have stated the case somewhat different from what you have done.

First, as to the suggested Conference,

I was of opinion that matters did not seem to me sufficiently ripe for such a conference. That as nothing could be done in the business without Mr Wesley, I should be glad to have some conversation with him upon the business before any such proposal could be made or the members of such Conference could be chosen.

[He then reiterates the condition that nothing be printed without consent.]

I wish in all my transactions to follow the Lord and not to run before him. Therefore I did not press at all for an interview with Mr Wesley but mentioned it as something that I thought might be useful to the important business to which you kindly led me. This observation arose from the repeated use you make of the phrase that Mr Wesley would grant me a private Conference.

The word Governors is not applicable (or at least not acceptable) to our Constitution. The Elders' Conference of the Unity do not govern but have a superintendency and are themselves subject to the established principles in the Unity and responsible to the Synods and the members may be changed. I know not who could have told Mr Wesley that the only condition upon which he could join the Moravians was that he must "implicitly believe and obey." I have been near forty years with the Brethren and have never heard nor read this condition unless it refers to our Lord and his Word. Among us order and subordination is established but implicit faith in any mans words and implicit obedience to any mans order exists perhaps in no well regulated Society less than in the Brethrens' Congregations.

Upon our conversations upon an union on the plan of the Tropuses, I pointed out to you the difficulty arising from your new church-constitution settled in America and in agitation here. You thereupon put the question to me, whether I thought upon it as a condition *sine qua non* that Mr Wesley or the Methodists should drop all thoughts of such a constitution if they and the Brethren should unite upon the tropus plan. To this I replied that I could not say that and that I hoped such a constitution would not take place in England.

It has appeared throughout the whole of our conversation that this last article has been much in our way and therefore we spent much time in discussing the two points, the National Churches and the proposed new Methodist Episcopal Church. I own that I wish that my arguments had convinced you that the National Churches have been a work of God's gracious providence for the benefit and salvation of millions and that the proposed alteration in the plan of the Methodists would be of very bad effects, by stopping the means of utility to which they seemed particularly called, and, by gratifying the ambition of many and hurting and stumbling others, be a means of destroying their own existence. Your reasons do not in the least convince me but in these two points we seemed to remain *toto cælo* different in our opinions. My influence, then, in this new plan (though no man can do much by his personal influence among us) can never be of use—I have been informed since I came here that Mr Wesley had declared in Manchester that no such new Church should be established in England during his life and that you had expressed yourself in the same manner. I was glad to hear it, but how far this report can be depended upon I cannot say.

Your affectionate Friend and Brother,

B. La Trobe.

Coke to La Trobe. Ballinrobe, Ireland, 7th June 1786

Mr Wesley writes to me in answer to the letter which I sent you a copy of, as follows :—

John Wesley to Dr Coke. Edinburgh, 17th May 1786

I see no possible objection to Mr La Trobe's proposal so far as you have gone yet. The steps you mention may certainly be taken without any manner of danger, and this is all that can be done at present. I am exceeding willing to have a private Conference with Mr La Trobe ; but it is certain that nothing that passes therein should be spoken out of it, inasmuch as the premature mention of anything might frustrate our whole design. Undoubtedly nothing is more desirable than a cordial union among the children of God. I am not conscious of having neglected any step which had a tendency to this. And I am as ready now as ever I was to do anything that is in my power to promote it.

[Coke continues to La T.]

I doubt whether Mr Wesley understood what I meant by desiring him not to publish anything that may pass in private. If you wish that I should mention anything more to him on that point as a preparation to your interview I will. It is not probable that you and he will be able to have a private Conference together before next October unless you happen to meet in Bristol. Favour me with an answer at the Preaching House in Dublin and dont forget to pray for

Your very affectionate Brother,

THOMAS COKE.

No. 9.

Loretz to La Trobe. 12th July 1786

[Translation from a Copy probably taken before despatch of letter.]

My Dearest Brother La Trobe,

We have heard with surprise of your conversations with Dr Coke and the Bishop of Chester and we hope these conversations will be of service to the cause of our Saviour. But as long as John Wesley lives and rules we have little hope. The acquaintance with Dr Coke may have results and be useful to the cause of the Lord. His agreement in the ground of our doctrine and his open and cordial declaration lead me to hope that we may come into a nearer relation with him in the future. At all events he is right in believing that the Tropus and Diaspora are our essential foundations upon which to build a Union. That is the standpoint from which we must set out if we are to achieve what is expedient. On that basis we could agree to collaborate and to serve the awakened souls in their party in accordance with the grace the Saviour will give us. The Methodists must permit the Brethren to continue to care for souls in their accustomed way ; we only seek to win souls for the Saviour and bring them into intimate relations with him and we would not upset the church-constitution in which they are. Therefore we can work with Methodists as with any other Protestant church. If you can agree in a preliminary conference we are willing to help for we are debtors to all men and will serve all men with the talents God has given us.

But I fear that Mr John Wesley will not be content with that and that he will fear to lose his influence and authority in his party. The difference in secondary matters (*Nebenideen*), *e.g.* that Coke and his friends will not recognize the value of the national church but hold such as a corruption of true Christianity, need not hinder our communion with them. We agree in the fundamental point (*Grundsatz*) viz., that we recognize as a Brother anyone who has faith in Christ and lives as his disciple even though he differs from us in lesser matters.

We will not fight over special opinions. It is enough that we give to everyone who asks for it our creed and let him judge whether it be well founded. Even the intention of John Wesley and Dr Coke—to separate from the Church of England—we must allow to be their conviction. It is an affair outside our circle. The Saviour will prosper that which is best for His purpose. The Methodists know that theirs is not our scheme and plan : we have said in all sincerity that we cannot help them by surrendering our own constitution. If that had been for sale there have been opportunities for many years—as when the Americans asked the Brethren again and again to give them a church-constitution. But we have always refused because we have not the commission to found new Confessions (*Religionen*) or to help thereto.

I cannot be offended if Dr Coke and other learned men in England hold that the English High Church has too much Roman error and superstition, because it is not according to Holy Scripture or sound Reformation principles that Clergymen have the *caracterem indelibilem*. . . . This is *opus operatum*, dead work and superstition. It will not be difficult for Dr Coke to prove that these and other errors are maintained by the clergy of the Church of England, if not in theory yet in practice, and that its worship is frivolous and objectionable (*leichtsinnig u. verwerflich*). But from such judgment comes contempt and it needs great insight not to reject the valuable with the worthless and to find the gold in the sand. I have read in a famous English author that if the English Church had not so many mundane advantages, only the most light hearted and degraded part of the population would be members of it—and I hoped that this judgment was not true.

That John Wesley is an arbitrary pope is proved by the Protocol of their Conference of last year communicated to you confidentially, he demands that his colleagues give an account but he himself will not give an account of his expenditure or of what he says and does. He is a Pope, as he said Count Zinzendorf was. But it must be doubted whether after J. Wesley's death, another man will be found to whom the Methodists will give so great power. More probably they will fall into parties. They must either remain connected with the Church or make their own church—that we must leave to the Will of God ; we have no call to help or hinder.

Your intercession for the Methodists to the Bishop of Chester I recognized as brotherly service and if all the English Church leaders were as he we might hope that your efforts to retain the Methodists in the Church would be recognized as meritorious. But I fear that the dear and venerable man has colleagues with different minds. I have not heard that the English bishops have taken care so to aid the children of their church that they have preserved the essence of Christianity in the country. This lack has lost many good people to the Church ; perhaps, happily, through the Bishop of Chester something may be done towards that good end.

We wish the help of our Saviour for you in all your efforts.

J. LORETZ.

INDEX